Temple Israel Library
Minneapolis, Minn.

Please sign your full name on the above card.

Return books promptly to the Library or Temple Office.

Fines will be charged for overdue books or for damage or loss of same.

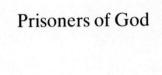

Prisoners of God

David Smith

PRISONERS OF GOD

*The Modern-day Conflict
of Arab and Jew*

QUARTET
LONDON

First published by Quartet Books Limited 1987
A member of the Namara Group
27/29 Goodge Street, London W1P 1FD

British Library Cataloguing in Publication Data

Smith, David
    Prisoners of God: the Modern-day
        Conflict of Arab and Jew
    1. Jews – West Bank
    2. Palestinian Arabs – West Bank
    3. Jewish–Arab relations – 1973–
    I. Title
    956.95'044 DS110.W47

    ISBN 0-7043-2607-8

Typeset by Reprotype Limited, Peterborough, Cambs
Printed and bound in Great Britain by
The Camelot Press plc
Southampton

For
Pamela, Mark and Matthew

CONTENTS

Acknowledgements.. ix

Introduction 1

Part One: The Prophecy Fulfilled

  1. The Spoils of Victory...17
  2. A City of Two Tales..41
  3. Possession is the Law 69
  4. The Eternal Triangle...97

Part Two: Between Two Truths

  5. The Palestinians are a Jewish Problem........................ 129
  6. Alienated Islands 151
  7. The Conspiracy of Conflict 171
  8. The Generation Gap.. 191

Conclusion.. 215

Notes.. 239

Index.. 245

Acknowledgements

I owe thanks to the many Israelis and Palestinians who gave me their time in the course of researching and writing this book. Rarely did I encounter anything other than courtesy, kindness and patience from members of both communities. At the request of a few, I have withheld names and personal details. In two instances I have assigned fictional names which have been placed in quotation marks on the first reference. Like every other figure in the book, they exist. It was always my intention to write a book based on the experiences and thoughts of real people. I regard the use of composite characters as a danger to the integrity of such a work. In the circumstances, I am indebted to those who agreed to be interviewed when it would have been easier to refuse.

David Nicholas, the Editor-in-Chief of ITN, kindly gave me leave of absence to take up a visiting Professorship at the University of Michigan. That enabled me to gather my thoughts and complete the manuscript.

During my years in the Middle East I relied heavily on colleagues in the Israeli media and the Palestinian press. I owe an enormous debt to Jamil Hamad whose insight, knowledge and editing of the first draft proved of incalculable value. It was a privilege to be given his time. Among my Israeli colleagues Avi Noam Ben Yosef of *Maariv*, Dani Rubenstein of *Davar*, Hirsh Goodman and Yehuda Litani of the *Jerusalem Post* were kind enough to offer suggestions and analysis; Israel Goldvicht was magnanimous in establishing contact with Israeli settlers in the territories. Hana Siniora, the Editor of *Al-Fajr*, Daoud Kuttab at the same newspaper and Zuheir al-Rayyes of *Al-Mawqif* provided both ideas and counsel on the Palestinian communities of the West Bank and Gaza Strip. All my Israeli and Palestinian colleagues could have written their own books on the subject; yet they generously shared their expertise.

Lina Majaj did most of the translating and interpreting from Arabic with skill and wit; my thanks as well to Miriam Shemoni who was responsible for the Hebrew translations and for keeping me up to date once I had left the Middle East. Outside Israel I was grateful for the assistance of Touma Hazous in Jordan, Antoine Touma in Syria and Alice Brinton in Egypt who arranged interviews and guided me on my many visits to those countries.

There is not sufficient room to mention all those who educated me during my time in the region, but I would like to single out the following: Yossi Beilin, David Hartman, Yossi Ohmert, Meron Benvenisti, Dedi Zucker, Daniella Weiss, Mustafa Natshe, Hanan Mikhail, Sari Nusseibeh, Tawfiq Abu Ghazala, Mary Khass, Fayez Abu Rahme, Hatem Abu Ghazala.

The major part of the manuscript was read and criticized by Jamil Hamad, Hisham Sharabi, Yehuda Litani, Walter Reich and Ehud Sprinzak. Their comments and amendments were invaluable. At the University of Michigan, Professor Richard Allen checked the final draft. I take sole responsibility for the result.

Last but by no means least, my gratitude goes to my wife Pamela. She cherished the concept and she saw me through the months of research and composition. This book would have been unthinkable without her love and support.

INTRODUCTION

'Golda, you remind me of a groom who wanted the dowry but not the bride.' – ISRAELI PRIME MINISTER
LEVI ESHKOL SPEAKING TO GOLDA MEIR, JUNE 1967

On Monday June 5 1967, for the third time in two decades, the Jews and Arabs of the Middle East went to war over Palestine. The world has lived with the consequences ever since.

In the Egyptian capital, Cairo, the state-controlled radio declared: 'The *Jihad*, the holy war, has started. Our people have been waiting 20 years for this battle! Arab armies have a rendez-vous in Israel!' In Jordan the sentiments were similar, the language even more strident. 'Kill the Jews!' Radio Jordan insisted. 'Kill them with your rifles, your knives, your bare hands!' From his command post in Tel Aviv, Israel's Defence Minister Moshe Dayan broadcast a concise, blunt message to his men: 'Soldiers of the Israeli Defence Forces, on this day our hopes and security rest with you.'

Israel struck the decisive first blow. In stunning pre-dawn air strikes across the face of the Arab world, Israeli jets all but eliminated Arab air power, and with it any chance of an Arab victory. Without any air cover, Arab tanks and infantry under the clear skies of the desert stood at the mercy of the Israelis. In a few

1

astonishing hours of incredibly accurate bombing and strafing, Israel brought its Arab neighbours to their knees. Streaking in ahead of the dawn, the first waves of Israeli Mirage fighter-bombers destroyed the main Egyptian airbases in the Sinai Peninsula. Only hours before, Egypt's President Gamel Abdel Nasser had proclaimed: 'We are so eager for battle in order to force the enemy to awake from his dreams and meet Arab reality face to face.' Now 200 of Nasser's front-line fighters, mostly Russian-built Mig-21s, were caught and destroyed on the ground. That morning, the Israelis hit Arab bases in Jordan, Syria and Iraq. They swept in from the sea to strike at Egyptian command centres closer to Cairo; landing only long enough to refuel, they hammered away until 20 of the most vital airfields in the Arab world lay smoking in ruins. It was a devastating display of air superiority. On that first day, some 400 warplanes of five Arab nations had been obliterated. Israel, boasting exactly that number of fighters, had lost 19 planes and pilots. Radio Cairo disguised Egypt's monumental defeat with a report of an Israeli airman who had been shot down near the delta town of Zagazig. Egyptian peasants had hacked him to death, the radio claimed with a pride that bordered on glee. Yet the outcome had already been decided; and Israel had won hearts and minds the world over with its expression of the Jewish will to survive against all odds.

That first day unleashed the emotions of the Jewish people scattered across the Western world. One taxi-driver in Manhattan marched into the offices of the Jewish Agency with two sturdy youths, announcing: 'I have no money to give you, but I'll give you my sons.' In a luncheon at New York's Waldorf-Astoria hotel, $1 million a minute was pledged during a single quarter of an hour. By the second day of the war, as the Israelis closed in on the Arab half of Jerusalem, thousands of American Jews volunteered to go to Israel, tens of thousands more demonstrating in support of the Jewish state. At a rally opposite the White House, a young girl student confided: 'I'm so happy to be Jewish. I feel so wonderful. I've never felt so wonderful in my life.' On the third night, with Jerusalem captured, British police had to quell a mini-riot at London's Heathrow Airport as hundreds of British Jews fought to get on board a flight to Tel Aviv. By the end of the week, as the Israelis completed the Arab rout by taking the Golan Heights from the Syrians, there were Jewish demonstrations in the major capitals

2

of Europe. 'This is our finest hour,' declared a demonstrator in Paris. 'I can't imagine a Jew anywhere who doesn't feel great pride in simply being Jewish.' On Saturday June 10, the final day of the war, California's Governor Ronald Reagan joined a galaxy of movie stars for a rally in Hollywood. Israel enjoyed the admiration and affection of the free world, Governor Reagan declared.

In six amazing days, the war was over, and when the guns fell silent, victor and vanquished alike recognized that what had been wrought amounted to a political and geographic earthquake. In the west, troops of the triumphant Israeli army stood on the banks of the Suez Canal. To the north, in Syria, Israeli armour stood at the gates of Damascus. To the south, their paratroopers had taken the fortress of Sharm el-Sheikh, commanding the Strait of Tiran and the southern sea route to Israel, after the bloodiest desert fighting since the Allies' victory at Alamein in 1943. In the east they had captured perhaps the most valuable prize of all: Jerusalem and the West Bank of the River Jordan, the Biblical land of the forefather Abraham.

Thus did the tiny state of modern Israel, 2.6 million strong and barely 19 years old, defeat the 21 nations of the Arab world and the 110 million people who threatened its survival. Thus did the Jews become the absolute masters of the Middle East. They needed to take orders from no one. They could dictate their own terms in the face of superpower inaction and Arab impotence. They had the unmitigated support of not just world Jewry but the public at large in Europe and North America. At the White House, President Lyndon Johnson voiced the admiration of a Western world dumb-founded by Israel's lightning victory. David, the President remarked, had slain Goliath.

In the years that followed, however, the world at large came to view Israel's most glorious hour in an entirely different light. Those six days in June led to further war, claiming tens of thousands of lives and drawing the superpowers ever closer to their own confrontation. The price of oil would rise dramatically as a consequence; the poorer nations would be afflicted with an economic crisis that stunted their development for generations; the industrialized world would suffer recession through the same process. The defeat of 1967 would spur an Islamic revolution in the Moslem world, a holy war against the Jewish infidel and its American ally. It would give mavericks such as Colonel Muammar

3

Gaddhafi of Libya a pretext for a campaign of world-wide terrorism. Among the Arabs, the sense of humiliation felt that June would produce the likes of Abu Nidal and Wadi Haddad, men who killed and maimed innocent civilians in the name of winning back the land lost then. More blood would be spilled and more resources spent in the aftermath of that war than on any other modern-day conflict. In so many hidden, at times invisible ways, the world would pay a price for the legacy of Israel's victory.

Yet the years after the 1967 war would defy a solution and spawn a new conflict between Arabs and Jews. In the tiny battleground of the West Bank – just 80 miles long and 26 miles wide – the two peoples would live together, contesting the same territory. Many on both sides would claim that it was granted to them by God. The Jews would cite God's teaching as they occupied and settled the land of Abraham, Isaac and Jacob. The Arabs would see God's will in the political, legal and military struggle that followed. In the process, Arabs and Jews would be locked in a modern-day secular conflict, fuelled by age-old religious zealotry and bigotry. They would be trapped together in a promised land. They would become prisoners of God.

To the Jews of the world, Israel is both a homeland and a state of mind. It is the Biblical land given to Abraham by God 1800 years before Christ. It is the territory for which Moses searched in vain 500 years later, spending four decades in the wilderness as he strove to lead the Jews back home from the desert of Sinai. It is the kingdom that Joshua, the successor to Moses, finally captured by conquering the people who lived there, the Canaanites. Joshua bequeathed a homeland but not security. For the next 700 years, the Jews suffered the first of many holocausts at the hands of the Babylonians, the Greeks and the Romans. After expelling nearly a million Jews in the first century A.D., the Romans called the land Syria Palestina after the Jews' most hated enemies, the Philistines, the first Palestinians. In succeeding centuries, Palestine was overrun by the Arabs (A.D. 636), the Crusaders (1099), Mamelukes (1250) and Turks (1517). Yet the Jewish people, persecuted minorities in the world outside Palestine, still considered the territory theirs. They clung to the hope of a return to the promised land. It proved an elusive dream until the 20th century.

In the 1880s, when the pogroms of Russia and Poland drove the Jews from their ghettos, the first Europeans came to the home of their ancestors. With money from the newly created World Zionist Organization and wealthy families such as the Rothschilds in France, the first pioneers bought land from the Turks, built kibbutzim or farming communes and began planning the revival of the Jewish state. By 1911, there were 85,000 Jews in Palestine and more than 500,000 Moslems. In those days, violence between Arabs and Jews was rare. Ironically, given the bloodshed of the subsequent decades, the Jews had always suffered far less under Moslem rulers than at the hands of supposedly more advanced Christian civilizations represented by Rome, the Crusaders, the Russian Tsars and the Germans. The 20th-century battle for Palestine destroyed the tradition that had protected Arab from Jew and vice versa.

During World War One, the British, entrusted with the League of Nations Mandate over Palestine, could not make up their minds to whom the land belonged. Cynically, at times chaotically, they sought to play Arab against Jew and so advance their cause in the Great War. In 1915, they promised it to the Arabs; two years later, Arthur Balfour, British Foreign Minister, pledged his government's support for a national home for the Jews in Palestine as long as it did not 'prejudice the civil and religious rights of existing non-Jewish communities'. Twenty years later, after Arab rioting and insurrection, the British awarded it to the Arabs again in a White Paper issued on the eve of World War Two. But that war swung the balance decisively to the Jews. Horrified by the ovens and gas chambers of Buchenwald, Auschwitz and Bergen-Belsen, the Western world took up the Jewish cause as its own. It closed its eyes when the displaced Jews of Europe began flooding into Palestine in defiance of a British immigration ban. It all but rejoiced when Jewish terrorists made it impossible for the British to stay in the Holy Land. The war for Palestine followed.

In 1947, when the British finally threw up their hands and turned the Palestine problem over to the United Nations, it took the General Assembly only a few weeks to partition the land between Arabs and Jews. At four o'clock on the afternoon of May 14 1948, the Jewish leader David Ben-Gurion read a 979-word pronouncement declaring Israel an independent state. He began: 'In the Land

5

of Israel, the Jewish people came into being.' Palestine had been inhabited for nearly 10,000 years; among its first tribes were the forefathers of the Jews and the Palestinians. Now, in the aftermath of world war, the modern-day Israelites had returned to claim the land promised to them by the Lord.

The Arab response was swift and violent. They claimed that the Jews had usurped the land granted to them by the Prophet Mohammed. They combined the armies of Egypt, Transjordan, Iraq, Lebanon and Syria, marching on Israel the following day, supported by bombers which attacked Tel Aviv. But the Arabs were humiliated. The Israelis, outnumbered by 20 to one, even so outfought, outmanoeuvred and outgunned the Arabs, who finally sought a ceasefire after eight months of fighting. Yet although the Arabs put down their guns, they refused to recognize the reality and existence of Israel.

With the war won, Israel soon became something of a modern miracle. From the camps of Europe, the remote wastes of Yemen, the middle-class suburbs of England and America, Jews poured into Israel, were declared citizens and went to work. In 16 years, the population tripled. Supported by massive donations from individual Jews, American aid and German reparations payments, the country sprang almost overnight from a picturesque wilderness into an enclave of dynamic purpose. Deep-water ports were dredged, power and irrigation plants built, modern cities and industries created. For more than a decade, its gross national product soared by at least 10 per cent. By the mid 1960s, Israel boasted a standard of living which rivalled that of Western Europe. Nor was the miracle confined to the Jewish homeland. 'Israel,' said Ben-Gurion in 1960, 'has created a new image of the Jews all over the world – the image of a working and intellectual people, of a people that can fight with heroism. The state has straightened the backs of every Jew in every country."

Arguably for the first time since the reign of Joshua, the enemy had paid the price of war with the Jews. During the campaign of 1948, some 750,000 Arabs or 80 per cent of Palestine's non-Jewish population fled from the land of their own ancestors. They filed sullenly into refugee camps across Israel's borders, becoming 'our Jews', as the Egyptians called them and constant symbols of what the Palestinians termed *al-Nakba*, the Disaster. For years the Israelis fostered the belief that the Arabs ordered mass evacuations

6

to clear the way for the invading armies. But, in 1986, a classified report, prepared by the Israelis in 1948 and kept secret for almost four decades, shattered that myth. It revealed how the majority of Arabs fled because the Jews intimidated them into doing so. One village would be attacked, the report explained; Arabs living nearby would run for their lives because they feared their homes would be the next targets. The threat of bloodshed, the Israelis learned, was as strong a weapon as violence itself. As Israel's first President, Chaim Weizmann, noted: 'It was a miraculous simplification of our task.' The war of 1967 provided no such instant solution for a problem that had afflicted the Jewish people since the time of Abraham: how to live with its neighbours.

The rise and fall of nations is an endless process of territories being joined and rejoined in changing mosaics, of people displaced and resettled, of power expanding and contracting. A new nation may be forged through conquest, as was England when the Normans defeated the Anglo-Saxons. Other countries have been born out of a combination of immigration and revolution: typically the United States and most of Latin America, where settlers cut loose from their colonial ties. Some modern states owe their emergence to a form of rebirth – a conscious revival of an ancient state of civilization harnessed to contemporary revolution. Present-day Greece fought for its independence from the Ottoman Empire partly in the name of its ancient, glorious incarnation; 20th-century Germany struggled for national unity, remembering its identity under the Holy Roman Empire. Most of those precedents can be found in the creation of modern Israel: conquest, war of liberation, rebirth, immigration and the chaos caused by the break-up of a colonial empire. Yet Judaism's unique blend of race, nationality and religion appeared to offer immunity from the laws of history. No other people had been dispersed for so long from its original home and maintained the memory of that land as a living reality. Until 1967 that distinct identity enabled the Jews to defy the past and imbue one generation after another with the righteousness of their God-given claim to Palestine.

After 1967, on the other hand, the lessons of history caught up with the Jewish people. Unlike 1948, most of the Palestinian Arabs did not flee from the land won by Israel in the Six-Day War.

7

Instead, in capturing all of Palestine, the Jewish state had assumed responsibility for most of the refugees who had left their homes 20 years before for exile on the West Bank and the Gaza Strip. In June 1967 some Arabs gathered whatever they could and walked towards the Jordan River as their armies retreated in disarray. Old and young, the tattered and the well-dressed, they trudged along the road from Jerusalem to Jericho and beyond in blistering heat: as in 1948, the Israelis did what they could to encourage them to go, picking up entire families along the road and driving them to the border. Yet the majority of Arabs stayed. The 400,000 people caught in the Gaza Strip had nowhere else to go, because the escape routes towards Cairo had been cut. Almost every man, woman and child hung on to their homes in refugee camps built in 1948. On the West Bank, almost 600,000 Arabs remained, over 70 per cent of the pre-June population. Their feelings were summed up by a young Palestinian interviewed by *Newsweek*. 'We will stay here until we can fight again and take back our land,' he said as the fighting ended. 'I will go back to my lands in Palestine, or I will die here,' remarked another. As for the Israelis, there was initial recognition of the painful problem the 1967 war had reopened – and the tremendous burden the Jewish state had inherited. The territory captured was among the least desirable on earth. It offered no ready assets, it was crowded and short of water. Nearly half the people living there were dependent on international aid and government-funded relief. 'I'm beginning to understand things I never did before,' said an Israeli army officer who was put in charge of refugees in the ancient town of Jericho, close to the Jordan River. 'The Arab refugees were always something political in my mind. Now I see them, and it's something else, something human.'

The result was that Israel's triumph in 1967 added both land and people to the infant state. In winning all of Palestine, Israel had acquired most of its Arabs. A Jewish nation of 2.6 million ruled an Arab population of almost 1.3 million, made up of West Bankers, Gazans and the Palestinian minority that had stayed in Israel after 1948. Ninety per cent of them were Moslem, the rest Christian. Levi Eshkol, Prime Minister in 1967, expressed concern bordering on paranoia about the new demographic situation. Others, such as his successor Golda Meir, emphasized the strategic advantages of having the army deployed along the borders of old Palestine. The debate between the two reflected the internal divisions with which Israel lived ever after. Golda Meir did indeed want the dowry, the land, but not the bride, the people: a short-term gain that flew in the face of long-term considerations. Yet she went further than that. 'It's not as though there was a people in Palestine considering itself as a Palestinian people,' she remarked, 'and we came and threw them out and took their country away from them. They [the Palestinians] do not exist.'

Such disregard for history rebounded on Israel in the decades after the 1967 war. Far from becoming a non-people, the Palestinians learned the first lesson required for nation building – a lesson the Jews had applied ever since they were driven out of Palestine by the Romans. In the defeats of 1948 and 1967, the Palestinians recognized they could count only on themselves. Just as the Jews had become a nation during the long years in exile, so Palestinian nationalism was born out of their own diaspora. Golda Meir might have doubted their right to be called a people – but the Palestinians grew to believe they were a nation and that that was all that mattered in the years after the June war. They rationalized their claim to the Holy Land. They argued that they had lived there for more than a thousand years; that the Prophet Mohammed had conquered the territory in their name during the seventh century; that they had been expelled because of alien Jews seeking justice for the sins the Palestinians had not committed. Amid the degradation and deprivation of refugeedom, they began to think almost like the Jews. They began to talk not of the Disaster but of *al-Awada*, the Return, the divine wish of God. By the 1980s, with the hindsight of 20 years of Israeli occupation on the West Bank and Gaza, they reinterpreted their history. They saw defeat as the seed of future victory. They insisted on staying in their land as a means of undermining the Jewish enemy and destroying the cause of Israel from within.

In this way, triumph in the Six-Day War presented Israel with the dilemma which had been the undoing of many young countries down the centuries. Conquest, sheer force was not necessarily enough to build a new nation. Sooner or later the seizure of land had to be legitimized, leading to an amalgamation of conquerors and conquered. Otherwise, history proved how the process of conquest could be reversed. Some Israeli historians, increasingly concerned about the country's future, pointed to the lessons of history Israel could no longer ignore. A classic example was the insurrection of the Netherlands against the rule of Spain in the 17th century. In the 19th century the Belgians rebelled against the regime of the Netherlands, creating the two modern states of Holland and Belgium. Others saw warnings for Israel in the experience of some European states during the days of colonial empires. Military rule abroad, they maintained, could erode the fabric of democracy at home.

Yet the Jews, always the exception to history, convinced themselves they had no option and little to fear. Their self-belief, born out of victory in war, blinded them to a reality which presented a far more serious challenge than the French had faced in Algeria or the Portuguese in Mozambique and Angola. Israel's colonization was taking place on its own doorstep: on land, the West Bank, which many Jews saw as the Biblical territory of Judaea and Samaria. Military rule demanded that virtually every Israeli male born after 1967 served a military regime which contradicted the ethics on which Israel had been built. It created a dependency within Israel on Palestinian labour and Palestinian assets such as water, land, farming. It allowed Jews to set up home in the territory just as the whites of Europe had done in black Africa. The difference was that such colonization happened only a few miles from Tel Aviv, Ashkelon, Netanya, the cities of modern Israel. The difference was that such settlement made it impossible for Israel to meet the price which peace entailed: the return of the land. The occupation became as unique as the Jewish identity. The world had witnessed struggles as to where the dividing line should be drawn between nations, but not two peoples living on the same land, both of them deeply conscious in their hearts and souls that it was their country given them by God. There could be no simple way out. It was either partition or war to the finish.

In the process, the Jewish state became bi-national in all but name, inhabited by an Arab population which grew to form almost 40 per cent of the total and which seemed destined to be a majority in the 21st century. As a result, the conflict became ever more complex and costly, the differences between the two sides ever more irreconcilable. In divorcing themselves from history, the Israelis embarked on a venture of conquest which ultimately threatened not just its survival but peace in the world outside. They became living proof of the maxim first articulated by the American philosopher George Santayana: 'Those who cannot remember the past are condemned to repeat it.'

In July 1982, I reached the besieged city of Beirut at the height of Israel's war in Lebanon. Docking at the port of Jounieh, which represented the only way in or out of the city, we were greeted by Israeli soldiers occupying an Arab capital and encircling thousands of Palestinian fighters trapped inside. Within minutes of arrival, in the dusk of early evening, the shelling began: a furious barrage of tank and mortar fire designed as much to demoralize the Palestinians as to kill them. It was Friday, the Jewish Sabbath, yet religious observance did not impede Israel at war. Indeed, when I mentioned this to the Israeli commander checking passports, he remarked in a strong American accent: 'There is purity in the gun and sanctity in war.'

In the weeks that followed, the Israelis achieved virtually all their military objectives in Beirut. As in 1967, thousands died. Unlike the Six-Day War many victims were civilians. Yet in the eyes of the Israeli government, although not necessarily its public, the days of bombing from the air and the war of attrition on the ground justified the end: the expulsion of the Palestinians from their last remaining stronghold in Lebanon. The battle for Beirut, said Israel's Defence Minister Ariel Sharon when he justified the actions of his army, would force a solution to the Arab–Israeli conflict. It did not. Just as 1967 had been the catalyst for further conflict rather than peace, so the war in Lebanon prompted more of the violence endemic to that most troubled of regions. The war may have assumed a different face. The United States as well as Israel became the target for Arab and Moslem extremists; almost as many Americans died as Israelis. Yet the heart of the crisis, the Arab–Israeli dispute, thwarted every search for a solution. In the vacuum that such stalemate invariably produced, Palestinian fighters returned to Lebanon and resumed terrorist attacks on Israel. By 1987, the Palestine Liberation Organization (PLO) had as many men under arms in that country as it did before the 1982 invasion: a testament to the futility of war in a region that had suffered two major conflicts before June 1967 and two since – the Yom Kippur War of 1973 and the Israeli invasion of Lebanon in 1982.

11

The world at large tended to view the very existence of Israel, the legacy of 1948, as the root cause of the Middle East's crisis. For much of the Western world, and most importantly the United States, the apparently eternal threat to the Jewish state justified increasingly one-sided support for the government of Jerusalem. Yet Egypt and Syria attacked Israel in 1973 not with realistic ambitions to destroy the Jewish nation, but rather as a last-ditch attempt to recapture territory lost in 1967. In 1982, the Israelis invaded Lebanon in the hope of crushing the PLO and so freeing themselves from the scourge of Palestinian guerrilla action, a direct consequence of their punitive occupation of the West Bank and Gaza. In short, the goal of most Arabs was no longer the pipe dream of somehow driving the Jews out of Palestine. At the same time, Israel's security rather than its survival was at stake. The legacy of 1967 had become an issue.

Yet the years after 1967 witnessed an unprecedented military build-up on all sides. Much as the superpowers publicly fretted over the possibility of direct conflict in the Middle East during the nuclear age, neither had many reservations about fuelling an arms race that made the region the world's principal stockpiler of weapons. The Middle East became the main arena for superpowers who tested each other through indirect conflicts rather than head-on confrontation. By the mid 1980s, Israel and its Arab neighbours had less than three per cent of the world's population, but they accounted for eight per cent of the world's military spending: an average of $350 per person annually for military purposes. They bought more than 42 per cent of the world's arms imports. The number of men under arms in those countries rose from 1.3 million in 1973 to 2.3 million in 1986. In Israel defence expenditure increased from 10 per cent of gross national product in 1967 to 30 per cent by 1987. In Syria, the main Soviet ally in the area, the military budget leapt from 15 to 60 per cent during the same period. The Israelis had developed a nuclear capacity; the Syrians had become the only country outside the Warsaw Pact to acquire Russia's most sophisticated long-range missiles, SS-22s and SS-23s. The results of conventional warfare may have been inevitable but the figures were staggering. One study, produced by Anthony Cordesman of the US Eastern Analytical Assessments Center in 1986, reported that 3.5 million people were casualties of various Middle East conflicts between 1979 and 1986; at least 300,000 had been killed. 'God is neither Israel's real-estate agent,' wrote Cordesman in the *Middle East Journal*, 'nor the Arab world's general.' It was of little consolation to anyone that the cause of the modern-day conflict lay in the status quo created by the 1967 war. With every escalation of the arms race, the stakes became that much greater, the potential for further conflict so much more dangerous to a world that had become a victim of its intractability.

For four years after the 1982 siege of Beirut I worked throughout the region: initially, on the repercussions of Sharon's invasion of Lebanon and the embroilment of the major Western powers in that country's misery. When I moved to Israel, early in 1984, I lived with the long aftermath of that earlier war in 1967. On the bright side, it provided an opportunity to know and try to understand both Palestinians and Israelis living on the front line of the conflict. On the other hand, it meant witnessing the bloodshed between Arab and Jew which had become so routine that their indifference was more shocking than the violence itself. Almost everywhere I travelled, I would hear the same sentiment. That 1967, not 1948, presented the obstacle to peace. That Arabs accepted the outcome of 1948, namely, the establishment of Israel; but not the legacy of 1967, the occupation of the West Bank and Gaza. There was a consensus that a solution lay solely in those territories. 'If Arabs could turn the clock back, it would be to 1967, not 1948,' confided President Hosni Mubarak of Egypt. 'I'm ready to accept Israel and make peace with Israel,' remarked King Hussein of Jordan, 'if we wipe clean the slate of 1967.' Even the Syrians, the most die-hard of Israel's enemies, came to terms with the facts of 1948. 'The aim to destroy Israel is a thing of the past,' explained the Syrian Foreign Minister, Farouk al-Shara. 'The issue is 1967. In our case, the return of the Golan Heights.' For their part, most informed Israelis understood that most Arabs no longer sought the destruction of the Jewish state but rather a return to pre-1967 borders. Yet as Shimon Peres, Israel's Prime Minister in the mid 1980s, admitted: 'The longer we stay the way we were after 1967, the more difficult it becomes to make peace.'

The Roman philosopher Seneca once wrote: 'Man investigates the outcome, rather than the cause, of war.' That, in a sense, has been one guiding principle for this book. I am neither Arab nor Jew, neither a Hebrew expert nor an Arabist. I am merely a Western reporter who has lived in the Middle East and witnessed the Arab–Israeli conflict with a mixture of sympathy and revulsion for both sides. At times I have felt both are right and, on other occasions, that they are wrong. Because I spent my working life reporting the aftermath of 1967, as every correspondent in the Middle East does at one time or another, I sought to understand the motives and aspirations that have guided both peoples in the years since. In doing so, I came to realize the undying legacy of the 1967 war and its impact on the future. I grew to appreciate that the experience of Arabs and Jews since those six days in June would shape the destiny of both for generations to come. In the words of the ancient sages, 'The best prophet of the future is the past.'

Palestine, or the Land of Israel, remains either the cue for another war, the like of which not even the Middle East has experienced, or the laboratory in which peace will be tried, tested and proven. In the event of war, all of us will suffer one way or another. Peace, on the other hand, would be a victory for humanity – much-needed evidence that nations can live together whatever their differences. But this book raises more questions than it provides answers. I have no solutions for the Arab–Israeli conflict. I offer few predictions for the future. What motivated me in the first place was the human dimension of the struggle: the mentality and emotions of two nations living side by side yet locked in battle for a small piece of land which has had such an extraordinary effect on all our lives: the claims and aspirations of people who turn to God for ultimate vindication of their conflict. As a reporter, it was my responsibility to talk and listen to all sides. It has therefore been my intention to let Jews and Arabs speak for themselves.

– D.A.S.
January 1987

14

PART ONE

THE PROPHECY FULFILLED

'The whole land of Canaan, where you are now an alien, I will give as an everlasting possession to you and your descendants.' – THE LORD'S PROMISE TO MOSES – GENESIS 17:1

'It is not because of your righteousness or your integrity that you are going in to take possession of their land; but on account of the wickedness of these nations.' – MOSES TO THE CHILDREN OF ISRAEL – DEUTERONOMY 8:19

1
THE SPOILS OF VICTORY

'Of one power even good is deprived, and that is the power of making what is past never to have been.'
– ARISTOTLE

In June 1967, he was Colonel Motta Gur, the swashbuckling commander of Israel's 55th Parachute Brigade. On the morning of June 7, the third day of the war, he led the first Israeli troops into the Old City of Jerusalem. In approximately 15 minutes, he buried nearly 2,000 years of Jewish history.

Shortly before 10 that Wednesday, Gur and his paratroopers burst through the heavy wooden doors of St Stephen's Gate in the eastern wall of the holy city. An elite unit from the most modern of armies had then driven their half-track vehicles furiously down the Via Dolorosa, Christ's path to Calvary. The air rang with the sharp whine of sniper bullets, followed invariably by staccato bursts from Israeli machine-guns and the crump of mortar fire. Moments later, Gur's men fanned out, past the burning hulk of a civilian bus, through a broken archway and into the city the Jews called Ir Hakodish and the Arabs al-Quds – 'The Holy Place'. Twenty yards inside the wall the great courtyard of the Dome of the Rock, from which the Prophet Mohammed was said to have leapt to heaven, opened up in front of them. Some soldiers, their fingers curled on triggers, crouched for cover. Others stood in awe before the ultimate symbol of Jerusalem, old and new, ancient and modern: the Temple Mount, with its sublime, golden mosque, the very heart of the Old City. For more than a thousand years, it had been a holy site for Islam. The medieval Crusaders had briefly turned it into a Christian church. But now, for the first time since the Romans burned the Temple in A.D. 70, the Mount was in Jewish hands.

With the guns momentarily silent, Gur and his men raised the blue and white Star of David, the Israeli national flag, over al-Aqsa mosque. Some of the brigade broke ranks, scrambling down from the courtyard to the Western Wall, popularly known as the Wailing Wall. During the centuries of exile, the Jews had longed for a return to this monument of worship. Fresh from battle, still carrying their weapons, many wept like children as they prayed before it.

For Gur, the emotion of victory was mixed with tragedy. Behind him lay memories of a battle that had claimed hundreds of casualties, scores of lives. Even in the final assault on the Old City two of his officers had been killed by sniper fire. Yet he was the one chosen to fulfil the dream that had sustained the Jewish people through the centuries of exile, persecution and genocide: to satiate the desire every observant Jew had voiced in daily prayer, to be next year in Jerusalem.

'The Wailing Wall is the heartbeat of every Jew, the place for which every Jewish heart yearns,' Gur told his men. 'The great privilege of finishing the circle at last, of restoring to the nation its capital, its centre of sanctity, has been given to you.'

He concluded: 'Jerusalem is yours – for ever!'[1]

In the early hours of that Wednesday, Anwar Khatib, lawyer, businessman, survivor, issued his last edict as Jordanian Governor of Jerusalem.

'All available weapons will be distributed to the civilian population,' he ordered. 'Every remaining Arab is under orders to shoot anyone who tries to leave Jerusalem. This time the Arabs will not run from the Jews.'

Proud, haughty, somewhat contemptuous of his underlings, Anwar Khatib knew defeat was probable from the moment the first shots were fired. Just two years before, he had attended an Arab summit in the Moroccan capital of Rabat. The verdict had been unanimous. The Egyptians under Nasser, the Jordanians under King Hussein, the Syrians, the Iraqis, all had agreed that war with Israel before 1970 would be a mistake. But Khatib had no idea how ill-prepared Jerusalem was when the King ordered the Arab Legion to attack the Jewish half of the city on June 5, the opening day of the war. Instead of the five brigades reportedly at his disposal Brigadier Ata Ali, the Jordanian commander, had just one. Fewer than 5,000 men would have to defend Arab Jerusalem. Khatib refused to believe him. He felt sure a ceasefire would pre-empt the capture of the Old City.

'Morale is high, we can hold out,' he reported to King Hussein in a telephone conversation that first morning. By that afternoon, all communication between Jerusalem and the Royal Palace in Amman had been cut. Khatib was forced to evacuate Government House and take refuge at army headquarters. In the early hours of the second day, he retreated to the inner sanctum of the holy city. Dressed in a dark, pinstripe suit, proceeding rather than running, he crossed the no man's land that led to Herod's Gate as round after round of automatic fire whistled past him. One tracer flew inches from his neck; his suit was showered with gunpowder. The next man across was shot dead as Khatib stood waiting by the gate, urging him to run.

For the next 24 hours, Anwar Khatib watched from the window of an office overlooking the Dome of the Rock as the Israelis advanced relentlessly on the city, taking the command posts at the police school and Mount Scopus, finally winning control of the high ground on Ammunition Hill after a desperate battle. In many instances, the Jordanians fought with extraordinary courage. Their resistance gave Ata Ali enough time to organize the withdrawal of much of his army, albeit in disarray. At 3 a.m. on Wednesday June 7, the Brigadier informed the Governor of his decision to pull out and urged him to do likewise. Khatib refused.

'If it is the will of Allah that I should die, I would not want to die anywhere other than Jerusalem,' he insisted.[2]

The first Arab brought to Colonel Motta Gur on Temple Mount was Anwar Khatib. There would be no further bloodshed if Khatib ordered his people off the streets until the curfew was lifted, Gur declared.

'I ask only that you take your flag down from the mosque,' replied the Governor. A few days later, Khatib reluctantly gave his approval for Israeli plans to evacuate Palestinians who wished to leave across the Jordan River.

After the battle for the police school, Sergeant Hanan Porat of the Parachute Brigade had prayed. Once they had stormed Mount Scopus, he had eaten. Following the capture of Ammunition Hill, he had written a note to his family, to be sent in the event of his death.

At Ammunition Hill, in the early hours of June 6, his men had fought bunker to bunker, trench to trench, one rooftop to the next. Some had vomited out of revulsion after hours of close combat, much of it hand-to-hand, which left the area littered with dead from both sides. At Ammunition Hill, his company commander had died in front of him. Only after the battle did he realize that he had defended the position standing on the corpse of his friend. 'My mind is preoccupied with Jerusalem,' he wrote. 'I think only of what it will mean to be in Jerusalem.'

The following day, Porat was among the second wave of Israeli paratroopers to follow the trail of corpses, shell holes and burning cars that led to Temple Mount. He had not slept for three days, but he felt no trace of exhaustion. Just 24, and fighting in his first war, Porat had driven his men forward with a passion than came close to fury.

'There is only a sense of exhilaration,' he noted. 'If I think about it, I suppose it seems shocking, rather inhumane. But it is pure joy. For me this battle is the beginning of a process I have prayed for all my life,' he added. 'After 2,000 years we are going home to begin again.'

At 11 o'clock on Wednesday June 7, Sergeant Porat trotted across the flagstone plaza in the courtyard of al-Aqsa mosque and down the narrow steps to the Western Wall. The large rectangular blocks of grey-rose stone, resting one on the other, were all that was left where Solomon's Temple had once stood. The long, narrow alley was crammed with dozens of heavily armed Israeli soldiers, most of them oblivious to the sniper fire that crackled through the streets around them.

Porat, still helmeted, armed and loaded with the paraphernalia of war, stood close to the wall and rocked back and forth in worship.

'Blessed is the Lord,' he prayed. 'Blessed is the King of the Universe who kept us in life and sustained us and enabled us to reach this time.'[3]

By that Wednesday morning, the Moghrabis had not eaten a full meal for almost three days. Hassan, the father, had gone out two nights earlier to try to buy food, but had fled back home when he heard shooting outside the Old City wall. By Tuesday afternoon they could hear the battle coming closer. Insaf, the mother, cursed the fact that all of them had refused to believe the war would really erupt. Then, once it did, they had refused to believe it would spread to their quarter of Jerusalem. The following day, Sergeant Porat and the paratroopers captured Temple Mount, less than a hundred yards from the small, three-room cottage where Hassan Moghrabi, his wife and five children lived.

Some time around 11 o'clock the shooting stopped, although they could still detect the sound of armoured vehicles rumbling through the narrow stone streets. Huddled together with his family in the kitchen, Hassan Moghrabi did not dare to voice the fear his neighbour had expressed the night before. The neighbour believed the Jordanians had left and that the Israelis were coming. There had been no mention of it on Radio Cairo; they were still boasting of Egyptian successes in the battles of the south. As for Jordan Radio, it had been silent since Tuesday morning. The neighbour thought this meant the worst. He had been told there were bodies lying in the streets of the Old City. The stench was terrible, his neighbour said. He had also heard about foreign troops coming into the city from the road north, the road leading to Ramallah and Nablus. The people had gone out to greet them, thinking they were Iraqis, maybe Syrians, as the radio had claimed. The way Hassan's neighbour told it, the people were stunned to discover they were Israelis. After that conversation they had both agreed it was wiser to wait indoors, for reliable information.

Around midday on June 7 1967, with Israeli flag-raising, prayers and victory celebrations well under way on Temple Mount, the

Israeli army finally relayed the news to the 135 families who lived alongside the Moghrabis. The simple announcement was broadcast by one of Motta Gur's paratroopers. Hassan Moghrabi wrote in his diary: 'They tell us we have nothing to fear as long as we follow the curfew. We are to wait for further orders.'

The Moghrabis, like most other families in the quarter, stayed indoors as the celebrations brought thousands to the Western Wall and Temple Mount. Out of sight but so close, sound provided the family with the only indication of what was happening. They heard soldiers singing, they listened to the wailing of those at prayer. They heard but did not recognize a trumpet volley from a *shofar*, the ram's horn that called the faithful to worship. It belonged to the army rabbi who had visited the wall declaring: 'I, General Shlomo Goren, chief rabbi of the Israel Defence Forces, have come to this place never to leave again.' The next time the Israelis spoke to the Moghrabi family, it was to order them out. On the night of June 10, at the end of a Jewish Sabbath which had seen thousands of Israelis visit the Western Wall, an Israeli officer marched through the narrow lanes of the quarter giving everyone three hours' notice to leave once and for all.

'Everyone gathered whatever they could, and loaded it up on carts, donkeys, bikes,' Moghrabi wrote that day. 'My wife has been beside herself. She has been so worried about the children that she forgot her purse on the kitchen table. It has all her jewellery.'

A chorus of screams and wailing rose from the Moghrabi quarter as families moved en masse to Zion Gate at the Old City wall. The Israelis illuminated the area with floodlights, then a giant bulldozer moved in, demolishing the houses with what Hassan remembered as breathtaking speed and efficiency. The Israelis searched every building before they knocked it down. Even so, at dawn, the demolition teams found an elderly Palestinian woman in the wreckage of her home.

Mahmoud, the eldest of the Moghrabi children, was five at the time of the 1967 war. A year after they had fled, he and his father returned to the ruins of their home. By then the Israelis were laying foundations for the piazza which ever since has welcomed world Jewry to the Western Wall. A Moroccan Jew was in charge of the construction. In Arabic more reminiscent of Casablanca than Jerusalem, he gave them permission to search the debris of the family home.

Hassan found what he was looking for, his small library of books, buried deep in the rubble. Close by lay the remains of the family cat. For a year, Mahmoud had refused to believe the cat was dead. The child would carry that memory through life; the bitterness he felt then led to hatred and militancy as he grew up.

Eighteen years later, on October 1 1985, and 2,000 miles away, on the coast outside Tunis, Palestinian rescue teams were digging through the rubble of Yassir Arafat's headquarters when they found Mahmoud's body. By then he had become a member of the PLO's Force 17, the elite commando unit that guarded Arafat. Force 17 had in turn become the target for the Israelis seeking revenge for a PLO attack on Israelis that had taken place a few days earlier.

Mahmoud Moghrabi was asleep when the F-16s, the American-made Phantoms of the Israeli air force, flew in low over the cluster of villas and apartment blocks that served as Arafat's command post. The building where he was billeted took a direct hit. He died instantly.

Beside him in the rubble, they found his diary. One entry, titled 'June 1977, 15 years old', said:

'My father tells me he has read about the Indian leader, Mahatma Gandhi. My father believes Gandhi had the right way. It is called passive resistance. I cannot accept that, for the first time I cannot accept what my father says.

'The only way the Zionists will listen is if we meet violence with violence. I have my own experience of that, so I have made my own mind up about it.'[4]

Twenty years stood between the Jewish ecstasy and Arab despair of 1967 and the political deadlock of the 1980s. In that time, Motta Gur had entered politics, Anwar Khatib had gone back to his law practice, Hanan Porat had become a leader of the Jewish settlers' movement on the West Bank. As for the Moghrabis, they had moved to the Mount of Olives just outside the old city. Each was a microcosm of the Israeli and the Palestinian experience in the years since 1967. Each represented the conflicting views of the Jewish and Arab societies thrown together by the Six-Day War.

Gur joined the Labour Party of Ben-Gurion, Eshkol and Golda

Meir. In spirit and deed he represented the traditional wing of the movement that had led Israel from independence in 1948 until its first electoral defeat in 1977, at the hands of Menachem Begin's Likud Party. By the 1980s, the soldier who had commanded the operation that so changed the map of the Middle East spoke as a politician who now must live with its consequences. He voiced self-doubt and misgiving.

'Looking back, I know we had no choice in 1967,' Gur recalled in an interview in 1986. 'The Arabs had opened fire first in Jerusalem. We had to counter-attack. It was bound to lead to us taking the Old City and then the territory beyond, the West Bank,' he submitted. 'But there was no time to stop. We didn't have time to consider what we were doing, or where it would lead us.'[5]

Instinctively, he went back to the early 1960s. The Israeli army had assigned him to produce a master-plan for the conquest of Jerusalem. He remembered how Ben-Gurion, Prime Minister from 1948 until 1963, had rejected the plan out of hand. In Ben-Gurion's view, the capture of Jerusalem would have signalled a quantum political leap Israel could not contemplate for generations. Israel, Ben-Gurion contended, had to establish itself first and gain inter-national acceptance before embarking on such dramatic expansion of its borders. Ben-Gurion had called in second opinions from economists, lawyers, even anthropologists to back him up.

'They all felt the same,' said Gur. 'Not that the capture of Jerusalem and the West Bank was implausible. Rather that Israel would not be able to swallow it, to absorb it, to digest it if you like,' he explained. 'That was the thinking until 1967. The belief was that Israel did not need more territory, more room to live. What we needed was three, four, five million more Jews, not more territory. Or more Arabs, for that matter.'

By his own admission, Motta Gur never saw the discrepancy between government policy and military necessity when he con-quered the holy city in 1967. Such issues were overshadowed by the emotion and exhilaration of victory. But in the years that followed, Ben-Gurion's prognosis came to haunt him. At the time, the belief of most soldiers was that Israel's victory would prove a decisive move towards peace. In losing the West Bank, the Gaza Strip and Jerusalem, the Arab world had lost all of Palestine. Surely that would bring everyone to their senses, to the negotiating table. Moshe Dayan, Defence Minister in 1967, had told his army to wait patiently for the telephone call from King Hussein of Jordan or President Nasser of Egypt, to say they were ready to talk peace. So as not to jeopardize a possible truce, Dayan ordered Gur to present the most acceptable face of occupation to the Moslems of Jerusalem. An open-hearted, forthright character, Gur was comfortable with such diplomacy. As a child, he had grown up in a mixed quarter of Jerusalem. His father had worked for an Arab company. His mother had taught her children Arabic. He counted Arabs as friends and as neighbours.

'In 1967 I felt that we were doomed to live together, and that we would find a way to do it,' he remarked. 'It was going to take a few weeks, at worst a few months, but it was going to happen. Yet if I am honest with myself today, I have to admit that time has worked against us, not for us as Dayan believed. That was our mistake.'

Menachem Begin, the stubbornly independent leader who ousted the Labour Party from power in 1977, did not approach the future with such *laissez-faire*. Labour prime ministers such as Ben-Gurion and Eshkol belonged to the old school of Zionism which sought a socialist state capable of limited co-existence with the Arabs. By contrast Begin had grown up as a protégé of Vladimir Jabotinsky, a Polish Zionist who preached self-defence above all else. Begin joined Jabotinsky's paramilitary youth organization in Poland at the age of 15 and the experience shaped his entire life. 'A new specimen of human being was born,' he later wrote, 'a specimen completely unknown to the world for over 1,800 years, the fighting Jew ... We fight, therefore we are.' Every member of Israel's first generation of statesmen had been deeply affected by the holocaust, but Begin seemed more indelibly marked by it, almost to the point of obsession. 'He felt an overwhelming duty to make sure Jews were safe,' recalled one of his aides. 'It was not just a question of Israel. It was a matter of every Jew.'

A man of unshakable beliefs, Begin showed from the start that he saw himself leading a mission on behalf of the Jewish people. As a result, the Bible dictated his view of the world. Within two days of his election in 1977, he redefined Israel's approach to the land occupied during the June war. He insisted on calling the West Bank by its Biblical names, Judaea and Samaria; he turned to the prophets of old to justify Israel's historical claim to the territory. He espoused the sanctity of 'Eretz Israel', the region that in Biblical times would have encompassed Israel and the West Bank.

'They are not occupied territories,' he claimed. 'From now on I hope you'll use the term liberated territories.'

In Begin's Israel, religious Zionists such as Hanan Porat flourished. For the first decade after the 1967 war, Porat fought the political establishment to secure the right to return to the Biblical land of the West Bank, where his parents had lived briefly during the 1940s before a terrible Arab massacre in the early days of the 1948 war of independence. As a founder of Gush Emunim or 'Bloc of the Faithful', the ultra-chauvinist settlers' movement, he persuaded, cajoled, bullied and blackmailed those in power to make his spiritual odyssey a reality. Under Begin, no such pressure was necessary.

'Being a Jew is a matter of religion, land, nation and spirit,' he said in an interview in his new home, on the West Bank site his parents first settled 40 years before. 'I can be a Christian on Mars but I can only be a real Jew here. Begin recognized that. He saw a new breed of Jew.'[6]

To most Israelis, settlers such as Porat presented an enigma: unassuming, even self-deprecating in public yet ruthless in the private exercise of political power. A moderate among Gush Emunim, he was nevertheless a radical by anyone else's standards. What set him apart was a deep, at times blind devotion to a cause he considered divine. He was, by his own admission, close to mysticism.

Like many others who fought in the Six-Day War, and then became West Bank settlers, Porat had studied at an Orthodox seminary in Jerusalem founded by the late Rabbi Avraham Ha-Cohen Kook, the first chief rabbi in Palestine at the beginning of the century. Kook created a new wave of thinking, both in religious and national terms, primarily because he linked the Bible, Zionism and politics into one consummate process that heralded the redemption of the Jewish people. By the 1920s, Kook had perfected a vision of the world and history as a step-by-step programme leading, inexorably, to the Messiah's coming and the return of Jews to the promised land. The pre-Messianic age explained the rise of modern Zionism, the emergence of its founder Theodor Herzl, the convening of the Basle Congress of Zionists in 1897 and its adoption of a programme aimed at the establishment of 'a home for the Jewish people in Palestine secured by public law'. Everything that followed – the Balfour Declaration of 1917, the migration of Jews from Europe to Palestine, the conflict with the Arabs – formed part of the process heralding redemption. By the 1960s, Kook's son Zvi Yehuda had taken up the teaching of his father. Hanan Porat, studying under him in the months preceding the June war, learned of one continuous chain of events to this era of the Messiah. The rabbi interpreted every Jewish disaster, from the destruction of the First Temple by the Babylonians, through the holocaust, to the massacre at Gush Etzion, as God's will. God's teaching, God's preparation of his chosen people, the Jews, for the Messiah.

So Hanan Porat had gone into the battle for Jerusalem not just as a sergeant in Motta Gur's brigade but as a soldier of God, repentant for the 'sin' of not taking all of Palestine in 1948. Within three days he stood on Temple Mount, the apotheosis of religious aspiration for any Jew. It convinced him that his rabbi had spoken with a genuine spirit of prophecy. In the years that followed, the disciples of Rabbi Kook became missionaries with unshakable confidence in the divine authority of their cause. They rationalized the capture of Jerusalem and the West Bank as yet another stage in the long, sometimes painful Messianic process foreseen by the rabbi. They interpreted the war as the cue to make their radical view the majority one. Hanan Porat's personal mission, back to the home his parents first built in 1943, became part of God's design. Settlement, in all of the Biblical land of Israel, became God's will. Porat cast himself as a disciple who no longer questioned the modern-day legality or ethics of such settlement – or the effect it had on the prospects for peace.

'I am fighting for what God gave the Jews,' Porat claimed. 'The war of 1967 wasn't like the Americans beating the Japanese, or the British defeating the Nazis. It was God's war and God's call to the Jews,' he added, momentarily pausing before completing his thought. 'If anyone tries to give back this land, then I see another war, among the Jews themselves.'

During Begin's years as Prime Minister, the government and settlers imbued Israel with such self-righteousness and self-belief. The fear of liquidation, the memory of the pogrom and the ghetto, provided the spur. The Bible lent the moral justification. Israel, Begin argued, marked the fulfilment of Biblical prophecy. Never again would the simple Jew be the victim of hatred and prejudice. Such thinking made the West Bank both a means to the end of

27

ensuring Israel's security and a divine mission leading to redemption. Such leadership gave free rein to those who sought to populate the territory with Jews and so pre-empt any exchange of land for peace with the Arab world. In the eyes of Begin, families like the Porats, born in Poland, represented the persecution every Jew had known. In his view, Hanan Porat voiced the desire of the nation at large to prevent a repetition of the holocaust. Begin's Israel made extremism acceptable, his leadership fostered a dramatic new climate in which the fanatic thrived. Tens of thousands of Jews, living in 'liberated territory' that was supposed to be only temporarily occupied, provided ample evidence that extremism paid off.

Only in the mid 1980s did the Labour Party of Motta Gur return to power, and then at the head of a coalition government which included Begin's successor, Yitzhak Shamir. By that stage the settlers had achieved most of their goals: more than 120 settlements in the West Bank and Gaza. Ever since 1967, the exchange of land for peace had been the accepted formula for a final settlement of the Arab–Israeli dispute. It had been seen to work in the agreement reached by President Anwar Sadat of Egypt and Begin, the Camp David Accord. In 1982, the Sinai had been handed back to Egypt in return for full, diplomatic relations between the two countries and an end to the state of war. On the West Bank, that formula was no longer feasible or practical.

Israel paid a price, however, for its extremists inside and outside government. In 1967, Motta Gur and Hana Porat had been members of the same brigade, dedicated to God and country. Twenty years later, they represented a society polarized by its policy on the West Bank. Gur repudiated almost everything Porat stood for. For his part, Porat called his former commander well-intentioned but hopelessly naïve.

On the Arab side, Anwar Khatib and Hassan Moghrabi symbolized the dramatic changes that took place within Palestinian society after the disaster of 1967. Unlike Israelis, Palestinians had enjoyed little political freedom under Jordanian rule in the years leading up to the war. A traditional hierarchy – a wealthy, land-owning, educated aristocracy – ruled with benign neglect and in deference to the Kingdom of Jordan. The working-class peasant or small farmer had no say in the running of his life. Policy was made in Jordan, it was executed by pro-Jordanian bureaucrats such as Khatib. Israeli occupation ushered in a new era. The after-shock of monumental defeat, and the oppressive nature of Israeli rule, brought about the rapid demise of old school leadership and the rise of the PLO. Just as occupation created Begin's new breed of Jew, so it spawned the Palestinian nationalist.

In 1967, the PLO of Yassir Arafat was a movement in its infancy, numbering just a few hundred students, academics and workers scattered throughout the Arab countries. Occupation made the PLO the vanguard of the Palestinian cause, capable of enlisting young recruits from the territories and the refugee camps of Lebanon, Syria and Jordan. The Israeli presence on the West Bank and Gaza Strip provided the *raison d'être* for a movement which preached the politics of violence as the only viable response to Jewish dictatorship. Personal experience taught people on both sides to vacate whatever middle ground existed between Israelis and Palestinians.

Typically, before the 1967 war, Hassan Moghrabi had faith in the Israelis and he believed in the possibility of Jew and Arab co-existing in the land of Palestine. His grandfather had come to Jerusalem from Morocco at the turn of the century. The family settled in the Moghrabi quarter of Jerusalem, taking its name from the area in which they lived: the Moroccan district of the city, teeming with families newly arrived from the Maghreb desert of North Africa. In the early 1960s, Hassan had inherited the hardware store his grandfather had started. One generation had bequeathed to the next a basic respect for the Jews. His grandfather had grown up alongside a Jewish community in Morocco. He had passed down his childhood memories of Jews in Casablanca who had been as resourceful as they were peaceful. A lively intellect in his own right, Hassan had read beyond the norm for a man of his education. His understanding of the Jews before 1967 made him believe that it would be possible to live together afterwards.

'I was not as gloomy as many of our neighbours when the Israelis came in 1967,' Moghrabi recalled during an interview. 'The Jews suffered so much in their lives, under Hitler and in Arab countries where things were not as good as they were in Morocco. I did not foresee great suffering for us,' he maintained. 'I saw no reason to

29

think it would be like 1948 when so many Arabs were made refugees. I did not believe that was the Jewish way of doing things.'[7]

The loss of the family's home destroyed that notion of compromise. For the first time in their lives, the Moghrabis became refugees. At first they moved to Jordan, but the dire poverty and deprivation of the camps forced them to return to Jerusalem. As their children grew up, watching parents trying to rebuild their shattered lives, the occupation took its toll.

The diary of Mahmoud, the son who joined the PLO and died in Tunis, provided a rare insight into why young Palestinians turned to militant nationalism in the years after the Six-Day War. As a child, he despaired for his family as they sought shelter in Jordan. 'Everywhere we went,' he wrote at the age of nine, 'Jordanian soldiers would shout at us. "Why did you run away from your country? We don't want you here." I think the Jordanians are cowards.' As a teenager, he believed passionately in demonstrating against the occupation. 'We have to make the Israelis aware of our grievances,' he wrote in 1975. 'Isn't that democracy?'

Arrested for the first time in 1976, at the age of 14, he acquired a dire cynicism about his future. 'There is a routine. Three times a day I get a beating, it comes with the meals,' he noted during an initial spell in jail. 'When I won't confess, they turn me over to the courts. I get a fine and a suspended sentence,' he continued. 'Within a few weeks, I'll be back in jail and it will begin all over again. They [fellow prisoners] tell me the food gets worse, so too the beatings.' His diary recorded 19 arrests in the course of the next two years.

Shortly before leaving Jerusalem to join the PLO, in the late 1970s, Mahmoud summed up his feelings towards the Israelis. 'We have now lived with the Jews for a number of years,' he wrote. 'They have eaten from my table and I have eaten from theirs. They have learned my language and I have learned theirs,' he explained. 'But time did not help. Time made the injustice of it all that much greater. Time planted hatred and vindictiveness instead of love and affection.'[8]

Mahmoud Moghrabi spoke for a generation that grew up under occupation, learning to despise the Jordanians almost as much as it loathed the Israelis. For this new breed of Palestinian, Jordan bore responsibility for the loss of the West Bank and the plight of the

Palestinians living there. Whatever control King Hussein had exercised before the 1967 war, it was steadily eroded in the years afterwards. Alone the King might have settled for an accommodation with Israel. With the PLO gathering such strength, however, he had no such option. Hussein, ruling a population comprised mainly of Palestinian refugees from 1948, lived with the constant nightmare of the Palestinians taking over his country. In 1970, he almost lost his throne during the civil war of 'Black September' with the PLO. In 1973, he refused to join Egypt and Syria in the Yom Kippur War against Israel. Much as he had learned a bitter lesson from the defeat of 1967, he was incapable of making peace with the Israelis as long as the PLO remained such a danger to his family dynasty and such a force on the West Bank.

In the circumstances, Yassir Arafat assumed the mantle of undisputed leadership. An Arab summit in 1974 anointed the PLO with the title that became its slogan: the sole, legitimate representative of the Palestinian people. For nearly a decade, Arafat reigned supreme. He raised billions of dollars from the oil-rich countries of the Gulf, he built an army lavishly endowed with Soviet weaponry, he created a mini-state in Lebanon close to Israel's northern border. Increasingly, Palestinians under Israeli occupation looked to the PLO for salvation. Yet the battle for Palestine became a trap for all concerned. The politics of guerrilla action gave the Israeli government a pretext for Jewish settlement: the more violent the tactics used by the PLO, the more brutal the Israeli reprisals. The endless cycle of violence on both sides enlisted more volunteers for the Palestinian cause while strengthening Israel's determination to stay on the land for ever. Few talked of partition any more, but rather of war to the bitter end.

In such a climate, moderate politicians like Anwar Khatib became relics of the past. By 1987, Khatib was still drawing a salary from the Royal Palace in Amman. He lived in the Governor's residence, paid for by the Jordanians. By an anachronism of history, he remained theoretically in charge of a bureaucracy loyal to the Hashemite Kingdom. His survival allowed the Israelis to foster the belief that occupation was temporary, the Jordanians to claim that they had forsaken neither territory nor people.

Yet the Israelis had long since stopped courting Khatib as a possible partner for dialogue; even King Hussein had ceased to look upon his Governor as a figure through whom to wield

31

influence. Always an advocate of compromise, Anwar Khatib had paid the price for doing what old-style Palestinian leaders had always done: co-operate with the colonial power of the day.

'If Motta Gur told you time was working against all of us, I have to say I agree,' he remarked in an interview at his home in 1986. 'Look at the new generation of Israelis, brought up in the image of supremacy created by the 1967 war. They're fed on the rhetoric of power. They are educated to believe Jerusalem and the West Bank were given them by God,' he explained. 'They are brought up on war against the Palestinians. That, after all, was what the [1982] war in Lebanon was about.'

In poor health, Khatib stopped to catch his breath before turning to his people. 'Then look at our Palestinian youth,' he added. 'They have been fed on the rhetoric of resistance. They have been educated to think no one else should have a share in this land. Their upbringing has been Israeli occupation.' His voice rose in despair rather than anger. 'Will these new generations ever negotiate?' he asked. 'You tell me.'[9]

It was supposed to be a secret, cloaked in a mystery all of its own, masked with instant denials on both sides.

Yet, in the years after 1967, the generation responsible for the war negotiated face-to-face in search of a solution. King Hussein met Israeli leaders, shook hands with them, exchanged gifts, spoke at length formally and informally. Sometimes it meant a clandestine rendezvous in Paris, the world's press having been given false leads in the hunt to track down a King or a Prime Minister who had disappeared out of public sight for a day or two. On other occasions, it was arranged by a helpful third party such as the British, the King using one of his many private visits to London to talk to the Israelis.

In extreme circumstances, at a critical moment in the secret negotiations, the King had been known to pilot his own helicopter into the small airport at Atarot, close to Jerusalem on the West Bank. On such occasions, as in the summer of 1986, the Israelis invariably offered to escort him to the Old City, promising special security arrangements to eliminate the fear of discovery.

But, down the years, King Hussein had always refused that which he acknowledged as his greatest wish – to see once again the holy sites of Jerusalem, to visit once more the Dome of the Rock. Dinner and discussion over, the King and his bodyguards flew back across the West Bank to the Royal Palace in Amman.

Still, whatever the secrecy, the risks, the disappointments and setbacks, the quiet diplomacy created an understanding of sorts. More than anything else, the covert meetings explained the remarkable similarity of opinion that developed in the 1980s between Hussein and Israelis such as Abba Eban: scholar, states-man, diplomat, Israel's Foreign Minister during the Six-Day War and a pillar of the Labour Party ever since. The two men had first met in September 1967, a matter of weeks after the war ended. To talk to them both twenty years later was to sense the common ground such politicians shared – and their mutual inability to reverse the process that began in 1967.

With the hindsight of 20 years, they both regarded the June war rather than 1948 as the turning-point for the Middle East.

'I feel now, as I felt then,' said King Hussein in an interview in 1986, 'that the war should never have taken place. It was one of those unfortunate moments in history when one loses control over events, and tragic developments tend to steer a course for them-selves, by themselves, ultimately leading to disaster.'

Contrary to what the Israeli leadership had believed at the time, Eban judged 1967 as the major obstacle to eventual peace, not the catalyst for negotiations.

'The totally one-sided nature of the war, with 100 per cent victory for us and complete defeat for the Arabs, made peace then impossible,' he said at his home outside Tel Aviv. 'It created excessive over-confidence on our part and excessively bitter frustration on theirs. For any Israeli to think that the shock of defeat would shake them into peace was a total misunderstanding of the Arab psyche.'

The years since, both men argued, had served only to deepen the hostility and suspicion between Arab and Israeli. Each looked to the other to make the first move and so break the cycle of bloodshed and war. Each doubted the willingness of the other to take the risks involved. Eban chided Hussein for not following the example of the late Egyptian President Anwar Sadat in seeking peace with Israel. Sadat's historic visit to Jerusalem in 1977, and the subsequent peace treaty with Israel, had proved that Israel was prepared to make concessions for peace.

'Frankly, I am amazed that over the years the King has not played the supreme card, the ace that is his,' he said. 'The only variable left in the Middle East equation is public opinion in Israel; it is the one factor that could change everything. Sadat showed that the Arabs control the Israeli domestic equation, they have it in their power to change the mind of Israel. In 1977, it was Sadat. Today it could be King Hussein and the Palestinians.'

Characteristically, the King displayed the caution that had ensured his survival for more than three decades. Israel, he acknowledged, needed help; the moderates within Israel such as Eban had to be encouraged before the extremists destroyed the prospects for a settlement. By 1986, however, he questioned Israel's ability to make the concessions peace demanded.

'The problem is not the belief in peace,' the King explained. 'It is what Israel is prepared to give in return. Perhaps Israel has been hardened by war. Perhaps Israel sees no interest in peace, unless it is on its own terms. I sometimes ask myself whether, after so many years, Israel is capable of peace.'

As for the situation in the occupied territories, where more than 1.3 million Palestinians lived under Israeli rule, they both diagnosed the dilemma facing Israel. The longer the occupation lasted, they said, the more difficult a negotiated settlement became. Israel, declared the King, had placed itself in a corner.

'What does Israel plan to do with the Arabs living in the territories?' he asked. 'Drive them out? Incorporate them into Israeli society? Treat them as second-class citizens and adopt a policy of apartheid? And, if so, where is the democracy Israel keeps boasting about?'

Eban was hardly more sanguine about the prospects. Israel, he maintained, could no longer contemplate the return of all the territory captured in 1967; yet the occupation had such a dramatic effect on the country's moral and political standing.

'How can we maintain the state of Israel against the wishes of a third of the population?' he questioned. 'We either give them a place in our system, at which point they hold the balance of power. Or we do not give them civil rights, and Israel becomes a South Africa. That is already the pattern in the West Bank and Gaza.'

Neither man acknowledged it openly, but they both recognized the fate that had been common to both in the years since 1967.

For his part, the King knew that he had become increasingly isolated from the people of the territories. Two decades of Israeli occupation there had indeed nurtured a sense of Palestinian nationalism that looked not to him for leadership, but to the PLO and Yassir Arafat. Since the Six-Day War, the King and Arafat had shared the gamut of political emotions: first, political marriage in the aftermath of 1967, then civil war in the wake of disagreement in 1970. In the 1980s, after Arafat was driven out of Lebanon by the Israelis, they united once again, only for it to end in acrimonious separation in early 1986. By 1987, and the 20th anniversary of the war, Hussein was trying to regain control of the West Bank politically, economically and diplomatically. His hope was either to force Arafat to heel or, if that failed, to create the kind of credible Palestinian leadership among the people of the territories that would enable him to take his case to the Israeli public and negotiate, as Eban had suggested. But the battle for the loyalty of West Bankers could not hide the fact that, after 20 years, the King faced exactly the same dilemma as in 1967. Then Palestinian refugees from the war of 1948 had made Jordan a country of two peoples, Jordanian and Palestinian. Then the King had chosen war as the way out, in the vain hope of winning back Palestine and so solving his Palestinian problem. The exodus of Palestinians after the 1967 war left his country with a Palestinian majority. By 1987, peace offered the only realistic way out for him and his people. Yet Hussein knew that to take Sadat's road to Jerusalem, as Eban had urged, would make him even more vulnerable to the wrath that cost Sadat his life.

As for Abba Eban, he had become a lonely figure both within his own Labour Party and the country at large. If he saw the Middle East equation as a paradox, then so too was his own career. In 1967, his Churchillian rhetoric had made him Israel's finest advocate abroad. More than anyone, he had been responsible for creating that image of the Israeli David facing the Goliath of the Arab world. He had preached the cause of peace with a passion that won hearts and minds the world over. 'Let us build a new system of relationships from the wreckage of the old,' he said during one memorable speech at the United Nations that June. 'Let us discern across the darkness the vision of a better and brighter dawn.'

Since Begin's election in 1977, however, Eban had been out of government and out of step with the fierce, earthy nationalism of modern Israel. Publicly, he insisted that Begin's leadership marked nothing more than a detour off Israel's main road since 1948. Privately, though, this elder father of the Jewish state suggested Israel had passed him by. His demise mirrored the transformation that had begun with the victory of 1967. Whenever he reflected on the spirit that had given birth to Israel, he voiced the same dismay. 'Looking back to the beginning, I feel a certain discomfort,' he said in 1984. 'We created a Utopian image. We predicted that our new state would be a light unto the nations . . . my speeches were replete with noble commitments, to democracy, equality, social justice,' he recalled. 'Now I wake up in the mornings with a twinge. Did I help create excessive expectations?'

Eban and King Hussein, whose reign was almost as old as Israel, belonged to the same generation of leadership. It came of age in 1948, it went to war in 1967. As the generation responsible for that war, they believed it was their responsibility to break the deadlock created in those six days of June. A solution, they argued, would be beyond their successors.

As the 20th anniversary of the war approached, they diagnosed the same threat – to themselves, to their countries, to the world at large.

'The continuation of the state of "no war, no peace" is a prescription for disaster,' remarked the King. 'The continued occupation of the West Bank is a time bomb. It has to be defused before it is too late. And we do not have much time left.'

'The worst possible scenario is the maintenance of the status quo,' concluded Eban. 'It makes Israel like no other country in the world, ruling a people who form more than a third of its population against their will. It gives the Arabs their only excuse for another war. It leaves us all living in a volcanic tranquillity. The only question is: how long is the fuse that will lead to the explosion?'[10]

The tragedy of the Middle East was that such a meeting of minds had never led to formal negotiations. Far from breaking the deadlock, the secret dialogue enabled both sides to maintain that status quo. In time, the state of 'no war, no peace' became the most attractive option for all concerned because there was no realistic alternative. The consequences were as frightening as they were predictable.

36

For Haim Albades, a commander of the Israeli police in Jerusalem, the demonstration at Temple Mount had become an annual ritual almost as old as Motta Gur's moment of triumph in 1967.

Every year a small group of Jewish demonstrators gathered at dawn outside the entrance reserved for Moslems and Gentiles who wished to visit al-Aqsa mosque. In 1986, the Jews could not muster more than a few dozen of the faithful. It had been the same the year before. Still, they formed a picket line in front of the gate. All of them wore the *kippa*, the skullcap that symbolized respect and fear of God. Most were shrouded by the *tallit* or prayer shawl. Many carried the *siddur*, not so much as a declaration of faith as of intent. One of them had a revolver, half-hidden in his back pocket; another had a sub-machine-gun slung over his shoulder. Commander Albades, a blunt yet affable character, faced the same chore each year: to keep them out and so maintain the peace between Jew and Arab in the holy city.

At 8.00 a.m. the battle of wills began. For the Jews it was Tisha Be'Av, the holy day of mourning for the Temple. They prayed in memory of the first synagogue, destroyed by the Babylonians 587 years before Christ. They grieved over the loss of the Second Temple, razed to the ground by the Romans in the first century A.D. And they claimed a God-given right to worship that day on the site where they envisaged a 20th-century replica. It was of no concern to them that the Moslem world revered the place as the holiest shrine after Mecca and Medina; that the Israeli government denied them permission to enter; or that their chief rabbi had taught that the coming of the Messiah, and only that, could herald the creation of the Third Temple in Jewish history.

> 'Because He who controls the Temple Mount,
>   controls Jerusalem.
> And He who controls Jerusalem,
>   controls the land of Israel.'[11]

On the other side of the gate, clearly visible from where the Jews assembled, activity was furious. From dawn the Mufti, the spiritual leader of the city's Moslem population, had assigned dozens of young men to guard the courtyard surrounding al-Aqsa mosque and the Dome of the Rock. According to Islamic legend, God took the prophet Mohammed up into heaven from this site. Modernists might have regarded it as a mystical exaltation, but Islam portrayed it as a literal journey, with the prophet transported on a white steed boasting a peacock's tail and a woman's breasts. Now the Mufti's guards defended the shrine against the so-called Jewish infidel. They carried no weapons, no copies of the Koran. They gave no hint of worship. Looking down on the entrance where the Jewish demonstrators waited, each was a study in concentration and barely disguised anger. For the Moslems of Jerusalem, the Jewish holy day of Tisha Be'Av had become an annual event in their calendar.

> 'Because Glorified is He who carried his servant by night
>   from Mecca to Jerusalem...
> A place to be blessed
> A place to be defended at all times.'[12]

For as long as he could remember, Haim Albades had spent the holy day on duty there. He too had a ritual to be observed. For the first few hours, he would keep the demonstrators back. Then, after a decent period of argument and insult, he would allow them to move up to the gate but no further. He shared a joke with his officers. Negotiating with these Jews, he said, was like dealing with the Arabs. Never give them what they want immediately, he submitted. Always make them wait.

'We are proud Israelis, devout Jews,' claimed Gershon Salomon, the well-dressed gentlemanly figure who led the demonstration. 'We have the backing of thousands of ordinary Israelis who think the way we do.'[13] That was not exactly a lie, nor was it quite the truth.

The Jewish demonstrators called themselves Neemanei Har Habayit, literally the 'Faithful of the Temple Mount'. Formed shortly after the 1967 war, they numbered about 150. Contrary to Salomon's definition, they were anything but representative of mainstream Israel. Many were veterans of the Jewish underground that had used terrorism to force the British out of Palestine in the 1940s. Others came from Gush Emunim, the group that spear-headed settlement on the West Bank. They were supported by an American rabbi, Meir Kahane, a self-confessed racist who advocated the expulsion of all Arabs in the name of creating a purely Jewish state. For many years they thought and acted like a new

38

Jewish underground. They kept their charter, a step-by-step programme for the Jewish take-over of the holy site, a closely guarded
secret. They covertly trained young Biblical students for animal
sacrifice, a rite practised during the period of the First Temple.
And in an undercover operation, carried out by young religious
zealots, they stockpiled building materials, religious artifacts, even
the pure linen costumes to be worn by the priests of their futuristic
Temple.

Ever since the Six-Day War Israel had dismissed the Temple
Mount faithful as a lunatic fringe of national life. To the average
Israeli, more concerned about unemployment and inflation, or
health and education, such campaigns were irrelevant nonsense.
Almost unnoticed, profiting from the public indifference, the
faithful enlisted the support of right-wing politicians, leading rabbis
and orthodox Jewish communities the world over. Menachen
Begin's philosophy had legitimized such crusades and the West
Bank had created a precedent: the settlers of 'Judaea and Samaria'
had set an example for other minorities, however small, to follow.
In the Israel of the 1980s, the consequences were no longer
necessarily as important as the principle of the Jewish return to all
the promised land. Not surprisingly, Gershon Salomon and the
Temple Mount faithful felt time was on their side.

'Legally, the precedent has been set. Philosophically, even
politically, the decision has been taken,' Salomon explained. 'What
has happened on the West Bank will happen here on Temple
Mount. What the Jewish people have won back in war, they will
make theirs in peace.'

On the other side of the gate, Jerusalem's Moslem leader,
Sheikh Saad al-Din al-Alami, responded fiercely. 'Any attempt to
build a synagogue on this site would be tantamount to a declaration
of war,' he said. 'And Moslems are prepared to die for this
place.'[14]

The demonstration served one purpose, it mirrored the stalemate of the past – and the danger posed by the future.

2
A CITY OF
TWO TALES

'Might is right, and justice in the interest of the stronger.' – PLATO, THE REPUBLIC

It took 10 minutes to walk from the Jewish settlement of Kiryat Arba to the centre of the Arab city of Hebron. Yet the three Israeli settlers who formed the 'supervision team' would not dare venture out on foot.

Piling into their open-backed jeep, their weapons in hand, they drove down past the checkpoint that marked the exit from Kiryat Arba and turned left on to the steep, winding road that led to Arab Hebron. Reaching the end of a half-made track, they turned right and began their descent into the Azzoun quarter of the city, a maze of backstreets and alleys where Arab children made a pastime out of pelting Israeli vehicles with stones. The 'supervisor' sitting in the rear raised his gun once every so often to let everyone know that the 'sheriffs in the grey jeep', the nickname given them by the Arabs, were in the vicinity. Only settlers had guns. That made them almost as impervious to attack as they were immune from the law.

Reaching the house of Zeyad Jabari, they found no one at home,

41

only two labourers busy at work on a simple, white stone cottage near completion. Referring to Israeli government maps which defined the precincts of Kiryat Arba, the supervisors decided on demolition of the Arab's property. This section of the Azzoun quarter, they reasoned, was designated for the future development of Kiryat Arba, specifically an extension of the settlement's all-Jewish industrial zone. They could not allow a new Arab house to be built, just as they had not tolerated the erection of electricity pylons nearby a few weeks before. One of the 'supervisors' called the command post at Kiryat Arba on the jeep's short-wave radio. That afternoon a huge, yellow bulldozer arrived from the settlement. Within an hour, the demolition team had reduced Zeyad Jabari's future home to debris and dust. After that, the 'supervision team' from the Kiryat Arba town council moved on to bulldoze down two freshly-laid pylons that connected scores of Arab families in the Azzoun quarter to the local grid. The 'sheriffs' of Kiryat Arba, their anonymity guaranteed by the refusal of local Jewish leaders to divulge their identities, drove back in the jeep to the settlement.

'Confusion reigns in Hebron,' reported Israel's leading newspaper, *Ha'aretz*, in recounting the incident on January 14 1983. 'It is a kind of helplessness, a form of anarchy, seasoned with the knowledge that there is no one to talk to, no one to ask for help.'[1]

Of all the cities of the West Bank, Hebron exposed the most extreme face of Jewish settlement and Palestinian nationalism in the years after the 1967 war. It spawned more bloodshed, hatred and emotion than any others. No other city symbolized the conflict that followed the Six-Day War quite like Hebron. Tension between Jewish settlers and local Arabs existed throughout the West Bank, but Hebron touched the raw nerve of that conflict because Jews tried to live alongside Arabs and to make it one city for two nations.

Beginning in 1968, Jewish settlers imposed their will first on the people of Hebron and then on the government of Israel. In the early days, they squatted, they demonstrated, they built illegally. They created what they called facts: settlements that no government could dismantle in the name of peace. In later years, they took the law into their own hands. The sheriffs of Kiryat Arba were representatives of a group of settlers taught by experience to take unilateral action and argue about it afterwards. In the process, this

42

sprawling, squalid city reshaped and redefined the hatred between Arabs and Israelis, re-enacting a tale as old as the Bible with a passion almost Biblical in its intensity. As a result, Hebron became the litmus test of Jewish intentions on the West Bank, the watershed for the Palestinian response to occupation – and the principal arena for the wider Arab–Israeli conflict.

The struggle for Hebron assumed such dimensions that it became a source of concern and dismay for not just the Arab world but Israel's allies in the West. Only the main Jewish protagonists seemed unconcerned. As early as 1976, Rabbi Moshe Levinger, the religious and extra-parliamentary political leader of the Hebron settlers, had spelled out his vision with brazen honesty. A devout follower of Rabbi Kook and his interpretation of the 20th century as the pre-Messianic period, Levinger viewed settlement as the Jewish renaissance. The Arabs, in his mind, had a straight choice – either to be absorbed into Israel or expelled. As for the question of Jewish democracy and peace with the Arab world, he was characteristically blunt.

'The Jewish national renaissance is more important than demo-cracy. Democracy can no more vote away Zionism, or settlements, than it can decide that people should stop breathing,' he declared in an interview with the *Jerusalem Post*. 'Peace is not in itself a goal ... Right now, the advancement of the Jewish people and the redemption process are more important than some hypothetical peace.'[2]

In the decade that followed, Levinger made Hebron the class-room for the settlers' movement. The victories he won here served as models for settlement elsewhere in the West Bank; the defeats he turned into lessons with which to refine the strategy of his followers. This gaunt, ascetic figure, so careless of appearance that he looked like a modern-day prophet, emerged as the arch-manipulator of government policy in the West Bank, and the arch-enemy of the Palestinians as well as many Israelis.

'He would sit in my office for hours and explain why he was going to riot in the streets,' recalled a former Military Governor of Hebron, Yehoshua Ben-Shachal, in 1984. 'The man had a vision. He was fighting for Hebron. It always worked out for him.'[3] Levinger's wife Miriam put it another way. 'Auschwitz we can't fix, what Khomeini is doing to the Jews of Iran we can't fix,' she said in 1982. 'But Hebron? Hebron we can fix.'[4]

On Wednesday June 7 1967, the third day of the Six-Day War, Hebron fell to an Israeli army that was able to advance on two fronts, from newly-captured Jerusalem and the south. At noon, just two hours after Temple Mount had fallen to Colonel Gur, the Jordanian army had withdrawn from the city. By nightfall the Israelis had arrived. The Palestinians offered little resistance.

The following day, Defence Minister Moshe Dayan headed south from Jerusalem to Hebron. His memories of that journey, he was later to recall, were filled with images from the Bible, images of ancient sites he had explored during his younger days as a scout and budding archaeologist. For him the territory was both a strategic prize and a host of potential digs. He thought of Shiloh, where the Israelites had brought their tabernacle under Joshua; of Tekoa, the birthplace of the prophet Amos; of Beth-el, the site of Jacob's dream, Samuel's judgement, and the place where Saul, the first king, gathered his army to face the Philistines; and of Anathoth, home of the sage Jeremiah.[5]

That morning, as he took the narrow, winding road that led from Jerusalem, past Bethlehem, and then down into Hebron, Dayan was struck by the tranquillity of this Biblical land. The hills that filled the horizon on either side were in full bloom. In the groves and vineyards, Arab farmers were working the rocky, terraced soil that had been their livelihood for centuries, as if unaware that a war had been fought. But the city itself presented a stark reminder of the conflict. Under curfew and the control of an army that had orders to shoot on sight, Hebron was deserted. In streets normally teeming with thousands of farmers, merchants and businessmen, the silence somehow shocked him.

When Motta Gur had captured Temple Mount, Dayan had joined the celebrations there the minute he heard the news. Now, in Hebron, he made straight for the mosque at the cave of Machpela: a site which, after Temple Mount and old Jerusalem, represented the holiest of shrines in the Holy Land to both Moslem and Jew. Abraham, the forefather of both nations, had reached Hebron with his family, his flocks and his herds two thousand years before Christ. Here he had built the first altar to his Lord. Here he had buried his wife Sarah, after buying the cave of Machpela from Ephron the Hittite for 400 shekels of silver. Abraham too had been buried here, in the tomb that later became the burial ground for Isaac and Jacob, Rebecca and Leah.[6]

For the next 3,000 years, Hebron had been the capital for monarchs ranging from Royal David to Herod the Great, a garrison for the empires of Egypt, Rome and Byzantium, the key to the ancient trade-route of the patriarchs running from Mesopotamia to Africa. In A.D. 638 the Prophet Muhammed had captured the city; and apart from the Christian Crusades in the 11th and 12th centuries, Hebron had remained in the hands of the Moslem world until the night preceding Dayan's arrival.

Dayan the soldier stood in awe of what his army had captured. Dayan the politician could feel an uncharacteristic humility. The amateur archaeologist, however, was less than overwhelmed. Down the centuries, Hebron's many rulers had converted the cave of Machpela from synagogue to mosque to church. Different architects had erected their own halls of prayer, added their own minarets, even fashioned the doors of every room to suit the style of their dynasty. Yet Dayan drew inspiration from the history he saw depicted all around him. Hebron, he reasoned, symbolized the integration of race, religion and creed under the regime of the time. Furthermore, Jews had lived there not just in Biblical times but from the Middle Ages onwards. In the 15th century, a small Jewish community fleeing from Christian persecution in Europe had settled in Hebron alongside Arabs, building their own schools, hospitals and even synagogues. Their enclave had survived until 1929, when Arabs killed dozens of Jews living in the casbah of the city and forced those who escaped to run for their lives. In Hebron, Dayan saw the chance to re-establish a Jewish presence as old as the Bible and as recent as British rule in Palestine.

For their part, the Hebronites, or Khalilis as they were known in Arabic, enjoyed the reputation of being supremely pragmatic, adaptable, far more so than any other Palestinian community on the West Bank. (In Arabic, Hebron is Khalil al-Rahman, Friend of Allah the Merciful, in reverence to Abraham, father of Ishmael, the first prophet recognized by Moslems, as well as the forefather of the Jewish nation.) Their hilltop city, so fertile with its gardens of olives and grapes, so isolated from the world outside by the Judaean mountains, had forged a unique identity based on self-sufficiency, tradition and religious faith. To the Arab way of thinking, the Hebronites seemed overly conservative, devoutly

45

religious, somewhat backward – and a suitable butt for the many jokes told about their naïveté and ignorance.

Yet, in the minds of Westerners and Israelis, Hebronites had proved masters in the art of survival. Resourceful farmers, astute businessmen, canny traders, they had successfully migrated to every corner of the territory and the Arab world. In Jerusalem, Nablus, Jenin and Ramallah, they formed the nucleus of commercial life. In the capitals of the Arab states, from Saudi Arabia to Yemen, the Hebronites had installed themselves as civil servants, factory managers and accountants directing the ambitious development plans generated by petrodollars. Their conservatism generated a rare dynamism. Their religious faith was the cornerstone of their success. That had made them, notionally at least, partners for the Jews in the past. To Dayan, they seemed natural allies in his attempt to make the city a laboratory for an experiment in co-existence.

Summoning the Arab leaders of Hebron a few weeks later, Dayan unveiled the doctrine integral to any understanding of what happened on the West Bank in the years that followed. Just as Hebron had been the dominion of others for 4,000 years, he argued, so now its fate would be decided not by its people but by Israel. If the Arabs behaved, there was the carrot of reward. If they resisted, there was the stick of heavy-handed occupation. Speaking personally, Dayan had stressed his vision of an 'invisible occupation'. The Israeli army would remain at hand but out of sight. Israel would use the West Bank for defence but not for settlement. Arab and Jew would learn to live with each other but not together.

On the evening of August 1 1967, Dayan and the then Mayor of Hebron, Sheikh Mohammed Ali Ja'abari, signed an agreement. It made the Tomb of the Patriarchs in Hebron the future gauge of the relationship between their two peoples in this city. 'All of us, Jew, Moslem, even Christian, have a claim to Hebron,' Dayan said. 'So no one's flag will fly over the Tomb of the Patriarchs. But all of us will have access to the holy site. Jews will have their appointed hours for prayer, so too the Moslems. Jews will be free to visit, but not to live in Hebron.'[7] Jew and Moslem had lived in peace here in the past, he concluded. Hebron would stand as proof of the common wish to do so again.

Neither man lived to see the next generation of Palestinians and

Israelis turn their model for living together into a breeding ground of discrimination, religious fundamentalism and terrorism. Yet, unwittingly, they were the architects of the plan that divided the city after their deaths. Paradoxically, their doctrine of compromise created hostility on both sides.

'Dayan's policy was no policy at all,' recalled Shlomo Gazit, the general's right-hand man in the territories during those first years after the war. 'It was a recipe for maintaining the status quo. It did that. But it also created a vacuum and opened the way for the extremists on both sides: Jewish settlers and the PLO.'

Nabil Ja'abari, the Sheikh's son and one of the heirs to the family dynasty, took that argument one step further. 'On the Israeli side,' he said in a 1986 interview, 'the vacuum was filled by cowboys carrying the Bible in one hand and a gun in the other. On our side, it meant the PLO, brandishing the olive branch of peace or the Kalashnikov rifle.'[8]

The Jewish settlers of Hebron and the PLO made unlikely partners, but they formed an unholy alliance that dictated the pace of the Jewish return to Abraham's city.

Ever since 1967, the PLO had made Hebron its prime arena for resistance to Israeli occupation. From the schools, factories and farms of the Hebron district, the PLO's network of underground leaders recruited young Palestinians for a cause that derived untold impetus from the behaviour of Rabbi Levinger's settlers. Armed with rifles, grenades and explosives smuggled across the river from Jordan, the military cadres of Hebron launched a wave of attacks on the Israeli army in the first years after the June war. Slowly but inexorably the pattern was set. For each guerrilla strike, Rabbi Levinger demanded a concession on settlement – and every killing deepened the divisions within the Israeli government on a policy for the West Bank.

Kiryat Arba, created in 1972 as an antidote to Levinger's campaign of squatting in Hebron, did not conform to Dayan's vision of co-existence. But it met the demands of cabinet colleagues who supported Jewish settlement as a line of defence against PLO insurgency from Jordan. 'The wall has been breached,' said Levinger as he moved his home to Kiryat Arba in September 1972. 'Those who believe they can turn back after this are fooling themselves and the Arabs.' Few Israelis believed him then. They would recognize the folly of their indifference a decade later.

For most of the 1970s, Levinger turned his attention elsewhere. First he spearheaded the drive to create settlements in Samaria, winning round after round of the legal and political battle to instal Jews in that northern sector of the West Bank. The sites that Dayan had recalled from the Bible – Shiloh, Beth-el, Sebastia – fell to Levinger's army of religious zealots and young pioneers recruited from *yeshivas*, Orthodox seminaries, both at home and in the United States. But by 1979 Levinger was ready to mount a sustained attack on the centre of Hebron. In April that year, he launched a campaign that, in time, would return scores of Jews to the city that successive governments had denied him. In the process, innocent civilians on both sides would be murdered, terrorism from both Arab and Jew would become a fact of life; and the PLO and the Jewish settlers became locked in a symbiotic relationship, each feeding off the extremism of the other, each providing the other with the excuse for perpetual conflict. In the process, the split personality of the Israeli government emerged into the open, shattering Dayan's naïve vision of peaceful co-existence. As Binyamin Ben-Eliezer, Military Governor of the West Bank at the time, noted: 'It was an unwritten alliance between the settlers and the terrorists. No one could stop it.'[9]

Levinger's campaign began with the settlers taking action as they had done throughout the 1970s: seizing a site, then squatting on it in defiance of government orders, and finally winning permission to remain there. The difference in tactics this time was that they occupied property in the heart of an Arab city on the West Bank: Hadassah House, a disused clinic that had been opened by the Jews of Hebron at the turn of the century. The difference in government was that, this time, they had the unqualified support of many cabinet ministers: among them Prime Minster Begin and Ariel Sharon.

'Abraham, Isaac and Jacob lived in Hebron,' wrote Miriam Levinger, the rabbi's wife, in her first newsletter after she and a group of women settlers broke into Hadassah House and set up barricades in April 1979. 'King David didn't live in a fenced-off Kiryat Arba. He lived with his wives and children in Hebron. There are historical truths that one cannot compromise on and

Hebron is one of them. Give it time. The government will recognize the truth.'[10]

Within a year, the government had indeed accepted the Levingers' literal application of the Bible to the 20th century and the PLO had provided both the excuse and the rationale. When a PLO gunman killed a young Jewish settler in the casbah of Hebron, Levinger turned the victim's funeral into a massive political demonstration, calling on the government to grant the settlers permission to set up permanent homes in the centre of the city. 'This young man's blood has given us life,' the rabbi declared. 'Can Israel turn its back on those who are persecuted for being Jews?'

A few weeks later, in March 1980, Moshe Dayan lost his increasingly lonely battle in government. The cabinet voted overwhelmingly for Jewish settlement in the centre of the city. That decision marked a volte-face Hebron lived with ever after. It gave the Jewish return to the city a logic as well as a momentum of its own. It transformed Miriam Levinger's sit-in at Hadassah House from an illegal occupation into a government plan for the re-establishment of the Jewish quarter of the casbah. It made settlement a direct consequence of Palestinian counter-attack. And it was only the beginning.

On a warm Friday evening in May 1980, four gunmen took up position on the rooftop of the Arab shops and houses across the street from Hadassah House.

They were led by Adnan Jaber, a young West Banker who had fled with his family to Jordan after the 1967 war and who had been sent to the Soviet Union by the PLO to train as a commando. The group also included Mohammed Shubaki, a young Hebronite who had been recruited to the PLO a few months before. Their orders came directly from Abu Jihad, military chief of Yassir Arafat's Fatah organization, then based in Beirut. They waited until a large group of Jewish worshippers, many of them Americans studying at Rabbi Levinger's *yeshiva*, were returning from Sabbath prayers at Abraham's tomb, and then opened up with automatic rifles and hand grenades. Six settlers died, 16 were wounded. It was the single worst incident in the city since the slaughter of 1929.

'I am sorry that the situation has reached this point,' Jaber later told foreign reporters allowed to interview him. 'But as a fighter I have to carry out orders.'

Within 24 hours, the Israelis had deported the Mayors of Hebron and neighbouring Halhoul, Fahd Kawasmeh and Mohammed Milhem. Both were outspoken supporters of the PLO, both were accused of inspiring violence by advocating armed resistance. Blindfolded and gagged, both were taken from their homes and driven to the Lebanese border in northern Israel. Arafat and the PLO celebrated their arrival in Beirut as a propaganda victory.

Within 48 hours, Begin's government, besieged by settlers demanding permission to occupy the centre of Hebron, gave the go-ahead for plans to move the settlers into two other sites close to the casbah. The outrage in cabinet was such that Begin authorized Rabbi Levinger and Gush Emunim to take action without recourse to government. For the next four years, the settlers enjoyed a freedom of action they had never known before. Yet such licence from the government was still not enough for some.*

Immediately after the mass funeral for those killed by the PLO, militant Jewish settlers called a meeting at Hadassah House. Those who attended were well-known figures among Levinger's movement. Menahem Livni, formerly a captain in the Israeli army, acted as the rabbi's chief lieutenant in Hebron; Natan Nathanson was head of security at Shiloh, one of the first settlements to be built in Samaria; Yehuda Etzion, from the Ofra settlement north of Jerusalem, led an underground group already planning to blow up the al-Aqsa mosque on Temple Mount in Jerusalem. Levinger was there, along with two other rabbis from Kiryat Arba, Eliezer Waldman and Dov Leor.

'We were incredibly tense after the funeral,' said Benzion Heineman, a businessman and prominent Jewish settler who joined the others. 'Livni and Etzion talked about taking revenge for the boys who had been killed.'[11]

The settlers agreed that retaliation was called for. They sought

---

*In a written reply to a parliamentary question in March 1984, Interior Minister Yosef Burg revealed that between March 1980 and 1984 the cabinet took no further decisions on Jewish settlement in Hebron. In those years, the settlers created two new bases in the city: one in the old Jewish quarter, close to the synagogue, the other at Beit Romano near Hadassah House.

the guidance of their rabbis. According to their confessions years later, they obtained the blessings of Rabbis Levinger, Waldman and Leor; indeed Waldman was said to have volunteered to take part himself. Instead of turning to indiscriminate killing, as the Arabs had done, this new Jewish underground decided to strike at the top. They selected three Arab mayors who were outspoken supporters of the PLO on the West Bank, then divided themselves into teams of three to carry out the attacks. The plan was to injure rather than kill. The victims, said Livni, would serve as living symbols of Jewish wrath for years to come.

Judaism calls for 30 days of mourning. Exactly a month after the killings at Hadassah House, Natan Nathanson and two other settlers drove overnight to a fashionable suburb of Nablus, parking their car in the shadow of a large stone house. Carrying a bomb attached to a magnet, they scaled the fence that led to the garage. Nathanson crawled under a pale-blue Opel parked in the driveway and strapped the bomb to a steel plate just above the clutch. At eight o'clock that morning Bassam Shaka'a, Mayor of Nablus and a passionate advocate of the PLO cause, turned on the ignition and depressed the clutch. The car exploded in a fireball, blowing his legs off. At the same time, another car bomb maimed Karim Khalaf, Mayor of Ramallah. The third intended victim, Ibrahim Tawil of al-Bireh, escaped unharmed, but an Israeli army sapper was blinded as he tried to defuse the bomb placed under Tawil's saloon.

In the years after 1967, Israel had rarely questioned the motives of Palestinian terrorists. It expected violence from a people pushed into a corner by the politics of occupation and settlement. Many Israelis did not express surprise at the emergence of a Jewish underground: in their view, it was an inevitable consequence of allowing de facto co-existence in a city like Hebron. But Jewish terrorism changed the nature of the struggle for control of the West Bank. It destroyed whatever claim the Jews had to sanctity of purpose, it made that struggle a murderous battle of wills between two nations living in one territory. From that point on, the Palestinians did indeed face the choice Rabbi Levinger had outlined years before – either to accept Israeli occupation, and so commit national suicide, or themselves take the exile the Jews had suffered so long. In opting to stay, the Palestinians suffered a crisis of identity. So too did the Jews.

51

In the years that followed the 1967 war, the lanky, exuberant figure of Elyakim Haetzni became the scourge of both the casbah of Hebron and the office of almost every government minister of the day.

In the casbah, he would bargain with the mixture of good humour and anger that typified the man, delighting in the haggling of fixing a price, be it for a kilo of fruit or a piece of property. In the ministry, his tactics were much the same. He argued good-naturedly with those in power but he also berated them. In the absence of agreement, he did not hesitate to use the politics of blackmail. A fine intellect, his lawyer's mind sharpened by his wide reading of philosophy, Haetzni instilled a degree of fear and respect among both Palestinians and Israelis. He wielded neither the gun nor the Bible, one of the few Jewish settlers who did not. Yet he was a maverick in every sense, a self-defined political urban guerrilla. Others, such as Rabbi Levinger, were the leaders of demonstrations and sit-ins, the champions of the cause. But the settlements of Hebron owed as much to the influence of Elyakim Haetzni as they did to Levinger.

Haetzni was born in the northern German port of Kiel in 1926, three years before the killings in Hebron, seven years before Adolf Hitler came to power. The two events were linked explicitly in his own mind. The massacre and the exodus from Hebron separated Jews from the second holiest city of their faith. Hitler and the holocaust served as catalysts for the return of the Jewish people first to Israel, and then to Hebron. His longing for Hebron was born out of the schizoid split suffered as a child under the Nazis.

'As a child, I would spend my mornings in a German school, the only Jew in a class run by the head of the Nazi Party in Schleswig-Holstein. I would be teased, then taunted, mentally tortured,' Haetzni said in an interview shortly after leaders of the Jewish underground had been arrested in 1984. 'In the afternoons at the Jewish school I would read of Hebron, of David's city, of Solomon's wisdom, of the victory over Goliath. In the mornings I was the scum of the earth. In the afternoons I was the proud son of King David.'[12]

Fleeing from Nazi persecution, his family reached Israel in 1938 and the young Haetzni served in the Haganah, the Jewish Defence Force, in the war of independence 10 years later. After 1967 he

52

gave up a villa and his law practice in Tel Aviv to become the self-styled ideologue of the settlers' movement throughout the West Bank, especially in Hebron where he and his family made their home. Rabbi Levinger provided the spiritual leadership for the campaign of political insurgency. Elyakim Haetzni added the other dimension: self-justification. His philosophy made no reference to the Messianic vision of the Rabbis Kook; its roots lay in the political Zionism of Theodor Herzl. The lucidity of his argument made it the rationale many settlers used to defend Jewish expansion on the West Bank.

The return to Hebron, he explained, was fulfilment of both Biblical prophecy and the aims of 20th-century Zionism. After the war of 1967, the Jews had not forced the Palestinians to leave: as for the land, they had occupied only empty territory and disused property. His moral vision portrayed the Jews as merely coming home to that which was once theirs, seeking only to live alongside the Arabs – not to remove them. That, claimed Haetzni, conformed to Herzl's vision of co-existence between two nations who would live together in Hebron just as they might in Tel Aviv, Jaffa or Haifa. To talk of giving back the West Bank, then, represented a betrayal of modern Zionism. If any government wished to negotiate with the Arabs over Hebron, he argued, then surely it should bargain over Tel Aviv as well: because the West Bank was as much a part of Herzl's Palestine as the coastal plain. For him, the struggle for Hebron was no longer an Arab–Israeli issue. The conflict, he said, was being waged only among his own people.

'We Jews have an identity crisis,' he said in a second interview, in the autumn of 1986. 'It is in our genes. We want all the land of Israel, yet we want to remain a democracy. We want to retain our independence, yet we feel the need to be accepted by the Arabs,' he added. 'We want peace but the price peace entails, giving up land, means war. War among the Jews.'[13]

A witty man, with a capacity few Israelis had for laughing at themselves, Haetzni pointed to a picture on his living-room wall. It was an oil painting of the Avraham Avinu synagogue in Hebron's old Jewish quarter. Built in the 16th century, it was destroyed during the attack on the Jews of 1929 and rebuilt by the settlers in 1976. Labour Party leader Shimon Peres had authorized the reconstruction, he said. Peres, Haetzni chuckled to himself, the politician who advocated giving back the West Bank for peace.

'Why would Shimon Peres do that?' Haetzni asked, his voice suddenly acquiring the stridency of a criminal lawyer about to deliver the incriminating evidence. 'I know why,' he said. 'Because in the heart of every Israeli, and every Israeli politician, there is a settler, a little Gush Emunim. Peres, like the rest of them, is easy prey for us. We simply played on his heart strings.' He paced the room, laughing loudly. 'You people don't understand,' he concluded, 'but in his heart Peres is one of us. Call it the Jewish schizophrenia.'*

Elyakim Haetzni knew Idris Hirbawi as an Arab businessman who worked with the Jews. Government ministers, such as Dayan, recalled his case with a mixture of dismay and despair. Israeli army officers who knew Hebron saw families like his as evidence of the opportunities for co-existence Israelis had missed since 1967.

Idris Hirbawi was born in Hebron in 1926, the same year as Haetzni. Too young to remember the massacre of 1929, largely ignorant of the genocide being perpetrated by the Nazis in Europe, he nevertheless inherited a family tradition of co-operation with the Jews. When visitors called at one of his stores in the casbah of Hebron, he proudly produced photocopies of Israeli government documents listing his father and grandfather as being among those Arabs who had given shelter to Jewish families when the killing started in 1929.

'As a child,' Hirbawi said, 'I was taught that living together with Jews was a necessity, a duty we had to fulfil in the name of our survival. My family had always believed we had nothing to fear from the Jews.'[14]

Unlike the Ja'abaris, or the Kawasmehs, the Hirbawis did not represent a major *hamula*, or clan, of Hebron. Still, they had land, they had farms, they had stores dotted throughout the old city. Their claim was based on 700 years in Hebron, dating back to

---

*As Defence Minister between 1973 and 1977, Peres did indeed authorize restoration of the Hebron synagogue, although not Jewish settlement in the heart of the city. In a 1986 interview, he said: 'We did not imagine Hebron would develop the way it has.'

forefathers who had come here from Iraq as followers of the legendary Moslem crusader, Saladin. Down the centuries, they had always exploited the business opportunities created by the colonial power of the day, displaying the flexibility that was the hallmark of so many Hebronite families. For them, the rise of Hitler and World War Two heralded a period of unprecedented prosperity. Fearing the Germans would move to use the Arabs as a surrogate for their designs in the Middle East, the British reinforced the army in Palestine and sought to strengthen their control over the mandated territory. The Hirbawis, like many others, moved quickly to do business with the British and to bolster their political fortunes under a regime that then needed their support. They had done much the same under the Jordanians in the 1950s, building up the family's hold on the import of manufactured goods and the export of farm produce from a Hebron region that supplied the markets of the Arab world with olives, figs, dates and grapes. Taking control of the family concern shortly after the 1967 war, Idris Hirbawi believed Israeli occupation could make Hebron a commercial centre dealing with both the Israelis and the Arabs, enjoying what he called the best of both worlds.

'Hebron had always stood apart from the rest of the West Bank,' he said. 'We controlled our own lives, we made a good living whoever was in charge of us. That gave me great faith when the Israelis came. But occupation brought humiliation. It didn't happen immediately, it took some years, it started when the settlers moved in. The result was we lost our sense of well-being, our self-confidence.'

A blunt, rather acerbic character who peppered his remarks with caustic references to his fellow Palestinians, Hirbawi represented an independent Palestinian voice on the West Bank, committed neither to the PLO nor the Jordanians. His thinking, however, reflected the view of many ordinary Hebronites. His judgement of the past and the present synthesized the beliefs of a majority of the city's Arabs. The Israeli victory of 1967, he argued, marked the final stage of the movement to drive the Arabs out of Palestine. The Jews, he insisted, had not returned to Hebron to live alongside the Palestinians, as they had done until 1929. They had come back to remove them from the land once and for all. He had heard of Haetzni's argument, equating Hebron with Tel Aviv in the event of negotiations for peace. Hirbawi's reaction typified the feelings of many West Bank Palestinians.

'If the Israelis want to say that Hebron is the same as Tel Aviv,' he remarked, 'then what choice do the Palestinians have but to claim both? Any businessman could tell you: to give up your claim to one would weaken your claim to the other.'

At the mention of Haetzni's warning of the divisions among Jews, Hirbawi's strong, weather-beaten face cracked a rare smile.

'There is, on our side as well, a crisis of identity,' he said, telling his son to stay out of the argument. 'Like the Israelis we want peace. But the price of peace, giving up our claim to virtually all of Palestine, means war among ourselves. What Haetzni says about the Jews is true of the Palestinians.'

He barked an order to his son to bring him the file from the cabinet kept in the nearby paint shop. He patiently leafed through the court records, the lawyer's bills, the Governor's letters. The file documents the legal battle he had fought ever since the terrorist attack on the settlers at Hadassah House in 1980. The gunmen had used the rooftop of one of his properties opposite Hadassah. He knew nothing about the attack beforehand, he said. The first news he received was a note from the Governor, telling him that two of his houses were being bulldozed down immediately because they had provided shelter for the terrorists.

Stopping to search through the file, he produced a cheque from the Israeli government, payable to him through the Hebron branch of Israel's Bank Leumi. The government had issued the cheque, in the winter of 1980, after Moshe Dayan scolded his colleagues for having destroyed the property of a family well known in Hebron for the rescue of Jews from the 1929 massacre. Idris Hirbawi had never cashed the cheque, even though at the time it was worth more than $100,000. It was, he said, a point of principle, a last vestige of pride, an expression of family honour.

Ever since 1967, Khalil Wazir, otherwise known by his *nom de guerre* Abu Jihad, had been the military commander of Yassir Arafat's PLO. The years of exile from Palestine had dulled neither the emotional attachment nor the commitment to the homeland he lost as a child in 1948. The memories of the Palestinian exodus that year lingered, sustaining his will to order attacks on Israel, justifying to himself the righteousness of further bloodshed.

56

'The world always sees the Palestinians as being the people who fire first,' he said in an interview in Amman. 'Yet none of this would have happened if the Israelis hadn't taken the land in the first place. The Palestinians are not on the offensive. That is not true. Always we have been defending what is ours.'[(15)]

Did that make attacks on Jewish settlers legitimate?

'To me there is no difference between settlers and the Israeli army,' he replied, his voice betraying just a hint of anger. 'They carry guns, they serve in the military, they are part of the occupation. In my view, Rabbi Levinger is a terrorist. But you will not call him by that name because he is a Jew. And the world refuses to see the Jews as terrorists.'

What was the point of terrorism when it provided the Israeli government with a pretext for settlement?

'Violence is like a cry from the heart,' Abu Jihad insisted. 'The world doesn't listen to anything else. It is only through violence that the world will be made to stop and look at Israel,' he added. 'Israel has already shown its true face to the Palestinians. Now Israel is proving to the world just who the Jewish people are.'

In the summer of 1983, Abu Jihad had ordered a singularly brutal killing in Hebron. Four Palestinians attacked and stabbed to death a young American Jew in the city centre. His body was then dumped in the main street opposite the crowded market. Even by the standards of Hebron, it was an act of callousness and brutality. It unleashed a familiar response.

Within weeks, the Jewish underground exacted bloody revenge. With the encouragement of their rabbis, and showing none of their earlier squeamishness about inflicting the sort of massacre the Jews had themselves suffered often enough in the past, the Jewish terrorists dressed up as Palestinians to launch a horrifying attack. Using their army weapons and hand grenades, Rabbi Levinger's son-in-law and two other settlers stormed the Islamic University just outside Hebron as students gathered for midday prayers. They killed three, wounded 33 others. The hundreds who witnessed the attack would never forget the cries of those who lay dying in their own blood. As the victims were buried, local Palestinian leaders called for a holy war against the Jews of Hebron. They were arrested. Only a year later did the army round up the 25 known members of the Jewish underground.

'How is it that government takes measures against any Arab who throws a stone,' said Israel's deputy Attorney-General, Yehudit Karp, 'yet fails to bring to justice settlers who open fire on Arabs?'[16]

That question, voiced by many Israelis, symbolized the crisis of principle and philosophy which occupation had created. Since 1948, Israel had lived with Arab hostility; indeed it had provided the moral base for violent reprisals against Arab states which gave shelter and support to Palestinian guerrillas. After 1967, the emergence of the PLO had enabled successive governments to justify the harsh treatment meted out to Palestinians on the West Bank. In Hebron, Arab guerrilla action had been the spur for settlement inside the old city. Israel was at war, its leaders had argued. The PLO resorted to violence and sabotage so Israel should show few qualms about meeting terror with terror.

Yet the growing realization of the cancer within Israeli society was finally prompting the heart-searching so noticeably absent when the Jewish underground first appeared. Liberal Israelis were appalled by the evident reluctance of their government to deal with the underground. Rightly, they feared a cycle of killing and counter-killing that would spread from the territories to Israel itself. With some reason, they held Menachem Begin's government responsible for creating a climate of hatred and hostility which legitimized the Jewish terrorist. Understandably, they questioned the morality of modern-day Zionism.

Throughout, Begin displayed only ambivalence. Once an underground leader in the last years of the British Mandate, he believed the modern Jewish identity had been forged through the politics of violence. He had routinely applied the Biblical maxim of blood for blood since coming to power. For every attack on Israel, he had sanctioned massive reprisals, culminating in the 1982 invasion of Lebanon. On the West Bank, some army commanders had celebrated the car-bomb attacks on the Arab mayors in 1980. One cabinet minister had gone so far as to praise the 'positive aspects' of Jewish terrorism: it removed those Arabs who incited violence, it fulfilled a need no self-respecting democracy could meet. Such blatant betrayal of democratic principles aroused despair rather than anger among those Israelis who cared. Jewish terrorism, they reasoned, was the inevitable by-product of an occupation based on discrimination between Arab and Jew – and the abuse of the Palestinian majority by the Jewish minority. When he was arrested in 1984, underground leader Menahem Livni showed little compunction about explaining his thinking. The Jews had descended into the jungle of the Palestinians, as he put it, because Jewish lives were at stake. He quoted Menachem Begin in his defence. Begin, he said, told us to live with the sword in our hands and faith in our hearts.

Moshe Arens enjoyed a reputation for being blunt and forthright. His clipped, American English, a by-product of a distinguished academic career in the United States, tended to make every conversation a lecture. Invariably, though, Arens was open-hearted, thoughtful, disarmingly candid. In presenting the hawkish face of modern Zionism, he always appeared to be reasonable. Looking back on his time as Defence Minister in the mid 1980s, he blamed the Palestinians for the violence that spawned the Jewish underground and the plethora of settlements in ancient Hebron. He dismissed out of hand the suggestion that the government's appeasement of the settlers had been ultimately responsible for the bloodshed.

'Who started the killing?' he asked. 'The Arabs did. That didn't give the settlers an open ticket to go and kill as they pleased. But it certainly didn't stop me from authorizing more settlement. It wasn't a case of giving in to anyone. It was a matter of executing what the government had decided and what I felt was right.'[17]

He chided all those who judged Israel by the standards of the Western world. Coming from a man brought up and educated in the West, that sounded like a convenient excuse. Yet he passionately denounced what he called the narrow Western view of Jewish history and Israel.

'You don't understand,' he declared. 'We are not living in the West, whatever our common heritage. We are living in the Middle East. We are living with an Arab mentality that doesn't place the same value on life as we do. What is a Jew supposed to do? Lie down and die?'

Did that mean Jewish terrorism was a legitimate response?

'No,' he answered. 'What it means is that the only language is force, the only currency is strength. I don't expect the Arabs to like us, as you seem to believe I should. The only thing I expect from the Arabs is respect.'

Was that modern Zionism?

'It is practical Zionism,' he said.

The pragmatic approach explained how a secular politician like Moshe Arens shared a common language and so much common ground with a religious zealot such as Rabbi Levinger. Their relationship, based on a mutual interest that bridged the philosophical gap between them, mirrored the uncanny link between so many settlers and government ministers after 1967. Between them they installed Jews in the centre of Hebron on a scale that would have been unthinkable before Miriam Levinger's sit-in at Hadassah House in 1979. The limited numbers did not matter as much as the establishment of Jewish homesteads in the city. By the summer of 1984, settlers had moved in to four sites in the old Jewish quarter of Hebron. They were laying plans for new roads that would link them to each other. There was even a proposal for a highway to the mother settlement of Kiryat Arba. Yet by that summer, with a new government about to take over and committed to a freeze on settlement, time was running out. Levinger hatched a plot. In his final days as Defence Minister, and with the active support of acting Prime Minister Shamir, Arens saw it through government. It served as a classic example of how a small group of settlers manipulated successive governments to create facts on the West Bank before the Israeli parliament and public could stop them.

In the early hours of one humid August morning, three young families from Kiryat Arba moved secretly into the ancient site of Tel Rumeida, high on a ridge overlooking Hadassah House and the Hebron casbah. Three caravans were brought in; running water and electricity were supplied by the Israeli army. Arab residents of the city woke to discover a new Jewish settlement on land that until then had been half burial ground, half olive grove.

'These settlers are here to claim the right of the Jewish nation to this Biblical site,' said Rabbi Levinger the following day, by which time the Military Governor had ordered the army to guard them. 'This is an ancient burial ground,' he explained, 'the tomb of Jesse, the father of King David.'

'There is a decision by the Israeli government to establish Jewish settlements in Hebron,' said Yitzhak Shamir, referring back to the cabinet's decision to settle the Jewish quarter in March 1980. 'And Tel Rumeida is part of Hebron.' Said Chaim Bar-Lev, a leading member of the Labour Party: 'The gall and cheek of these people knows no bounds. Whatever happened to the rule of democratic government?'[18]

Familiar as such tactics were, this time the connivance of those in government could not be disguised. A few weeks before, the Justice Ministry department responsible for settlement had issued a secret memorandum, advising the settlers that any move on Tel Rumeida should be carried out 'secretly, in the dark, at night'. It was hardly surprising, since the same department had ruled in 1981 that settlement on the site could not be permitted since ownership was in doubt. The same department had warned then that Tel Rumeida was an ancient burial ground and that its potential as an archaeological dig would make settlement there 'unduly contro-versial'.[19] Now the secret memorandum had given Rabbi Levinger the green light to take action, what settlers called 'a nudge and wink to move'. They created a fact. They obtained the relevant authorization. They made Tel Rumeida government policy. The parties to the plan were Moshe Arens; the Israeli army officer who acted as Mayor of Hebron, Zamir Shemesh; and Yuval Ne'eman, Science Minister and chairman of the all-important cabinet committee dealing with settlement. Having moved in secret, at the government's suggestion, Levinger put the coalition to work.

Minister Arens gave his personal permission for the settlement. Mayor Shemesh sent in the army to guard it. Chairman Ne'eman called an emergency meeting of the cabinet committee. He alone attended. By himself, he passed a motion granting authority for the Jewish settlement of Tel Rumeida. In accordance with government procedure, as defined by the cabinet's decision of March 1980, it was legal. But that did not satisfy a Labour Party that was just days away from forming the next government.

'There has been no government decision allowing these people to stay here,' Bar-Lev said when he subsequently visited Hebron as Police Minister in the new cabinet. 'The only democracy in the Middle East didn't take a democratic vote on this.'

Moshe Arens was characteristically abrasive at the mention of Tel Rumeida. He denied any part in the plot, suggesting such language was insulting. Was it not evidence, though, of a split personality in government when ministers legitimized a settle-ment that had once been deemed illegal by their own Justice Ministry?

61

'I would acknowledge a certain schizophrenia in all of us when it comes to the territory,' he said. 'Settlement is a practical matter of security, and a political statement. There is as well an emotional factor no minister can deny,' he added. 'After all, we waited 2,000 years for this. We didn't wait 2,000 years to go to Uganda. We waited all that time to come back to Israel. And Hebron is part of Israel.'*[20]

April marked the anniversary of the Jewish return to Hebron. In 1968, Rabbi Levinger had infiltrated the city with 20 followers and taken up residence at an Arab hotel on the pretext of celebrating Passover. Many years later, Gush Emunim organized a massive celebration, bringing thousands of Israelis to Hebron, turning it into living proof of the slogan the settlers used: Hebron, a Jewish city with an Arab majority. By then the city which Moshe Dayan once saw as a symbol of future hope had become the microcosm of future struggle.

The buses bringing Rabbi Levinger's supporters came from the development towns in the north and south, the new cities of Ofakim and Netivot, Beit Shean and Kiryat Shmona, the places David Ben-Gurion had once seen as the future of Israel. Others had travelled in convoy from the poor neighbourhoods of Tel Aviv and Jerusalem, communities where the first generation of Israelis came from Asia and Africa. One huge contingent arrived from a city in the heart of Ben-Gurion's Israel, Afula, where family ties more often than not went back to Iran or Iraq, Morocco or Tunisia, North or South Yemen. They did not represent Israeli public opinion. Rather they symbolized the constituency Menachem Begin had nurtured and courted as he swept to office in 1977: Oriental, working-class, with a standard of education as low as their level of income. They formed what Begin called his 'working majority' – what his Herut coalition labelled 'the poor, the suffering, the oppressed'. They lived in Ben-Gurion's Israel. On that anniversary, they demonstrated in Begin's promised land: a measure of the dramatic transformation that Israel had undergone

---

*In 1900 the British offered Theodor Herzl a Jewish homeland in the East African colony of Uganda. He refused before the British proposal became an official offer.

since the days of Ben-Gurion, living proof of Begin's commitment to making all of Palestine the land of Israel.

In long lines, Rabbi Levinger and his settlers led the crowds from one site to another. First they visited the tomb of patriarchs, the Moslem and Jewish shrine that had imbued Dayan with his vision of future co-existence back in 1967. There they were met by a British-born settler, Rachel Klein. 'You can call it a mosque, a cathedral, whatever you like,' she said. 'As far as I am concerned, it is now a synagogue.'

The crowd, many of them laden down with children and picnic baskets, moved on to Hadassah House. Their guide was Avraham Ben-Yosef, an academic from Brooklyn, New York, now security officer for the dozen families who lived here in the main street of Hebron. 'The question is not who is in the majority here, that you can see for yourselves,' he said, pointing down the street to the crowded Arab market. 'The question is: what do we put first? The Torah (the Bible) or democracy?'

They stopped next in the original Jewish quarter of Hebron, directly behind the casbah. Fifteen families had returned here, excavating their homes from the sheer rock face of the ancient city wall. Chief among them were the Levingers, Moshe, Miriam and their 11 children. 'Who are the Palestinians?' asked Mrs Levinger. 'They have no history books, they have nothing like the Bible, they have no heritage. Who was their last Prime Minister? Who was their last King? They have no credentials.' She added: 'As someone who has credentials going back 4,000 years, I know that we are the ones to whom this land belongs.'

Escorted by the army, the crowds climbed the steep, narrow path that led to the final Jewish stockade in Hebron, Tel Rumeida. The sightseers had their first questions as they jammed into the small caravan that was home for Ettie Meidad and her two children. What was the point of being here, asked an elderly lady from the Negev town of Ofakim.

'Just as you settled the south,' replied Mrs Meidad, a strikingly attractive woman in her early twenties, dressed in a long, ankle-length skirt and headscarf, 'so we are now settling Hebron. We are sending a message out to Jews the world over just like you did.'

Was it safe? The question came from a young man who lived in Kiryat Shmona, on the exposed northern border with Lebanon. 'I shop in the Arab market, I take my children there,' said Mrs

Meidad. 'But I always fear the worst from the Arabs, I'm always conscious of their eyes. That's the best way to avoid being attacked. You see,' she added, consciously taking the crowd into her confidence. 'I don't expect the Arabs to give in to us that easily. If the roles were reversed, and I was in their position, I wouldn't. I would fight.'

The buses took the sightseers on a tour of the Arab quarters, then up on to the hill of Kiryat Arba. Driven round the settlement, shown its three schools, health clinic, orthodox seminary and shopping centre, they stopped at the industrial zone on the edge of the housing estate. There they were introduced to the latest converts to the cause of Jewish settlement, all of them Ethiopians, *falashas* or 'strangers' as they were called in their native Amharic. Most of them had been airlifted out of the famine-stricken Horn of Africa in 1985 under the secret government operation code-named 'Operation Moses'.

'Until I arrived in Israel, I had never heard of Hebron,' said one Ethiopian, a tall, handsome worker named Gideon. 'Now I understand that Hebron was the first Jewish city in the land of Israel. I do not think of history,' he confided, 'I cannot imagine what 4,000 years means. I can only understand my own experience, I can only relate to my own life. I know only that coming to Hebron rescued me from being a refugee in Africa.'*

Throughout the day, the Israeli army manned every entrance to Hebron. Hundreds of troops patrolled the casbah to pre-empt any Arab demonstration. Late that afternoon, they sealed off the city centre, forcing shopowners to close down and pedestrians to get off the streets. As dusk fell, Yitzhak Shamir, successor to Menachem Begin as both leader of Herut and Prime Minister, arrived as the climax to the celebration. After a plain orthodox meal, at the settlers' restaurant close to Abraham's tomb, Shamir reiterated his claim to the ideals and the constituency of Begin.

'Just as Jaffa was liberated in the war of independence in 1948 and was not given back,' Shamir said, Rabbi Levinger at his side,

---

*In the aftermath of the airlift, it was estimated that 100 Ethiopian families were settled on the West Bank. It was not a new policy. In the late 1970s, a number of Russian families allowed to emigrate from the Soviet Union were encouraged to settle there.

'so Hebron was liberated in the Six-Day War of 1967 and will never be given back.' He concluded: 'Hebron will be a leading city in Israel, in the land of Israel. Always.'[21]

As the Israelis toured Hebron, the city's 60,000 Arabs watched, unwitting guests at another nation's celebration: strangers, it seemed, in their land. With the army on every corner, the sullen, silent majority had turned away, displaying an indifference they did not feel, keeping their thoughts to themselves. As so often with the Palestinians on the West Bank, initial dismay turned into frustration. As the day wore on, frustration became acceptance of yet another fact. Only briefly, at Tel Rumeida, had anyone raised the murmur of a protest, an elderly Arab shouting at the sightseers as they had trampled across an olive grove.

'What do you expect me to do?' he cried as the soldiers marched him away. 'When a Jew walks on your land, he thinks about confiscating it.' It had been a wretched sight, an old man dragged away from a crowd that had no way of understanding his grievance. Some even cheered when he was put in the back of an army jeep and driven to army headquarters.

In the centre of the city, the storekeepers had tried to entice the visitors to buy, their Hebrew ringing out through the crowded alleyways of the fruit market and the casbah. For some, the reluctance of their guests to stop at a stall or step inside a store was irony itself.

'My family came originally from Iraq, following the Moslem crusade,' remarked Jawad Hanini, watching the crowds pass his shoe store on the edge of the casbah. 'Many of these Jews we are seeing today come from the same place. I can tell that from the little Arabic they speak. Yet do they stop and talk? Do I want to listen?' He paused, pondering the matter as though he did not wish to admit it. 'Do we recognize each other for what we once were, neighbours?'

In his house on the outskirts of the city, Abdullah Ahmed al-Suiri made his decision the moment he saw the first busload of visitors arrive. That day he had not worked in the small vineyard that had been in his family for five generations, more out of personal choice than fear. Whenever he could, he avoided contact with the Israelis.

'If I could, I would leave,' he said, reciting a list of families in the area who had moved out in the past few years as first the settlement of Kiryat Arba and then the neighbouring estate of Ramat Mamre were built around them. 'Much as you will hear Palestinians saying they will never leave, that is not the truth. Many have gone, many more wish to go. We do not have the heart or the stomach for this occupation.'

Suiri's three-room house, in which he and his two wives lived, stood on the main road that linked the two Jewish settlements. Throughout the day, thousands had walked between the two, passing his house and the building site that lay directly across the road from it. The site belonged to Suiri, it was part of the land his father bought during the British Mandate in 1936. Three years before, he had started a new home on the site. He had since been stopped by the Israelis. They had refused to give him a building permit.

'I go to the courts, I have a lawyer who is costing me almost as much as the new house would,' he said, busily searching a dimly-lit bedroom for the papers. 'We will lose, I know that, it is part of our belief as Palestinians that always we will lose. It is pride that makes me do it.'

Khaled Ossaileh was at home, far from the crowds and the soldiers surrounding one of his stores in the city. Sitting in his large, beautifully furnished apartment on a hill with a magnificent view of Hebron, he had been watching soccer from Europe on television with his children. With his open-necked shirt and shock of ginger hair, he could easily have passed for an Israeli. Calling in the maid to serve bitter-sweet coffee, Ossaileh presented a very different face of Arab Hebron.

'You don't have to like people to do business with them,' he said, recounting the number of Jewish agents through whom he imported everything from Pyrex glass to Sony stereo systems. 'When it comes to business, I have no problems with the Israelis.' Interrupted by a telephone call, which he answered in fluent Hebrew, he picked up where he had left off. 'But we have a saying in Arabic,' he added, 'that doing business is like a marriage. Both partners have to be satisfied or it is heading for divorce. On a business level, we can be satisfied. But on a political level, we cannot. So there is no marriage.'

Ossaileh was extraordinarily even-handed about what had

happened in Hebron since 1967. The Palestinians, he suggested, had wallowed for too long in self-pity. The Israelis, he countered, had lost control of the small minority represented by the settlers. The majority on both sides no longer cared because it saw no way out of occupation. The image that had come to haunt him was of two societies both facing a mental break-down.

'Look at Hebron today,' he said, walking to his balcony window. 'We have Jews from America, from Russia, from Iran, even from Ethiopia. Is this a Jewish return, or a Jewish invasion? Either way, I'm not sure the Jews know who they are any more.' He pointed to a group of Arabs below, making their way home from work, some of them riding donkeys, others bent over with bundles of firewood on their back. 'And who are the Palestinians?' he asked. 'Are we the *fellahin* [peasant farmers] of Hebron, are we the elite of the Arab world? Or are we the PLO, with guns in our hands?' He turned away, his voice dropping as his temper cooled.

'This is one city with two nations,' he concluded, 'leading each other to catastrophe.'[22]

3
POSSESSION IS
THE LAW

'I dream of more Jews, not more territory.' – DAVID
BEN-GURION TO CHARLES DE GAULLE – PARIS, 1960

For Ariel Sharon, Independence Day was always a moment for looking back and looking forward. Usually he spent the eve of the national holiday at remembrance ceremonies for the dead of the five wars Israel had fought since 1948. From the War of Independence to the invasion of Lebanon, Sharon had played a major role, first as a soldier, then as a general, finally as Defence Minister. His last battle, for Beirut in 1982, had made him the most controversial politician of his day in the Middle East.

Sharon cherished those holidays when he could retire to his farm in the Negev desert, one of the largest private homesteads in the country. Here he would adopt the role he enjoyed most, that of country farmer. His ranch was both home and a sanctuary from a world outside in which he was often an uncomfortable participant in the endless round of committee meetings, receptions and political rallies. Far from the political arena, Sharon assumed a private persona that bore little resemblance to his public image of perennial warmonger. As he relaxed over coffee and a cigar, there were glimpses of the warm good humour and charm which once made him so popular with his troops. As he reminisced about past successes on the battlefield and in government, Sharon once again became the commanding officer of his youth. Characteristically, he was intensely loyal to those who had supported him and scathing about anyone who had stood in his way. Left to his own devices, though, Ariel Sharon invariably became an unconscious parody of that public image of reckless adventurer and belligerent democrat. That evening was to prove no exception.

His focus was on the territories Israel captured in 1967: the Gaza Strip, where in 1970 he led a merciless, bloody campaign against the PLO; and the West Bank, where he had spearheaded the drive to settle up to 100,000 Israelis by 1987, the twentieth anniversary of the war.

Ariel Sharon had always been legendary for his maps. As a young field commander, seeking authorization for a typically bold, decisive strike against the enemy, Sharon had fought his first battles with the military establishment over maps and plans of attack. He had done much the same in cajoling, bullying and intimidating Begin's government into the siege of Beirut in 1982.

Now he had called for his son to fetch the map he had presented to Begin and the cabinet in August 1977. It was 10 years old, he said, but as relevant as ever. With that he laughed mischievously, then hauled himself out of his chair with the enthusiasm of a man savouring a moment he knew he would enjoy. Taking the map from his son, he spread it out on the coffee table and picked up a swagger-stick from the fireplace. With the presentation about to begin, it seemed impossible to forget the picture painted by his critics in cabinet during the Lebanon war of 1982. Some had accused him of tricking his colleagues into the siege of Beirut by drawing vague battle plans on the maps he brought to cabinet, then ordering his troops to overstep the line the government had agreed.[1]

Already Sharon had begun setting the scene in cabinet 10 years earlier. Begin's first government was then little more than a month old. He was Minister of Agriculture, his first portfolio. The map was his original master-plan for the West Bank. Sharon pointed out a cluster of blue and red dots around Jerusalem and Hebron. There were only 25 settlements on the West Bank when he took over at the ministry, he said. What he had proposed was 150 settlements with 100,000 settlers within a decade.

'Some laughed at me,' he said scornfully, nodding towards his wife Lily as though she too had had her doubts at the time. 'A few ministers thought it was preposterous. I remember one colleague who went as far as to call it madness.'[2]

For once there was a simple, genuine smile and then an expansive laugh that resounded through the room. Sharon's face, so much younger than his build suggested, bore witness to his satisfaction. 'Yet today we have almost reached those targets,' he said, returning to his map to show the mass of yellow dots marking settlements created since. 'Not quite as many settlements or settlers as we had hoped. But a lot more than some of my colleagues thought feasible in 1977.'

The Lebanon war, and the public criticism of his tactics in cabinet, came up inevitably. On the issue of the West Bank, his opponents had charged him with illegally seizing land for settlement. Indeed, for many years that had been the position of successive American governments. He brusquely dismissed such criticism, not out of anger, more out of boredom with what he and Lily called the same old lies.

'Contrary to what my critics say,' he continued, 'I have never taken any map, any plan into cabinet that was not realistic or achievable.' He went back to the map on the table, picking it up once again. 'This is proof of that,' he added. 'What we have achieved in the past years has been a miracle. I would say it has been a miracle comparable to the creation of Israel. We have won the only battle that is important in the Middle East, the battle for land.' He sat down, as if to say that was enough.

'And it's all been legal,' he added almost as an afterthought. 'If you're looking for criminals, you will write a very thin book.'

To the newcomer, settlements often stood out as the most striking feature of modern Jerusalem. Whatever the point of entry or exit, these large, impressive housing estates captured the imagination and dominated many first impressions of the holy city. The trunk road north to Nablus was lined with the settlements of Neve Ya'acov, French Hill, Ramat Eshkol. At the side of the highway east to Jericho and the Jordan River stood the future city of Maaleh Adumim. Heading south towards Bethlehem and Hebron, the visitor would find the township of Gilo. Together they formed the human and concrete ring the Israelis had built around Jerusalem since 1967 on land taken during the Six-Day War. Militarily, as tourist guides liked to point out, they offered a first line of defence. Diplomatically, they presented a negotiating obstacle that few politicians dared to mention when peace plans were discussed. Architecturally, they stood as monuments to Sharon's strategy, their façades more reminiscent of a Crusader castle or a medieval fortress than a new Israeli town. The Palestinians had long since given up the idea of demanding their removal. For their part, the Israelis had come to look upon these settlements as extensions of the city of Jerusalem; and Jerusalem, they said, was no longer negotiable.

Until 1967, the land of Gilo had been the predominantly Arab village of Sharafat. At the beginning of the June war, it had marked the dividing line between Israel and Jordan; the railway junction had defined the point where Israel ended and the Hashemite Kingdom began. The city boundary of Jerusalem stopped at the barbed wire that separated the Israeli army from the Jordanians. When the war broke out, Sharafat was designated the West Bank. Within two weeks of the war ending, however, the Israeli government formally annexed the Arab half of the city. Jerusalem, said Prime Minister Levi Eshkol, was being reunited after 2,000 years and would never be divided again.

To make it indivisible, the Labour government embarked on a campaign of building new neighbourhoods around the city. For that it needed land beyond the boundaries inherited from the Jordanians. In January 1968, the Israelis confiscated 1,000 acres of privately owned Palestinian land, some of it expensive real estate, to create two new suburbs north of Jerusalem, French Hill and Ramat Eshkol. In August 1970, they moved south. At a stroke, they seized nearly 2,000 acres of land belonging to the villagers of Sharafat. Within months, Jewish settlers were moving in to the first of some 10,000 apartments under construction in the newly proclaimed suburb of Gilo; and Gilo, the Israelis ruled, would be part not of the West Bank but of Jerusalem.

Hundreds of Palestinians fled the area, taking the compensation offered to get a new start elsewhere. A few stayed. Within the next few years, they were surrounded by tens of thousands of Israeli settlers. By the 1980s, they were living in the modern Israeli suburbs of Jerusalem, which boasted Orthodox schools, all-Jewish clinics, Israeli shopping centres and sports centres that few Arabs dared to use. By then the settlers' movement had undergone a radical change of both thinking and policy.

Rabbi Levinger's religious, right-wing nationalists no longer invaded the Biblical heartland of Israel, setting up camp wherever they could. Settlement had become the migration of young Jewish couples in search of nothing more complicated than a house with a yard and a two-car garage. They were secular, white-collar professionals, lawyers, accountants or government employees who carried briefcases rather than Armalite rifles and who chose their homes not on the basis of a Biblical map but by commuting times to Jerusalem or Tel Aviv. Just as the first generation of Israelis had converted the Arab land around Tel Aviv into the affluent, middle-class suburbs of Herzliyya, Ramat Hasharon and Ra'anana, so the second and third generations had transformed the territory around Jerusalem into the new dormitory towns of Maaleh Adumim, Gilo and Neve Ya'acov. Two generations before, the rapid expansion of Tel Aviv had pre-empted any attempt at a solution of the Arab–Israeli conflict. In the 1980s, the Jewish exodus throughout Jerusalem and the West Bank presented an apparently insurmountable obstacle to any peace plan hammered out by the Israelis themselves, the Americans and the Arab states.

'We never fooled ourselves that after us everyone would still be coming here waving flags,' said Israel Harel, a founder of Gush Emunim and chairman of the Council of Jewish Settlements. 'Our biggest success has been making settlement here such a natural thing that people, no matter what their political views, don't think of it as a dilemma any more,' he added. 'We have made the settlement process routine.'[3]

Michael and Naomi Grunzweig judged themselves to be typical residents of Gilo. Both native Israelis, he was a civil servant, she a computer programmer at the Hadassah Hospital in Jerusalem. Michael Grunzweig took some pride in driving around the township and pointing out the architecture. The fortress-like façade, with six storeys and flat rooftops that could be converted into ramparts, was designed for strong defence. The interior courtyards, with their attractive hanging gardens and oval arches, were built to give the army a clear field of vision in the event of a terrorist attack. He pointed out the slits in the iron grills that covered the windows. There was no room for a window-box of flowers, he suggested, but enough for a gun.

Together with their three children, the Grunzweigs lived in a spacious, well-furnished apartment of five rooms in the centre of Gilo. The children attended schools in the township; their parents had a short ten-minute hop into Jerusalem to their offices. With parks, cinemas, youth centres and shops at hand, Gilo offered a standard of living and a quality of life they could not afford in Jerusalem. They had moved here from another post-1967 suburb, Neve Ya'acov, because it meant more space each at a price that was unthinkable in the city.

'I do not consider that I am living on the West Bank,' remarked Mrs Grunzweig, a quiet, thoughtful woman who said she disapproved of the way settlers such as Rabbi Levinger behaved. 'I would never live on the West Bank. Gilo is Jerusalem to me.'

Her husband, a courteous, easy-going man in his early 40s, was not so sure. A geographer by training, he had served in the Israeli army as a guide in 1967; his job was to show troops the terrain that would be the battleground in those heady days of June.

'Where we are living now was, in those days, the West Bank,' he said to his wife. He added: 'Twenty years ago I could not have seen us living here, I would have thought it was too dangerous. But today it is part of Jerusalem. I suppose I could question the legality of it all. But down the years that has become blurred by the reality of a place like this.'[4]

Unlike their counterparts out on the West Bank, the Grunzweigs voiced no spiritual, ideological or emotional commitment to living there. In contrast to other settlers, they expressed a certain idealism, believing their presence in Gilo was not an obstacle to peace, but rather a catalyst for negotiations.

'If there is a purpose in living here, beyond meeting the needs of a family,' said Michael Grunzweig, 'then it lies in reminding the Arabs that they will lose their land if they refuse to recognize us and negotiate with us. I see settlements like this as a double-edged sword to be used against the Arabs,' he concluded. 'It shows them that there are consequences for starting the war of 1967, and losing it. It shows them as well that if they don't come to the table, then they will lose everything.'

Less than a hundred yards from where the Grunzweigs lived stood a small terrace of three houses whose original foundations were laid in 1949, the year after the birth of Israel. Each house had three rooms: only one had a bath and a kitchen. This amounted to home for peasant farmer Musa Salameh, his wife Fatima, their four children and twenty-five grandchildren.

The Salamehs fled to the West Bank in April 1948 after their village on the other side of Jerusalem was overrun by the Jewish Defence Force, the Haganah. The father, a cook in the British army in the days of World War Two, used the family's entire savings of 140 Palestine pounds to buy a two-acre plot in Sharafat.* They planted olive and apricot trees on most of the land, building the houses on the rest.

Musa Salameh, a gregarious, good-humoured figure dressed in an immaculately-tailored white *kefiya* and black gown, chuckled as he produced the papers that told his family's story. These were the deeds to the property and a Jordanian lawyer's contract stamped July 1949, notarizing the sale of seven *dunams* (almost two acres) owned by one Yussuf Saba to the Salameh family. Like most other villagers, he remarked with a rare frown knitting his brow, he never filed the deeds with the Jordanian land registry. His claim, and that of tens of thousands like him, rested solely on these documents.

The papers provided no defence as the Israelis expanded the new Jerusalem in the years after 1967. Musa Salameh's land was declared state property and he was offered compensation to make way for the settlement of Gilo. In 1973, with the village of Sharafat being levelled to the ground and Gilo already under construction, Israeli surveyors paid a first visit to his home, assuring him he had nothing to fear. But, in June 1976, the bulldozers came at first light. He and his wife were arrested that morning for standing in front of the demolition teams. By the time they were released, late that afternoon, the olive grove and apricot orchard that had been the family's livelihood for a generation had been destroyed. In the years that followed, the Israelis transformed their farm land into high-rise apartment blocks housing dozens of Jewish families, among them the Grunzweigs. The government spared Musa Salameh's home because he refused compensation and decided to stay.

---

*£140 sterling was approximately $300 US at the time.

'I suppose I knew this would happen,' he said, casting a glance outside at the huge housing complex that towered above his single-storey home. 'There was no point in going to court. They gave me a paper saying all this land was theirs. If I had gone to court, I might have lost this house as well.'[5]

If he had a regret, he said, it was that he did not move further away from the Israelis in 1948. His natural inclination was to become a refugee once again, to close his property, take compensation and make a new home beyond Bethlehem towards Hebron. But at 70 he was too old. His sons now had jobs as labourers on the Israeli settlements around Jerusalem. Each year brought another grandchild. His family felt trapped.

By the summer of 1986, the Salamehs were among a handful of Arab families still clinging to their homes in Gilo, defying warnings from the army to leave or face eviction. As the township grew and more Jewish families arrived, most had accepted compensation and left. In some cases, the Israelis had destroyed the houses of those who refused to make way for a suburb of 30,000 settlers. In June that year the bulldozers had demolished a property belonging to an elderly Palestinian widow named Halima Abdul Nabi. She had refused offers of $75,000 to leave her three-room cottage in the centre of the township, close to the reception centre where new Jewish immigrants were living as they waited for their apartments to be built. While she was in hospital, Israeli troops emptied the house and destroyed it. They needed the land for a parking lot.

'We went to watch it happen,' said Fatima Salameh. 'It was like going to a funeral. To me, it meant that we could expect the same thing to happen to us.' Said her husband: 'You know, from the Israelis' point of view, it no longer makes sense to leave us here.' He smiled to himself, toying with the irony of the thought that had crossed his mind. 'The Israelis always say that they are living in a sea of Arabs. So now we are living in a sea of Jews,' he explained. 'I know what the Arabs would do in this situation, they would get rid of us. Why should I expect the Israelis to act any differently?'

He stood up to look out of the window at the apartment blocks opposite his home. 'I have always felt Israel was fate for the Palestinians,' he said. 'Gilo was fate. It descended on us like some ancient God taking revenge on his enemies.'

The Jewish settlers of the West Bank saw Plia Albeck as something of a heroine, a constant symbol of the political will expressed down the years by Menachem Begin, Yitzhak Shamir and Ariel Sharon. To Palestinian landowners, she was responsible for the seizure of their land, living proof of Israel's desire to possess the territory at all costs.

The middle-aged lady at the Israeli Justice Ministry in east Jerusalem looked more like an orthodox Jewish housewife than a key figure in the history of the West Bank since the 1967 war. Yet, as the lawyer responsible for settlement of the territory, she had indeed played a major role for nearly 20 years. Since 1967, her office had approved the expropriation of more than 50 per cent of the West Bank. She had prepared the ground for over 130 Jewish settlements and she had defended the government in court against scores of Arab families suing for illegal seizure of land and property.

'I believe in the Bible and I believe in the process that returns the Jewish people to this land,' she remarked at the beginning of an interview in 1986.

Until Menachem Begin came to power in 1977, the Labour governments of Levi Eshkol, Golda Meir and Yitzhak Rabin had regularly seized land on the West Bank under special military ordinances as at Gilo, and to meet 'military needs', the euphemism used for creating a defence line out of Jewish settlements along Israel's eastern border with Jordan. That was the ostensible rationale behind settlements such as Kiryat Arba outside Hebron. In doing that, the Israelis had observed the Hague Convention of 1907 which permitted an occupying power to requisition land temporarily to meet military necessity. They may have been paying lip service to international law. But it left the door open for negotiations because, by the definition of the Israeli government, Rabbi Levinger had occupied Kiryat Arba temporarily. All that was to change, however, when Israel's supreme court ruled against Begin's government on one of Levinger's satellite settlements, at Elon Moreh, near Nablus, in 1979. The court declared that the army had presented no pressing, military need for land that had been taken from Arab farmers.

'It was clear to all of us that we could no longer continue to work in the way that had been used ever since 1967,' said Mrs Albeck. 'It was a watershed for settlement on the West Bank, forcing us to look elsewhere. And from now on, the need was no longer temporary. Mr Begin and Mr Sharon wanted a permanent basis for settlement.'

Mrs Albeck had subsequently become a self-styled investigator of land laws throughout the Middle East. In the months following the Elon Moreh judgement, she scoured the land charters of Palestine for an answer, or what others might call a loophole. She found it in the land law passed by the Sultans of the Ottoman Empire in 1858.

In common with British land law and that of most European states, the Ottomans had defined all land in Palestine as the property of the occupying power to be distributed at the discretion of the Sultans. The British had stuck by it during the Mandate, as had the Jordanians between 1948 and 1967. There were some restrictions, she noted drily. Anyone who had worked land for ten years could claim ownership. She claimed the basic premise of the Ottoman law entitled Israel to seize all land that had not been registered or farmed for a decade – and to declare it state property. Her interpretation provided a legal basis for Begin and Sharon. After the setback at Elon Moreh, their government seized vast tracts of the West Bank with little compunction and declared it state land for Sharon's master-plan. The Jordanians had registered just one-third of the territory before 1967. Sharon ordered Mrs Albeck to view everything else as Israeli unless proven otherwise.

The US government might have called it illegal, European states might have deemed it a violation of the Geneva Convention of 1949 and even Israeli lawyers could denounce their government for flouting international regulations.* But Mrs Albeck stood by her reading of history and the law with all the pride of an empirical scientist.

---

*The Geneva Convention specifically forbids the transfer of a civilian population of any occupying power to occupied territory. Israel denied it applied on the West Bank, saying sovereignty over the territory was not defined in 1967 and that the reference to the transfer of civilians was intended specifically to prevent a repetition of Hitler's transfer of the Jews. 'In other words,' said Palestinian lawyer Raja Shehadeh in 1986, 'the Israelis refuse to accept an international law which, by their own definition, was made in the common interest of preventing another holocaust.'[6]

'As a lawyer, I feel no qualms about what we have done,' said Mrs Albeck. 'We have built our case on the statutes we inherited from the Ottomans, the British and the Jordanians. To my mind it was always debatable whether we should take the land for military purposes and so deny the Palestinians a recourse to justice,' she added. 'This way they have a right of appeal.'

She concluded: 'I know of no case in which we have knowingly deprived any Palestinian of land rightfully his since Begin came to power.'[(7)]

Mid August marked the beginning of the harvest season. Like his grandfather and father before him, Fathi Ismail Subeih left home at dawn for the land they once worked. Along with his two wives, Zaimab and Mariam, and their mules he walked the four miles to the small vineyard that lay at the side of the main road linking Bethlehem to Hebron. They chose the same day every year, August 15, to begin the annual ritual. Ahead of them stretched three months of harvesting, eight hours a day, six days a week. As his father had done, he would then send his crop of grapes to the markets of Bethlehem, Jerusalem and Hebron and live off the proceeds until the next harvest. Unlike his father, though, Subeih had just eight acres to pick, half the land he inherited. The rest belonged to the state of Israel, which in turn had sold it to the Americans, South Africans and Israelis who lived in the West Bank settlement of Efrat.

A timid, nervous man, looking much older than his 50 years, Subeih had been disarmingly phlegmatic as he began work just a few yards from a site where Israeli bulldozers were clearing land for a new row of Efrat's custom-made villas. 'I'm grateful we still have something,' he said. 'They might have taken it all.' There were hundreds of small farmers like Fathi Subeih. Like many others, he had appealed; like virtually all of them, he had lost the case. Whatever the technicalities the simple, honest farmers of the West Bank judged it to be theft.

In 1979, the military government of the West Bank had made its first move, informing the leading families of Subeih's village, al-Khader, that land nearby was being requisitioned for 'military purposes'. The Governor informed the *mukhtar*, the village chief, and showed him the land in question. It bisected Fathi Subeih's vineyard. As no appeal was possible, work began on clearing the chosen land almost immediately. By June 1980, the Israelis installed a unit of religious students, who were combining their studies with military service, in a dozen prefabricated homes. In August 1980, Ariel Sharon visited what he called the new Judaean town of Efrat. It would, he said, be part of a chain linking Jerusalem to Hebron, securing for ever the Jewish identity of both cities.[8]

By then, however, the Elon Moreh decision had forced the Israelis to change the pretext on which Efrat was to be built. In January, the Governor informed the villagers of al-Khader that the authorities were taking possession of more than 100 acres of abandoned land for 'state purposes'. That meant more land was being seized on a site adjacent to the original one. It also gave the Arabs the right to appeal. Some 21 families from al-Khader did so, citing the fact that they had started registration procedures with the Jordanians in 1964 and had papers to prove it. Among them were the Subeihs. Like the others, they had documents from the Jordanians, dated August 1964, showing that they had applied for the title to the land they had worked for three generations.

Before the appeals commission delivered its verdict in late 1980, the Israelis had cleared most of the land, often with villagers throwing themselves in front of the bulldozers that were mowing down their vineyards and olive trees. The commission rejected the claim, saying the appellants had no registration documents that had been completed by the Jordanians. It also cited the evidence of an Arab agronomist who had been called in by the Arabs as an expert witness – to prove that they had cultivated the land for more than the 10 years required by Jordanian law. He had found no evidence of cultivated land on the building site, and had said so.[9]

'How could he,' asked Fathi Subeih, pointing up the hill from his vineyard to Efrat, 'when the Israelis had been clearing the land with bulldozers for months before?'

At the Justice Ministry, Mrs Albeck reviewed the case with what she called a satisfied conscience. One family that had lost land, she said, had received compensation in kind on a site nearby. At every stage the ministry had observed the rules laid down by the government. 'It is not that Palestinians lie,' she said laconically. 'It is just that often they do not tell the truth.'

The Israeli lawyer who represented the villagers, a well-known advocate named Felicia Langer, looked back on the case as just one of dozens she had handled. 'It was a typical example of Israel finding a way round the law,' she said. 'But it wasn't justice. It was robbery. Theft is legal here, you know.'[(10)]

As for the Subeihs, the 1980s yielded a succession of meagre harvests. When Efrat was being built, Fathi Subeih had seen what was coming and had put his savings into a small food store in Al-Khader. In 1986, he closed it due to the parlous state of a local economy suffering from the economic ills that beset Israel and the Arab world.

They had first met in New York when Shlomo Riskin had been a popular rabbi with the new generation of 'yuppies' and Marvin Goodman a successful, southern businessman attending syna-gogue. The relationship between rabbi and worshipper had become a lasting friendship, expressed every day as they jogged together through the streets of Manhattan. In the summer of 1986, after a number of years apart, they were reunited in the settlement of Efrat. And to see them then running side by side in sweat suits was to believe what Rabbi Riskin had prophesied: the Jews of Manhattan would indeed move to the Biblical land of the West Bank.

'This is proof that the Jewish exodus is coming to an end,' said the rabbi, a short, stocky figure who exuded a zeal bordering on the Messianic. 'In Efrat, Jews from Manhattan, Johannesburg, London and Tel Aviv have finally found home.'

'To me,' said Goodman, a tall, deliberate man whose slow Texan drawl reflected a far more languid approach to life, 'this is proof of one man's dream coming to fruition for the many who have followed him, recognizing in him the spirit of God.'[(11)]

Rabbi Riskin had first visited the West Bank in 1975. For more than a decade, he had been rebuilding the Lincoln Square Syna-gogue in Manhattan, making his temple the most dynamic Jewish community in New York by blending the energetic and innovative teaching that was his speciality. The sight of the Biblical land had imbued him with a sense of awe, wonderment and humility.

'For years, I had considered my vocation was to bring Jews back to religion,' he said during an interview in Efrat. 'So I had worked on a cross-section of Manhattan life, yuppies, singles, lawyers, academics, business people, the whole works. But I knew that many of them were coming to temple to worship Shlomo Riskin as much as God. It created a void. The minute I saw the West Bank, I knew what my mission was. It was to bring those people here, to bring them home.'

By 1981, with the settlement approved by government and construction under way, Riskin had raised nearly $5 million for the West Bank town that had now become his calling in life. Politicians such as Yitzhak Rabin, Shimon Peres and Yitzhak Shamir came to New York to speak from his pulpit. He personally toured the United States, Britain and South Africa to raise the other component of the equation: settlers.

'It became a remarkable expression of the Jewish identity,' said the rabbi, who did not underestimate his ability to work a crowd. 'I gave them all the same message. I told them there could be no accommodation with the world after the holocaust. When push comes to shove we have to look after ourselves, go it alone.'

By 1987, 250 families lived in Efrat. Many of them were middle-class, business folk with jobs in nearby Jerusalem. Many had left successful careers behind in America and South Africa to build new lives here. Some would undoubtedly have been classified as yuppies had they still been living in New York.

'We are old-fashioned pioneers with a microwave oven,' said Sima Schnell, a mother of four whose husband Chaim worked as an accountant in Jerusalem, 30 minutes away. 'For us, there was no further point in pursuing the American dream. The only dream worth having was the Jewish one.'

'In Texas, we say: no guts, no glory,' remarked Marvin Goodman, who had been a wealthy consultant to the sports clothing industry in New York. 'To me the West Bank is all about seizing a moment of glory that is uniquely Jewish.'

Despite making appeals to Jewish Anglo-Saxon communities the world over, however, Rabbi Riskin had raised more money than volunteers. He might have fulfilled his dream, but a number of his fellow New Yorkers had followed him to the West Bank, tasted briefly and then returned home disenchanted with the reality of his prophecy. Their departure left Efrat with grand plans for its future but a shortage of settlers to execute them. It was a familiar story among the Jewish communities of the territory. Day-to-day life in the closed world of the settlement did not match up to the high hopes with which they had set out. The pioneers of modern Zionism struggled to sustain the sense of purpose they heard from the pulpit. The lack of co-existence with the Palestinians around them, and the prospect of no dramatic change in that relationship, made many question the move from New York or Johannesburg.

In reality, the pioneering spirit had died. The settlers of Efrat survived, in comfortable homes and with guaranteed incomes. But they were divorced from the world around them – however hard their resourceful rabbi and the Israeli government tried to graft them to the land.

By the mid 1980s, the Palestinians of the West Bank had to make a choice as difficult as any these people had faced in the years since 1948. They had offered minimal resistance when it came to the seizure of land and the building of settlements. Now they faced a decision which they alone could take: whether to seize the opportunities for business presented by their new Jewish neighbours or to boycott them in the hope of driving them out. Such dilemmas had been common in Palestinian history. Every colonial power, from the Ottomans to the British and the Jordanians, had raised the same issue. Traditionally, the Palestinians had compromised, putting self-interest above any nationalist goal, freeing them to work for the occupying power and do business with the local administration. Historically, though, that had always proved their downfall. In supplying labour, produce and expertise to the regime of the day, they had created divisions among themselves, reducing their ability ever to present a common front against the occupier.

'There might not have been an Israel,' Yassir Arafat once said, 'if many of our people had not been seduced by the first Zionist settlers at the turn of the century. We have always faced these choices in our history. Whether to look after ourselves or our nation.'[(12)]

That comparison with Palestine of the 1920s and 1930s was a striking one. In the 1980s, the Israelis did indeed settle the West Bank rather as Jews had migrated to Galilee and built Jewish quarters in the cities of Haifa, Acre and Jaffa. Now, as then, they had more resources, financial and spiritual, than the Palestinians.

Once again, the Jews enjoyed leadership. Begin, Sharon and Shamir had replaced Herzl, Chaim Weizmann and Ben-Gurion. The difference this time was that the Palestinians faced a government, a bureaucracy well versed in dealing with the Arabs, an army coloured by the experience of five wars: and an Israeli machine that had long since practised a policy of keeping the peace by undermining the will of the enemy.

'The instinctive reaction to settlements was to boycott,' said Farah Araj, the Arab Mayor in the town of Beit Jala near Bethlehem and a man known for his belief in compromise. 'But we couldn't afford to. The Israelis knew that and so they exploited the differences between our people. We have been responsible for many of the divisions amongst us. But so too have the Israelis. They have a policy similar to the one the British used here. It is divide and rule.'[13]

In the first years after the settlement was built, Rabbi Riskin's settlers in Efrat developed a relationship with the local Arab population that typified many West Bank settlements. The Israelis had made little effort to appease the hostility felt in villages such as Al-Khader, where the loss of land had alienated opinion and created a lasting sense of bitterness. Instead the settlers focused attention on those neighbouring Arab communities which had no such grievance. They offered work, trade and access to the facilities Efrat enjoyed, be it the health clinic or a Hebrew class for Arabs. Equally importantly, Rabbi Riskin could intervene with the military government to obtain permits for the Arabs to build new homes, instal telephone lines or improve water supplies. The Israeli system, born out of Dayan's original policy of rewarding friends and punishing enemies, deliberately encouraged such favouritism. In some instances, it worked.

The village of Beit Fejar, which nestled in the hills adjacent to Efrat, had been spared when the settlement was built. Unlike Al-Khader, no one there had lost property. Unlike Fathi Subeih's experience with his village shop, the stone-cutting industry that had been Beit Fejar's livelihood for generations had prospered with the coming of Efrat. By the mid 1980s, almost half the village had worked at one time or another for the Jewish settlers, reaping the benefit of full-time employment that was rare elsewhere in the territory. The villagers had acted together, voting on the issue in 1982 when Efrat was no longer a hilltop outpost for the Israeli army

84

but a settlement bringing Jews from all over the world. That summer, villagers called a public meeting to elect a new *mukhtar,* village chief. A businessman, Ali Murshed Taqatqah, was the only candidate. Everyone knew that he represented compromise, conciliation and a collective approach to the settlers. Indeed, given his longstanding relationship with the local military Governor, he represented Israel.

'What I wanted was for us to face the reality of Efrat, not to fight it,' he said at his palatial home in Beit Fejar. 'I wanted us to grow, like Efrat has grown, not squander our future by dwelling on the past.'[14]

A tall, gentlemanly figure, immaculately dressed in a suit and a silk *kefiya,* Taqatqah listed his achievements with the conviction of a politician running for office in the Western world. In the past few years, he said, the village had built a new mosque, a new school, a new council building. Every home had electricity, more than 80 per cent of families had television, nearly 40 per cent a car. With Rabbi Riskin's help, he remarked, the Israelis had installed telephones as well. With the Israeli military government, he enjoyed what he called a 'sensible relationship'. He never made demands that he knew could not be met; he discussed and agreed everything with the Governor of Bethlehem district before he put in his proposals. Again, Rabbi Riskin's support was usually forthcoming.

'The result is that we usually get what we want,' Taqatqah said. 'You should note that this is now the most progressive village in this area. Unlike others, we do not live in the past. We live for today and tomorrow.'

Such satisfaction with Israeli occupation presented a stark contrast to the village of al-Khader. There the *mukhtar* produced a file of requests for new roads and new schools, most of which had been rejected by the Israelis. The *mukhtar,* a fiery, abrasive character named Samir Othman, bitterly accused other village leaders of betraying the Palestinians with what he called the politics of subservience.

Taqatqah said he had severed relations, as he put it, with the village council of al-Khader some time ago. There was, he added, no point in meeting to agree on the many matters about which they disagreed. In conclusion, he referred to his speech in Efrat in 1984, when Shlomo Riskin had been sworn in as chief rabbi of the settlement.

'Now I come to you as a neighbour,' Taqatqah had told the Jews of Efrat. 'But I hope in the name of the God of both of us that I may soon come to you as a cousin. Once that happens, we may even come together as brothers.'

Rabbi Riskin and his settlers chose to view such Palestinians as leaders capable of making others follow them. Yet to most Arabs on the West Bank such men as Taqatqah were 'collaborators'. In seeking to build bridges to the Arabs, the settlers created as much opposition as friendship.

As a family, the Cohens of Efrat remembered the profound impression Rabbi Riskin had made on the Jewish communities of Johannesburg, Durban and Cape Town. In speech after speech, the rabbi had hammered home the same message. The Jewish people had a choice, he had told them: either to stay where they were, and so face annihilation through assimilation into a country such as South Africa, or move to Israel and participate in the coming of the Messiah.

'How will you live with yourself, what will you tell your children, if you ignore this calling?' Rabbi Riskin had asked during his visit to the Cyril Dean Synagogue in Johannesburg in May 1982.

By that summer, Selwyn Cohen, his wife Merle and their four children had made the move. His wife's parents had followed soon afterwards. Now they were living in a row of tidy, spacious town houses inhabited solely by South African Jews. Selwyn, a rabbi, taught in a religious school in Jerusalem. His father-in-law, Ramon, an insurance agent, had found work there too as a broker. Like so many settlers on the West Bank, they voiced differing opinions about Israeli rule in the territory. In many instances, disagreement stemmed from the clash of different cultures endemic to all settlements that attracted Jews from abroad. In their case, the experience of growing up under apartheid created an unspoken tension as they built new lives on the West Bank.

'Every time I see the army get on board a bus here, pick out the Palestinians and demand their identity cards,' said Selwyn, a serious, contemplative man in his early 30s, 'I think of South Africa. It hurts me here the way it did there. There I didn't see it as my problem. Because I did not identify with the white community.

I always saw us leaving eventually. But here it is my problem. And that hurts.'

His father-in-law, the son of Lithuanian Jews who emigrated to South Africa in the 1920s, saw the same similarity but had an entirely different reaction.

'I didn't believe in one man, one vote in South Africa and I don't believe in that here,' he said, his English assuming the stridency of the Afrikaner accent. 'For me there is no tension. I see it as the same issue. Could we give South Africa to Nelson Mandela and the African National Congress? No. Can we now give the West Bank to Yassir Arafat and the PLO? No. Of course not. It is the same equation, and there is the same solution. If you want to call it separate development, that's fine. I see nothing wrong with it.'

The Cohens were symptomatic of many Jewish settlers. Unlike the Palestinians, they could agree to disagree and they could unite on the overall purpose of their mission. Yet they recognized within themselves the change in philosophy brought about by their isolation from the Arabs around them. Merle Cohen, a level-headed young woman, explained how her views had shifted to the right since moving to the West Bank. In South Africa, she said, she had been on the liberal wing of politics; she had supported the aims of Helen Suzman's Progressive Federal Party and its calls for equal rights for blacks and whites.

'Here I find myself becoming more and more extreme,' she admitted with a candour rare in a Jewish settler. 'Partly it's because so many of the settlers are that way. But mainly it's because I sense a rift of hostility and hatred between us and so many Palestinians. It can never be bridged. I find that very depressing at times.'

Said her husband: 'I don't have so many problems with it. I tend to think that what we have done here is comparable to what the whites did in South Africa. We too have imposed the rule of conquest.'[15]

'Give or take a few cases of theft, I think you could classify Israel's take-over of the West Bank as the perfect crime.'

Meron Benvenisti, a blunt, irascible figure in his early 50s, sat in the small, chaotic attic that served as his office in west Jerusalem. Dressed in his usual attire of jeans, open-necked shirt and sandals, he gave the impression of being an ageing student who had grown up in another age and had never quite accepted getting older. Yet in the 1980s the experience which had matured him had come to haunt many other Israelis. Much as he disliked the label, such outspoken criticism of Israeli policy on the West Bank made him the conscience of his country.

To Israelis who knew of his research, Benvenisti was either an embarrassment or a cheerleader for that sector of public opinion which still believed in compromising with the Arabs. Palestinians read his findings with mixed feelings. To some, his denunciation of what Israel had done was an inspiration. Others viewed him as a dangerous Zionist, whose prophecy was designed to make the Palestinians believe they no longer had a hope. A native Jeru-salemite, and a third-generation Israeli, Benvenisti had once been a prominent figure in the mainstream of national politics. In the years after the 1967 war, the Jewish Mayor of Jerusalem, Teddy Kollek, had groomed him to be his successor. For more than a decade, Benvenisti had served as Kollek's deputy and chief adviser. But both men were known for their tempers. Typically, they had quarrelled over two issues: the succession and the wider question of Israel's policy towards the Arabs of the West Bank.

'The arrival of Menachem Begin was a watershed for the West Bank and for me personally,' Benvenisti said in an interview in 1984. 'From that point on, settlement was to assume a permanency it had never had before. I wanted no part of it.'

Leaving the Jerusalem city administration, Benvenisti founded a research unit to monitor what Israel did in the occupied territories. In the years that followed, he became an authority on Israel's evolving policy, monitoring every stage of land expropriation and settlement. His first-hand knowledge and painstaking analysis made him a leader of extra-parliamentary opposition to both government and settlers; he represented a new Israeli left which, at first, was taken seriously even if its message was unpalatable.

'For a long time I, like so many other Israelis, was inclined to dismiss the settlers as a small group of unrepresentative Jews who would be in short supply after the initial flurry,' he explained. 'But when Jews started making commuter suburbs and dormitory towns out of settlements, the whole thing changed. For me that was the real threat.'

He added: 'The Jew who went to live in a suburb of Jerusalem such as Gilo was not ideologically committed, he just wanted a better lifestyle, a bigger home, clean air. But living there was bound to make him committed to a system that was based on exploitation, discrimination and two classes. It was a fatal trap for him and all Israelis.'[16]

As a historian, Benvenisti saw painful analogies for Israel. By 1986 the racial unrest in South Africa led him to draw a comparison with Israel. The Sharon plan, Plia Albeck's legal footwork at the Justice Ministry, Rabbi Riskin's mobilization of world Jewry: all came together to form one diagnosis for him.

'It is precisely the way the Boers in South Africa have worked and are still working,' he said, noting that few Palestinians on the West Bank had been dispossessed of land to which they had any formal, judicial claim. 'Everything South Africa does, however distasteful, is legal. So too Israel. But it is not the rule *of* law, which presupposes immutable values like justice. It is rule *by* law. In other words, it is legal but it is not just.'

By 1986, Benvenisti had avid readers throughout the Arab world, the United States and Europe. In the Royal Palace in Amman, visitors would see a well-thumbed copy of Benvenisti's work on King Hussein's desk. When foreign leaders visited Israel, as Britain's Margaret Thatcher did that spring, they used his findings as the basis for urging compromise on the Israeli government.

His was an increasingly isolated voice, however. During a final interview, he remarked that he was considering closing his research unit and turning his back on what had become a lonely crusade. 'The battle for the land is over,' he said, citing his own findings that Israel has now seized more than 50 per cent of the West Bank. 'We have reached the point of no return. We can never give back the territories captured in 1967. It is too late for that.'[17]

If so, the struggle for the West Bank no longer centred on land, rather its people.

Ron Nachman, aircraft engineer turned West Bank politician, was fond of telling visitors to his settlement of Ariel that he had an offer few Israelis could refuse.

'You can live an hour from Tel Aviv, Haifa or Netanya,' he would say, taking his script from the advertisements he was using on Israeli television. 'You can buy a five-bedroom villa, or a smaller apartment, for a quarter of the price in any of those cities,' he would declare, delivering that script just as he did on the air. 'You can live in the fastest-growing city of Israel,' he would add. 'Ariel, the capital of Samaria.'

His conclusion brought the same heartening smile that had made him a familiar face to the nation at large.

'And, on top of that,' he added, 'Ariel is different. Ariel is a model for living together with the Arabs.'

Until 1977, Ron Nachman had been a member of middle management at Israeli Aircraft Industries (IAI), working at Lod Airport near Tel Aviv on the next generation of fighter planes for the air force. A devout follower of Ariel Sharon, he had recruited 200 workers from the plant to present their case to the government for a West Bank settlement. What they had in mind was neither Rabbi Levinger's vision of a Jewish return to the promised land, nor Shlomo Riskin's magnet for drawing the Jews of America and South Africa home to Israel. Nachman's concept had been far simpler and far more ambitious. What he envisaged was a settlement that would attract Jews who wanted to live on the West Bank and to continue to work in Israel: a settlement that would create a permanent link between Israel and the territory.

'Ariel Sharon didn't need much persuading,' recalled Nachman. 'He saw Ariel as a model not just for the West Bank but for settlement throughout Israel. And, for him, the timing was just right.'

In November 1977, President Sadat of Egypt had visited Jerusalem, taking a political gamble which challenged Menachem Begin to make peace. For Sharon, who was publicly committed to the peace process but privately sceptical about its chances, Sadat's visit crystallized the need to settle the West Bank before the government would be obliged to negotiate with the Arab world. Just a few weeks after Sadat's historic address to the Israeli parliament, Sharon engineered the seizure of 60 acres of land near the Arab town of Salfit in Samaria for Nachman's pioneers. In legal manoeuvring reminiscent of Efrat, the government claimed that 'military purposes' were the reason for expropriation. Nachman and 12 colleagues from IAI moved in shortly afterwards. They set up homes in tents, getting protection and supplies from the army. Sadat and Begin meanwhile inched their way towards the Camp David Agreement, which was finalized in September 1979.

90

By then Sharon had pushed through a proposal to claim 750 acres more for Nachman's settlers. They defined it as uncultivated, untitled land belonging to the state. Days after Israel and Egypt formally signed the Camp David Accord, building began on the new city of Ariel.

'It's fair to say that Ariel was originally designed as a kind of road-block to peace,' said Nachman, whose use of cliché was habitual. 'But it became something else: a beacon of light for all of Israel.'

As Agriculture Minister, Sharon was responsible for both development of the West Bank and new towns of pre-1967 Israel as well. Built during the time of Ben-Gurion, those farming settlements of the Negev Desert, the Galilee Triangle and the northern border had become a national cause for concern in the 1970s. Ben-Gurion's dream, of making deserts bloom with Jewish expertise, had required lavish government investment in the 1950s and 1960s. But their remoteness had prevented both growth and cost-effectiveness. A drain on the country's resources, and a burden for the taxpayer, the development towns of Israel had become the white elephants of an ailing economy. In contrast, Nachman's concept of a settlement just 45 minutes from the cities of the coastal plain promised minimum investment for maximum return, both politically and economically. Sharon easily persuaded his colleagues in cabinet to provide the kind of support that made Ariel a favoured project even by West Bank standards. As a result, Ron Nachman was able to offer property at prices that undercut the market elsewhere by up to 80 per cent. He built schools, clinics, shopping malls, even a country club. Ariel promised as much as its advertising suggested.

'The equation is a simple one,' said Avi Boim, one of dozens of unemployed Israelis who moved here and was immediately absorbed into the growing municipal staff running Ariel. 'The land belongs to the government. The government sells it to private contractors at a tiny fraction of its real value. The contractors employ relatively cheap Arab labour to build. And we, the residents, are able to raise high government loans at almost no interest, with tax breaks thrown in as well. For me, the West Bank makes the impossible possible.'

Ron Nachman, who was elected Mayor in 1986, proved characteristically expansive about his achievements.

'Ariel is a real plus for Israel,' he said, producing plans that outlined building programmes to house 70,000 settlers by the year 2000 and to create a Jewish city that would absorb the neighbouring Arab town of Salfit. 'We have,' he maintained, 'identified that large portion of Israel that is not persuaded by the claims of the Bible or the coming of the Lord. People who want a quality of life they believe they should have as Israel grows.'

Few settlers in Ariel seemed to doubt the judgement of their leader. Most saw the expropriation of land half the size of Tel Aviv not as a necessary evil but as a positive benefit to both Jews and Arabs. The Palestinians, they said, enjoyed a quality of life that would have been unthinkable before the settlers came. Arabs worked in the settlement, earning good salaries by local standards. A few brought their children to Ariel's health clinics. Some settlers taught Hebrew and English to Palestinians in the Arab community of Salfit.

'Ariel is different,' remarked Naomi Loney, a black American teacher at the settlement's high school and one of the few foreign Jews who had moved here. 'This place is spiritually divorced from most other settlements on the West Bank. Its attitude towards the Arabs is an enlightened one.'[18]

That claim was a familiar one among the second generation of Jewish settlers who transformed the West Bank from occupied Arab land into bedroom suburbs – almost as easily as New Yorkers once moved from Manhattan to Scarsdale, Londoners from the East End to Chigwell or Romford. But Ariel's claim was different because it carried a degree of truth.

Wajiha Abdul Khader was 28. She lived in a small, sparsely-furnished cottage buried in the maze of narrow alleyways running off the main street of Salfit, less than a mile from Ariel. With an income of $60 a week, life was a struggle. But she expressed the feeling of many Salfitis: without the settlement of Ariel, their plight would have been considerably worse.

'At the beginning, when the settlers first came, I was truly frightened, I think everyone was,' said Mrs Khader, pouring coffee into a family heirloom, bone-china cups, as she talked in a living-room that doubled as her children's bedroom. 'But like most people here, we have benefited from the Israelis.'

A frail, wispish figure who constantly apologized for the chaotic state of her home, Mrs Khader explained that her husband Yusuf had been in and out of work until the settlers came. For the previous eight years, he had been employed as a tiler in Ariel. She hoped the settlement would grow because that would secure their future. Not in the least naïve, she defended her thinking as the only realistic option.

'The problem with so many of our people,' she added, putting her youngest to bed on the family sofa, 'is that we feel a duty to reject the Israelis. We have tried to keep our minds open. My husband knows what he is doing. He is helping to build somewhere that the Israelis will live in for many years.' She paused, choosing her words carefully. 'But there is something in that for us. After all, our parents got nothing from Jordan.'

When the Jordanians ruled the West Bank, in the 1950s, Salfit had been known as Little Moscow. Communist Party leaders like Fahmi al-Salfiti, Hamza al-Zirr and Arabi Awad had been born there. The party Secretary-General Fuad Nasser had used Salfit as a base from which to direct the most powerful political party the Hashemites tolerated in those days. In 1954, the people had staged an infamous demonstration against the young King Hussein. The King had sent his army in, the soldiers had dragged demonstrators through the streets behind their stallions. During the crackdown afterwards, the Jordanians had arrested and exiled communist leaders. The King's justice had offered a lesson no one forgot when the Israelis captured the West Bank in 1967.

'There was no longer the spirit for a fight,' said Hassan al-Zir, Salfit's Mayor from 1966 to 1986. 'Ever since then, people of Salfit have buried their heads and got on with surviving.'

'Today opposition lies below the surface,' explained Raja Ghanem, a prominent Communist Party member in the 1950s who tried unsuccessfully to block the construction of Ariel in the Israeli high court in 1980. 'It is no longer communism, rather the PLO. Scratch the surface here and you will find that people take what they can from occupation. But they're as disillusioned with the Israelis as they were with the Jordanians.'

Living with occupation had nevertheless brought some prosperity. Nearly 50 per cent of Salfit's men worked in Ariel, the town depending heavily on customers from the settlement shopping on Saturdays, the Jewish Sabbath. As a result, the Arabs enjoyed a

93

building boom. On average they constructed 50 new homes every year after the settlers arrived. The Israeli policy of reward or retribution singled out Salfit for improvements in schools and health care, the introduction of electricity and telephones. An administrative centre in the days of the Ottomans and the British, Salfit slowly regained its influence. Ron Nachman's formula seemed to be viable, even irresistible. Yet many had their doubts.

'Those who have gained out of the settlement accept it. Those who have not do not,' said Abdullah Ahmed Ayesh, a shopkeeper well-known in the town because one of his sons had joined the PLO. 'The mistake the Israelis make is to think that offers a solution. You don't change people by bribing them with a job or a telephone.'

Aware of the increasing dependency of the Arab town on the Jewish settlement and the measure of acceptance, the PLO launched a rare attack on Ariel in 1986. An Arab worker named Jihad Addik died when a bomb he was about to plant at the entrance to the settlement exploded prematurely in his car. Before his death, Addik told friends in Salfit that he could no longer tolerate the humiliation he felt in dealing with the Israelis. The attack, said Force 17, Yassir Arafat's elite commando unit, was designed to prevent development of the settlement, specifically to pre-empt plans for an industrial zone that would offer work to both Jews and Arabs. As a result of the abortive attack, relations between the two communities cooled noticeably. Few Israelis visited Salfit while Arabs were allowed into Ariel only for work.

The PLO had been powerless to prevent settlement and defeat in the battle for land. The more that conflict focused on hearts and minds, the clearer it became that the struggle would be fought between two peoples and two movements: modern Zionism and Palestinian nationalism.

When Ariel Sharon sent the Israeli army into Lebanon in 1982, he envisaged a total realignment in the Middle East. The invasion, he argued, would create new leadership in Beirut, and settle the issue of what to do with the Palestinians of the West Bank once and for all. He foresaw that the PLO would be forced to seek sanctuary in Syria, so losing any vestige of independence. Cut off from the West Bank, Yassir Arafat's support among Palestinians there would be steadily eroded. In time, he maintained, moderate Arabs from the occupied territories would step forward and negotiate home rule with the Israelis on terms which the government would dictate. Those Palestinians who sought an independent homeland would have to look to Jordan to fulfil that hope: a threat to King Hussein's future. A successful invasion of Lebanon, Sharon predicted, would guarantee Israel 30 years of peace and enough time to establish as many *faits accomplis* as it wished on the West Bank.

Many Israelis blamed Sharon for the most disastrous chapter in the country's history. They denounced his Lebanon war as a monumental strategic blunder. But, years later, Sharon would have none of it. He defended his action as part of a search for peace. By destroying the PLO as a military force, he declared, Israel had given West Bank Palestinians the chance to decide their future without the fear of PLO intimidation. Jewish settlement and the invasion had worked in tandem to raise the issue and induce a solution.

'The world saw Lebanon as a setback for Israel, but it wasn't. It was the second half of a two-pronged attack,' Sharon insisted. 'Palestinians could decide whether they wanted to stay and live in peace or join what was left of the PLO in exile. We made that choice clear to them by settling the land and neutralizing the PLO.'

The years since the war were highly productive for Sharon's original master-plan on the West Bank. More land was confiscated, dozens of new settlements were built, thousands of settlers migrated to the territory. Sharon enumerated the achievements accomplished since his siege of Beirut. Townships such as Gilo, he said, had secured Jerusalem for ever, providing homes for tens of thousands of ordinary Jews who served in the army as well as working in the nation's capital. Efrat formed part of a continuous line of settlements linking Jerusalem to Hebron, separating one Arab village from another along the way, breaking down the structure of Palestinian society. As for Ariel city, Sharon depicted it as his vision of the future: a West Bank in which hundreds of thousands of Israelis would impose a solution to the age-old issue of how Jews and Arabs would live together.

'All my life I have lived with Arabs,' Sharon claimed, consciously pre-empting the questions his strategy raised about the prospects for co-existence. 'It is not the Jews who have a problem in living together. It is the Arabs. We have to find solutions for them.'

To underestimate him would have been naïve. Disgraced by the war, forced to resign from defence by the massacre of Palestinians at Sabra and Chatilla, he had fought his way back into the mainstream of political life against all the odds. He remained the pivotal figure in the Likud Party of Begin and Shamir, eminently capable of making or breaking any of their heirs apparent: indeed in a position to be Prime Minister himself one day. As one of his rivals admitted in 1986, 'Every day Sharon moves closer and closer to his real goal.' Sharon owed his survival to his unrivalled reputation on the one issue that had dominated Israeli life since 1948, namely security. For Begin's majority of working-class, Oriental Jews, he was still the one leader who knew how to deal with the Arabs. As Israel approached the 39th anniversary of its independence, and the 20th anniversary of the 1967 war, he read a special significance into both landmarks.

'You have to recognize that Israel has now lived longer with the West Bank and Gaza than without. When you listen to those bleeding hearts, like Benvenisti, remember that they are right on one thing,' he said. 'It is too late for us to give back land for peace.'[19]

Did he see himself as a future Prime Minister? He would try, he remarked, looking at his wife as though to question whether he should say any more. And what if he succeeded? Then, he replied, the Palestinians would have to choose between Israel and Jordan.

More than most Israeli politicians, Sharon believed his own rhetoric. Yet it blinded him to the reality of the post-1967 era in the Middle East. However much land was expropriated, confiscated or simply stolen, the nub of the problem remained the people. Whatever damage he inflicted on the PLO militarily, he could not destroy its political influence on Palestinians. Israel might have gone beyond the point of no return when it came to land for peace, but it was also too late to force more than a million Arabs into tame submission or exile. Sharon's war in Lebanon, and its aftermath, proved how contemporary Zionism and Palestinian nationalism were locked in a battle which neither could win.

4
THE ETERNAL TRIANGLE

'What a beautiful fix we are in now: peace has been declared!' – NAPOLEON I, AFTER THE TREATY OF AMIENS, 1802

The procession at Beirut's derelict soccer stadium looked more like a victory parade than the final act of a war that had claimed thousands of lives. Hundreds of armed men hopped aboard trucks plastered with pictures of PLO leader Yassir Arafat and signs saying 'Palestine or bust.' Arafat's second-in-command, Abu Jihad, shouted a defiant tirade of a speech into a bullhorn, women wailed nationalist songs, wives and children burst into tears. As the trucks fanned out slowly through West Beirut, creeping along the devastated remains of streets reduced to rubble by the Israeli air force, the city came alive with cheering crowds tossing flowers and rice on to the motorcade. Gunmen saluted by firing bursts from their automatic rifles, even pedestrians yanked out pistols and blazed away aimlessly into the air. Every now and then a swish and huge boom could be heard as the celebration became young men firing rocket-propelled grenades which soared half a mile into the air and then exploded in clouds of inky smoke.

At two o'clock on the afternoon of Saturday August 21 1982, the convoy reached the port of Beirut. At 2.15 the first boat sailed for Cyprus. Twelve years after the PLO had moved to Beirut, 76 days after the Israelis had invaded Lebanon, two weeks after the Americans had finally hammered out an agreement, the Palestinians began leaving Lebanon with all the parties to the dispute claiming victory.

'The PLO has suffered a crushing defeat,' said Ariel Sharon, watching the evacuation through binoculars from a rooftop overlooking the harbour. 'We have destroyed their kingdom of terror.'

'We are the first Arabs ever to emerge from a war with Israel with our heads and our weapons held high,' remarked Yassir Arafat when he sailed for Greece a few days later. For the Israelis Beirut has been what Stalingrad was for the Nazis – a decisive defeat.'

'This has been a victory for reason and diplomacy,' added Philip Habib, the American mediator who had negotiated the evacuation. 'It is proof that common sense can sometimes stop the killing and the bloodshed.'

In those balmy, exuberant days of August 1982, it did indeed appear that the parties to the Middle East conflict had come to their senses. The final, freeze-frame image of the battle for Beirut, which for so long seemed destined to be Israeli tanks in the streets of the city, instead became Palestinians with Kalashnikov rifles under one arm and a new suitcase under the other. At the beginning of the month, no place was safe from the incessant air raids launched by the Israelis. In its final week, soldiers from both sides sunbathed, read books and hung out their laundry within range of each other's guns. The hatred lingered but exhaustion proved stronger. The accumulative attrition of 10 weeks of siege in Beirut had sapped the strength of both the Israelis and the PLO. Sharon might have claimed victory, but the Palestinians sustained the sense of an honourable retreat, with flags flying and the endless cannonades and thunderous volleys of rockets. The fanfare of their departure, and the rapturous welcome they received on arrival in other Arab capitals, symbolized both their military demise and their new-found political strength.

Ariel Sharon had destroyed the PLO as a military force, but he had made the Palestinians a far more potent threat on the diplomatic front. Instead of winning Israel a 30-year respite, the invasion restored the Palestinian issue to the top of the international agenda. Sharon had sought a climate for peace on Israel's terms. Unwittingly, his war built up momentum for a settlement that could somehow include the PLO. The years that followed would show whether peace was truly the goal – of Israel, the PLO, Jordan and the United States.

For the United States, the war in Lebanon had provided stark evidence of how a headstrong ally such as Israel could drag its superpower partner into a regional conflict. In the summer of 1982, President Reagan intervened personally on several occasions to stop the bombing of Beirut. On Thursday August 12, the final day of Israeli air attacks on the city, the White House finally located Prime Minister Begin after an hour. The US President, increasingly frustrated by the half-truths coming from Israel, was reduced to shouting his outrage and shock down the line to Begin's office in Jerusalem. The attacks, said Reagan, were causing 'needless destruction and bloodshed'. Begin promised to have them stopped. But that acrimonious exchange symbolized the sorry state of relations between Washington and Jerusalem. As the President remarked to an aide: 'That man [Begin] makes it awfully hard for us to support them.' Just a few months earlier, the expression of such sentiments in the Oval Office would have been unthinkable.

In 1981, Ronald Reagan had assumed the presidency with a Middle East platform designed primarily to win votes and capitalize on the humiliation suffered by Jimmy Carter at the hands of Iran. Whereas President Carter had made a solution to the Arab–Israeli conflict the priority, his successor viewed the Middle East primarily as an arena for the East–West conflict. Carter saw a PLO role as the only way out; Reagan refused to countenance an administration negotiating with Arafat. Carter had come to see the relationship with Israel as a potential threat to US interests in the region; Reagan looked upon Israel as the bulwark against Soviet intervention in the Middle East.

While much of it was campaign rhetoric, Reagan had defined his position en route to his landslide victory over Carter in 1980. He placed emphasis almost totally on strategic concerns, giving low priority to the Palestinian issue. The Soviet Union had seized the opportunity presented by the fall of the Shah in Iran to re-establish itself in the region, he argued. President Carter was accused of rewarding America's enemies and betraying its friends. A Reagan administration would redress the balance. And once he was President, Reagan voiced an unequivocal commitment to Israel.

'Israel is the only stable democracy we can rely on in a spot where Armageddon could come,' he told the *New York Times* in March 1980. 'If Israel were not there, the US would have to be there.'[1] As for the PLO, Reagan saw a Soviet puppet. 'President Carter refuses to brand the PLO as a terrorist organization. I have no hesitation in doing so,' he said at one point on the campaign trail. 'The PLO is said to represent the Palestinian refugees. It represents no one but the leaders who established it as a means of organized aggression against Israel.'[2] Less than two weeks after his inauguration, in January 1981, the new President even redefined American policy regarding Israeli settlements on the West Bank. Ever since the 1967 war, successive administrations had held that settlements were illegal under the Geneva Convention; but no longer did Washington adhere to this. 'As to the West Bank,' Reagan told a news conference, 'I believe the settlements there – I disagreed when the previous administration referred to them as illegal, they're not illegal.'[3]

To Menachem Begin and Ariel Sharon, the Reagan agenda offered a virtually free rein for their plans on the West Bank and in Lebanon. Unfettered by the constraints felt during Jimmy Carter's administration, the Israeli government sanctioned increasingly ambitious plans for the settlement of the territories. At the same time, Sharon prepared for a final assault on the PLO in Lebanon. When the Israelis seized the opportunity presented by the attempt to assassinate Ambassador Shlomo Argov in London in June 1982, and invaded, Sharon claimed he had forewarned the Americans. Secretary of State Alexander Haig did not condone the war, nor did he condemn it. Israel's patience had been sorely tested, he remarked. The President, visiting Europe shortly after the invasion began, declared that all parties should work towards stamping out the 'scourge of terrorism': a clear reference to the PLO.

'The thinking at the White House was ambivalent,' recalled a veteran Middle East hand at the State Department years later. 'We may not have agreed with the means used in the Lebanon invasion but we approved of the aim. Overriding everything was the special relationship with Israel.'[4]

Yet, as Sharon's quick, surgical strike against the PLO turned into the bloody siege of Beirut, the Reagan White House could no longer ignore the challenge to its credibility both at home and abroad. Just as Sharon was manipulating his colleagues in cabinet, so the Israeli government was deceiving the most supportive of Presidents. As the battle for Beirut became prime-time television, and the media highlighted Israel's use of American weaponry against innocent civilians, Mr Reagan had to act. Twenty months into his presidency, he launched his two-pronged attack on the Middle East crisis that was rapidly becoming a threat to the administration. First, he dispatched the marines to Beirut as part of a peace-keeping force with the French and the Italians. Then he produced his blueprint for peace in the region. No longer could he argue that the Palestinian issue was secondary to concerns about the Soviet Union's global strategy; that Israel represented America's interests in the region; that the PLO was the prime architect of terror in the Middle East. Instead, the President had to seek the solution that had once been Jimmy Carter's goal – a settlement of the Palestinian problem, a homeland for the people whose exile and occupation fuelled the crisis that had spread from Beirut to Washington that summer. On September 1 1982, White House aides unceremoniously took over a television studio in Burbank, California, removing the cast and crew of a new comedy show to prepare for an unscheduled address to the nation by the President. His speechwriters had worked on the text until minutes before he spoke live, but none of their patchwork showed. The speech was as well crafted and lucid as any that the masterful communicator who occupied the White House had ever delivered.

'Tonight I am calling for a fresh start,' the President said. 'This is the moment for all those directly concerned to get involved – or to lend their support – to a workable basis for peace.'[5]

What followed amounted to a passionate plea for urgent treatment of the festering sore that lay at the heart of the Middle East conflict. Dropping the habitual US role of anxious and often baffled mediator, the President outlined a future for the Palestinians of the West Bank and Gaza Strip. In essence, he proposed self-rule in conjunction with Jordan; a halt to any further Israeli settlement in the territories with an eye to eventual Israeli withdrawal; and Arab recognition of Israel's right to exist. The lessons of Lebanon were clear, he argued. The defeat of the PLO had not diminished the burning desire among Palestinians for a just solution while Israel's victory had proved that military might alone could not bring peace.

'In the aftermath of Lebanon,' he concluded, 'we now face an opportunity for broader peace. This time we must not let it slip from our grasp.'[6]

Israel's invasion of Lebanon had wrought momentous changes in the complex equation that had defied a solution of the Middle East conflict since the war of 1967. Every major actor in the regional drama had been deeply affected. Israel had suffered not just the loss of hundreds of men but a dramatic erosion of its reputation world-wide. Syria had endured a humiliating defeat at the hands of the Israelis, calling into question its ability ever to challenge the military supremacy of the Jewish state. Egypt had felt obliged to distance itself from Anwar Sadat's peace with Israel, withdrawing its ambassador from Tel Aviv and denouncing Begin's government. King Hussein feared that the PLO would return to Jordan, sowing the seeds of chaos that had almost cost him his throne 12 years before.

'When you looked at the players,' recalled Geoffrey Kemp, then a member of President Reagan's National Security Council and a specialist on the Middle East, 'you had to believe that both the Israelis and the Arabs had been sobered up by the experience of war in Lebanon.'[7]

An emergency Arab summit, held at the Summer Palace of Morocco's King Hassan a few days after the Reagan plan was unveiled, offered immediate proof of that wind of change. Only a few months before, Arab leaders had tried unsuccessfully to hold a meeting in the same city of Fez, but it had broken down after just five hours amid bitter interchanges between Arab moderates and radicals. Now the Arab world put on its most impressive display of unity in years. In the magnificent dining-room of the Royal Palace, Syria's hard-line President Hafez al-Assad shared a lunch of goat meat and couscous with his sworn enemies, President Saddam Hussein of Iraq and King Hussein. Arafat and King Fahd flashed 'V for victory' signs as they posed for photographers under a bedouin tent. The brotherly spirit reflected a seismic shift in the political geography of the Arab world. No longer did the radicals, such as Syria or the absent Libyans, dictate the direction being taken. The Saudis shrewdly wielded their economic clout to produce both a show of harmony and concessions to both the US and Israel. In particular, King Fahd exploited Syria's need for Saudi loans to win Assad's support.

The result was arguably the most revolutionary step the Arab world had taken in years. The so-called Fez Plan declared that 'all states' in the region had the right to live in peace. In the coded language of Arab diplomacy, this suggested the acceptance of Israel – the issue which had stalled any movement since 1967. It called on Israel to withdraw to its pre-1967 borders: again implicit recognition of the Jewish state. 'Ever since 1948 the West has demanded that we accept Israel's right to live,' said Arab League Secretary-General, Chedli Klibi. 'That is what we have offered.'[8]

'That is a breakthrough, a genuine breakthrough,' said Secretary of State George Shultz as the news reached Washington. Shultz, appointed after Haig's resignation in June, added: 'That may not sound like much to you. But that is a big piece of movement in people's attitudes – very, very important.'[9] As one of his advisers at the State Department remarked: 'It brought us a long way from the days when all the Arabs ever did was declare holy wars against the Zionist entity.'[10]

Within a day of the Reagan plan being announced, Menachem Begin had publicly castigated the President, calling the initiative 'stillborn'. In an angry speech to the Israeli parliament, Begin had shouted: 'For you, Mr President, this is a political matter. You need to get closer to Saudi Arabia. Maybe you need to shake hands with King Hussein. But to us it is our life! Our homeland! The land of our fathers and sons!' Now, within hours of the Arab summit ending, the government in Jerusalem dismissed the Fez proposals out of hand.

Yet, two days later, Israel's invasion of Lebanon came to its bloody climax. More than 800 Palestinians were massacred in the Beirut refugee camps of Sabra and Chatila. As evidence emerged of Israel's tacit complicity in the wholesale slaughter of men, women and children, President Reagan remarked that Israel had been transformed in the public mind from David to Goliath. A few days later, he took the remark back – evidence, if any was needed, of the administration's inability to divorce itself from Jerusalem.

'How do you deal with an ally you no longer trust?'

President Reagan raised the question at an emergency meeting of foreign-policy staff three days after the Red Cross started clearing the bodies from the streets in Beirut. He himself supplied the answer. That night he ordered the marines back to Beirut to keep the peace. He effectively shelved the peace plan launched with such determination at the beginning of that September. The massacres had provoked the most open rupture between the US and Israel in years. Initially, Mr Reagan had angrily demanded that the Israelis leave Beirut and insisted on recognition of 'the legitimate needs of the Palestinian people'. But he backed away from any decisive confrontation with the government of Menachem Begin.

'Begin was always watching for Reagan to go soft,' said one veteran Middle East hand at the State Department years later. 'After Sabra and Chatila they stared at each other almost as enemies. It was the President who blinked.'[11]

In the subsequent months Begin's government exploited the vacuum that Reagan's prevarication and preoccupation with Lebanon created. In September, within days of the President's call for a freeze on West Bank settlement, Ariel Sharon won approval for eight new homesteads costing more than $18 million. In November, the government authorized five more settlements and Sharon said Israel would push ahead with plans to instal 400,000 Jews in the territory within five years.

Publicly the President scolded the Israelis. The new settlements, he said, constituted 'a hindrance to what we're trying to accomplish in the peace movement'. Privately he supported a 20 per cent increase in economic aid to Israel which was approved that December. The policy planners at the State Department did not disguise their dismay. Deputy Secretary of State Kenneth Dam warned that any increase in aid could only appear to endorse and reward Israeli policies in Lebanon and on the West Bank. It would, he said, raise serious doubts about US commitment to the peace process. Worse still, the State Department believed the Israelis were deliberately stalling their withdrawal from Lebanon to focus the administration's attention on the crisis there and so divert it from the expansion of Jewish settlement on the West Bank.

Mr Reagan's grasp of the Middle East had always been limited.

104

In the months after the war ended in Beirut, it proved disastrous. In tackling the crisis of the moment – Lebanon – he lost sight of the Palestinian issue which he himself had defined as the core of the region's conflict. Key advisers at the State Department looked back on that period as symptomatic of the Reagan presidency regarding the Middle East: high on rhetoric, low on commitment, concerned more with appearances than results, downright wasteful of the opportunities created by the 1982 war.

According to those same advisers, the carnage of 1983 served Israel's aim to scupper the President's peace plan. More than 250 marines died in Lebanon, trying to keep peace amid the chaos fuelled by Israel's continued occupation; US warships and planes bombed Syrian targets in eastern Lebanon, making the Reagan administration look like Israel's surrogate in the region; and, in February 1984, the President withdrew the marines from Beirut with the country lost to America's enemies in the region, Syria and Iran. In that period, more than 20 new Jewish settlements were established on the West Bank. The massacres at Sabra and Chatila might have forced Ariel Sharon to resign from defence and persuaded Begin to retire from political life, but, by 1984, Israel had almost reached the target for settlements Begin and Sharon had agreed back in 1977.

As for the President, he had readopted the philosophy that led him to the White House in 1980. Late in October 1983, he addressed the nation on the aftermath of the bombing of the marines in Beirut and the invasion of Grenada. 'The events in Lebanon and Grenada, though oceans apart, are closely related,' he said. 'Not only has Moscow assisted and encouraged the violence in both countries, but it provides direct support through a network of surrogates and terrorists.' The President added: 'Israel shares our democratic values and is a formidable force any invader of the Middle East would have to reckon with.'[12]

'In retrospect,' explained Geoffrey Kemp years later, 'we missed our opportunity in the immediate aftermath of the siege in Beirut. After 1983, the parties to the conflict had to come to the President with the basis of a settlement. We are not going to initiate any more.'[13]

Given this particular US position on the region, the Israelis, the Jordanians and the Palestinians had to look to themselves for a solution. With Begin's departure from public life, and the open disillusionment of many Israelis with the Lebanon war, the Labour Party seemed set to regain power in Jerusalem. Despite their long-standing differences, Yassir Arafat and King Hussein were about to re-establish their alliance.

What the Arabs and the Israeli Labour Party needed was a common denominator. Together they looked to the West Bank: to the tens of thousands of Palestinians who lived with the aftermath of the 1967 war: to the only people who could realistically sustain the months and years of diplomatic wrangling that lay ahead. That common interest led them to the largest city in the territory, Nablus, and a businessman named Zafer al-Masri.

The al-Masri family had started their flour mill back in the 1950s, in the days when King Hussein had been running the West Bank and entrepreneurs loyal to the Hashemites enjoyed the benefits of a monopoly granted by the royal court. It represented just one branch of the al-Masri network, but an important one. Almost every town and village in the region bought from the Nablus mill. As the importer of wheat, with a choice of suppliers in Jordan, Syria, Iraq, even America, the mill-owner could negotiate a favourable deal when it came to buying, and then fix a price that guaranteed a handsome profit when it came to selling the flour.

By 1967, when the young Zafer al-Masri had returned from Beirut with a degree in business administration, the mill was part of a multi-million-dollar family empire. The al-Masris produced everything from matches to the olive-oil soap that carried the name of Nablus to every corner of the Arab world. They sold everything from flour to Volkswagen cars. The consortium made Zafer, the youngest of seven brothers but the one groomed to be managing director, a millionaire at the age of 21.

After the June war, the West Bankers and the Israelis shared a honeymoon of a kind. Zafer, a quiet, diligent figure more at ease in the accounts department than the front office, viewed Israel as yet another market for al-Masri products. Like so many businessmen on the West Bank, he believed that co-existence with the Jews was not just a necessary compromise but an opportunity to be ex-ploited. 'We learn from them, they buy from us,' he once said: a dictum for much of the ruling class on the West Bank during the

106

early 1970s. Personally, he had few qualms about dealing with the Israelis. Articulate, broad-minded, sophisticated, his education in Beirut had given him a taste of the world outside the West Bank; his travels in Europe, North America and the Far East nurtured a natural affinity for the West. The Palestinian future, he believed, lay in maintaining links to the Arab world abroad and peace with the Israelis at home. For many years after the 1967 war, his optimism was rewarded by the steady growth of the al-Masri empire.

By the early 1980s, however, the family's fortunes had dipped. Nablus, the industrial hub of the West Bank, was suffering a recession, born out of Israel's economic crisis and years of occupation, that had cut the city off from its age-old markets in the Arab world. The cold facts on the business ledger showed the extent of the decline. Exports of traditional products like soap and matches had been halved. Israeli import taxes had forced the price of a Volkswagen up tenfold in as many years. In the meantime, Israeli producers, who were competing with Arabs for the local market, often undercut them in price through mass production and the latest Western machinery. As for the mill, wheat could be bought only from Israel; and the Israelis demanded payment in advance. The West Bank market could not tolerate higher prices for flour because of the general recession. By the end of 1984, when the mill had lost nearly a million dollars, al-Masri closed it.

'For Zafer, for all of us,' explained his business partner Izzat Azzul, 'the writing was very clearly on the wall. We were wealthy men, none of us would starve. But we had to do something.' He concluded: 'We either made a deal with the Israelis, or we retired. We were too young for that.'[14]

Al-Masri had been a reluctant politician when he served as deputy Mayor in the late 1970s. Yet he came to believe the city had to regain control of the town hall from the Israelis, who had installed an army officer as Mayor following the removal of the PLO supporter Bassam Shaka'a in 1982. The alternative, he believed, was economic suicide. An astute, thoughtful man, he saw the danger but was ready to take the risk involved in working with the Israelis.

'It's a triangle, made up of Jordan, Israel, and the PLO,' he explained. 'My feeling is that the Palestinians of the West Bank

107

must add their voice to the equation. If not, we will always be victims of the triangle of interests that can never be squared.'[15]

'The question that stands before the whole nation is the question of Israel facing itself, Israel facing its history, Israel facing the truth of the Jewish experience.'

With those words, Shimon Peres, leader of Israel's Labour Party, had spelled out the challange to Israel in the days after the massacre at Sabra and Chatilla in September 1982. Two years later, almost to the day, Peres formed a new government of national unity which included not only his own party but the heirs to Menachem Begin's Likud, Yitzhak Shamir and Ariel Sharon. For Peres, that government signalled an end at last to the long, frustrating years in opposition to Begin. Peres assumed power with a domestic agenda dominated by an economic crisis at home and the occupation of Lebanon abroad. But Peres, more than any other politician of his generation, voiced the conviction that his country could obtain peace without signing away its future security.

'It is not just a dream, it is not just wishful thinking,' he remarked during an interview a few weeks before the election of July 1984. 'It was the reality Anwar Sadat presented when he came to Jerusalem. Peace,' he added, 'is the aspiration of most Israelis and most Arabs.'[16]

More than any other single event, the visit of Sadat to Jerusalem had made a lasting impression on Peres. As his biographer once noted, Shimon Peres felt mocked by history at the coming of the Egyptian President.[17]

Through his behind-the-scenes work as deputy Defence Minister in the 1960s, Peres had been largely instrumental in building the war machine that was so successful in 1967. After the setbacks in the 1973 war, he had rebuilt the army. By 1977 the nation once again felt the sense of security and well-being that had typified the years following the 1967 war. After the resignation of a bitter rival, Yitzhak Rabin, in the wake of a family scandal in 1977, Peres had rehabilitated the Labour Party. As on previous occasions, he had succeeded through the combination of hard work, intellect and political ruthlessness that had always been his hallmark. Yet Begin had won the election of May 1977, and Peres had been cast as the first Labour leader in the history of Israel to lose at the polls. The following November, Sadat had come to Jerusalem. In a depression that bordered on the irrational, Peres stood in line to receive the Egyptian leader that Saturday evening in November, feeling the whole world was against him. Even Sadat.

Inevitably, the marriage between Begin and Sadat quickly became an acrimonious separation. To fill the vacuum, and to pressure Begin into concessions, Sadat sought out Peres. By 1978, Peres was conducting his own diplomacy with the Egyptian leader, sensing the meeting of minds that Begin was never able to feel. By the time Begin and Sadat had signed the Camp David Agreement, at the end of the year, Peres had come to believe that a Begin could never make lasting peace with the Arab world, but that a Shimon Peres could. For him, that was the hidden significance of Sadat's visit to Jerusalem.

Seven years in the wilderness, another election defeat in 1981 and the trauma of the Lebanon war separated Shimon Peres from waiting in line to receive Sadat and election as Prime Minister in 1984. He was no longer the pessimist, even though the narrowest of election victories that summer had forced him to create a coalition of bitter rivals. Instead, Peres saw a place in history beckoning. He might be the man to convert Menachem Begin's fragile truce with Egypt into a solution for the West Bank and Gaza, the problem that lay at the heart of the Middle East's perennial crisis. He was not, as his enemies suggested, naïve or foolhardy. Peres knew the limitations. He recognized that Israel would never sanction the return of all the land captured in 1967. He acknowledged that the bitter American experience in Lebanon had sapped the political will of the Reagan administration for new initiatives. As a man who had lost two elections, he sensed that his days as head of his party were numbered unless he came up with a fresh approach to the problem that lay at the root of all else.

What Peres wanted was an arrangement with King Hussein, the PLO and those West Bankers who sought a peaceful relationship with Israel. In time, he argued, a measure of home rule or autonomy for the Palestinians in the territories would become a solution, enabling Israel to pull out gradually with little fear of further war. Such thinking made Zafer al-Masri a prime target for Shimon Peres as he sought to build a coalition that would defy the indifference of the United States and present the kind of formula for peace that no American administration could ignore.

Security Council Resolution No. 242 read like an anachronism of history even as the United Nations adopted it on November 22 1967. The day before, the Israeli air force had crossed the Jordan River for the first time since the June war and knocked out Jordanian tanks firing from the East Bank. Two days later, President Nasser of Egypt dismissed 242 as irrelevant. 'What was taken by force cannot be recovered except by force!' Nasser declared in an address to his people on Radio Cairo.

Yet, down the years, Resolution 242 had survived as a landmark statement from the world at large on the Middle East conflict. It enshrined the belief that the only route to peace in the promised land lay in Israeli withdrawal from all the territories captured in 1967 – and Arab recognition of Israel's right to exist. In the years that followed, the Resolution came to mean different things to different players, but the formula of land for peace remained, the core of all thinking in the region and the starting-point for all those who attempted to forge a settlement. Many of the Arab states followed Nasser's lead in rejecting it. The PLO had always refused to accept it because it symbolized recognition of Israel. For their part, the Israelis supported 242 in the comfortable knowledge that it represented no threat to their rule in the territories as long as the Arabs boycotted its principles. Instead of providing a first, positive step towards peace, the UN resolution therefore became an obstacle to negotiations.

For many years, King Hussein had privately despaired of his Arab allies ever crossing what he called 'the Rubicon of 242'. But early in 1985, a few months after Peres had become Prime Minister in Israel, a brief statement from the Royal Palace in Amman suggested that Jordan and the PLO had done just that. After three days of negotiations, the King and Yassir Arafat had agreed on a joint framework for talks with Israel. The declaration was full of ringing phrases, many of them the staple language of previously abortive Middle East diplomacy. It defined a just, peaceful settlement as the goal. It made a solution for the millions of Palestinian refugees a priority. It called for an international conference to be attended by both superpowers. Crucially, it echoed President Reagan's proposal for some form of federation between Jordan and the PLO instead of repeating the longstanding demands for an independent Palestinian state. Lastly, the statement maintained

110

that land for peace, as in 'all UN Resolutions', offered the only solution.

'My clear understanding,' said King Hussein during a visit to Austria a few weeks later, 'is that we both accept Resolution 242. It is a momentous decision. It is a challenge to the United States and Israel to make peace.'[18]

The timing could hardly have been more delicate or more auspicious. The Saudi King Fahd, who had been instrumental in working to bring Hussein and Arafat together ever since the Fez summit, was visiting Washington that same week in February to stress the urgent need for US involvement in the search for peace. President Reagan's Middle East envoy, Richard Murphy, was holding the first talks in years on the region with the Soviet Union. Israel was completing the first stage of its withdrawal from Lebanon. The President remained sceptical about the PLO's willingness to carry out the pledge to recognize Israel. Secretary of State George Shultz termed it 'kind of fuzzy'. But senior officials at the State Department thought otherwise.

'Hussein had embarked on a serious course,' reflected one official in 1986. 'His goal was freedom to negotiate with Israel. The question was: did we have the courage to make it work? Could we seriously take the PLO on board and make Israel follow?'[19]

As always, the PLO and Arafat personally presented a baffling enigma for the Israelis and the Americans. Calculated ambiguity had long since proved the main feature of Arafat's diplomacy. Yet Arafat had pressing reasons to seek a compromise with Hussein. As Ariel Sharon had predicted, the siege of Beruit in 1982 had sparked off civil war among the Palestinians in its aftermath. Arafat's one-time allies had become his enemies. Founding fathers of the PLO, such as George Habash of the radical Popular Front for the Liberation of Palestine (PFLP), denounced Arafat as a traitor.

'Arafat misread the situation after Lebanon,' Habash said in an interview in Damascus in November 1984. 'He seemed to think Lebanon changed everything...he believed Israel and the US would make peace...but you don't make peace with a man like Sharon. You make peace on his terms. And you betray the Palestinians. That is what Arafat is doing.'[20]

Stung by such criticism, and desperate to put his house in order,

Arafat had two aims: to retain a major say in any peace process with the Israelis and to buy time to rebuild his army. The agreement with King Hussein gave him both. With characteristic cunning, Arafat re-established a PLO presence, initially in Amman, so obtaining a credible base from which to supply moral and financial support to his supporters on the West Bank. By the end of 1984, he was pouring money and men back into Lebanon as well. Militarily speaking, Arafat was making the PLO a threat once again to Israel. Diplomatically, he was content to call the bluff of the Reagan administration. In Cairo the following year, he said: 'Our agreement with Hussein allows us to overcome the three American no's: no to the PLO, no to a Palestinian state, no to an international conference.'[21] Those who looked for a miraculous conversion, from fighter to peacemaker, misjudged Arafat. He was still practising the philosophy of the gun and the olive branch.

When he invaded Lebanon, Ariel Sharon could not have foreseen the coalition of Arab and Jew that was forming in the summer of 1985. There was Israel, exhausted by a Lebanon war that had cost billions of dollars and over 600 lives, led by a Prime Minister who believed he could break the cycle of conflict. There was King Hussein, seeking a compromise that would secure his future. And there was Yassir Arafat, searching for survival. For all of them, Zafer al-Masri held the key to success. If a figure of his calibre could step forward to take control of a city the size of Nablus, then other Palestinians on the West Bank would surely follow. Without progress in the territories, there could be no movement from the superpowers. Ironically, given the deadlock ever since 1967, time was working against them. Under the terms of Israel's coalition agreement, Shimon Peres had to hand over the premiership to Yitzhak Shamir in the autumn of 1986.

'It was take it or leave it,' said al-Masri. 'If you understood the way Shamir and Sharon thought about the West Bank, then you could understand it was no choice at all. All of us were in a corner.'[22]

Al-Masri voiced the simple, at times naïve, hope of people who sought an alternative to perpetual occupation. Others had less altruistic, far more cynical motives. Like any politician, Shimon Peres had half an eye on the next election. King Hussein wanted to restore his influence on the West Bank. Yassir Arafat sought to retain a veto on any process that might exclude his PLO. The

Reagan administration looked upon the Middle East as a grave-yard for foreign policy.

Of all the participants in the so-called peace process, only Palestinians such as al-Masri could not be blamed for its eventual failure. Responsibility for that rested with King Hussein and Yassir Arafat, with Washington and Jerusalem.

Much as she enjoyed such a good relationship with Ronald Reagan, Margaret Thatcher expressed a degree of impatience with American thinking on the Middle East.

The British Foreign Office, like Washington, saw the potential for the troika embracing Peres, Hussein and Arafat. But, unlike the Americans, the British did not feel as many inhibitions about talking to the PLO. As far back as 1980, a special envoy, Sir John Graham, had been sent to Beirut to see Yassir Arafat. Such recognition of the PLO was in line with the European Common Market's stated policy, the Venice Declaration of 1980, which effectively called for the PLO's involvement in any peace talks. After the Lebanon war, the belief in Whitehall was that the Americans were failing to make the most of the opportunities the siege of Beirut had created. The British did not doubt the intuition and understanding of the Middle East displayed by President Reagan's envoy Richard Murphy, a skilled diplomat with lengthy experience as an ambassador in the Arab world. But they knew Murphy lacked firm support from the White House for a fresh American initiative. They concluded, rightly, that Washington sought only the appearance of progress. The impasse presented a situation tailor-made for a Prime Minister who had long since believed in the power of her own advocacy and a personal philosophy: 'no risk, no progress'.

In September 1985, Mrs Thatcher, the first British premier to visit Jordan, arrived in Amman. King Hussein, an old and trusted friend, appealed for her to make the move at which the Americans balked. He asked her to meet members of the PLO; in effect, to give the PLO the very legitimacy which the Americans refused. The British Ambassador to Amman, John Coles, had briefed the Foreign Office on the possibility during the build-up to the visit. Coles, formerly a key member of Mrs Thatcher's personal staff at Downing Street, lent his voice with the backing of the Prime

Minister's adviser on the Middle East, Stephen Egerton.

The Prime Minister deferred her final decision to the penulti-mate day of the trip, when she visited the Palestinian refugee camp of Baq'aa just outside Amman. Surrounded by crowds wherever she went, Mrs Thatcher was led through the squalid backstreets and open sewers of a camp housing 65,000 people. Frequently, she was harangued by those who reminded her of Britain's responsi-bility to the Palestinians. At first somewhat taken aback, she was visibly moved by children presented to her as the orphans of those who had died in war against Israel. By the time she returned to Amman that evening, Mrs Thatcher had made her decision. The British would meet two senior members of the PLO's executive committee in London the following month. From Washington, Secretary of State George Shultz gave his private unpublicized approval. But closely as the British had consulted the Americans throughout the week, the Reagan administration showed itself both unenthusiastic and highly sceptical.

The stage was set for the British to engineer a breakthrough in the Middle East. However irrelevant and marginal it may have come to seem just a few weeks later, no one underestimated its significance at the time. The Foreign Office had designed the meeting to prompt the Americans into action, and, as one of Mrs Thatcher's advisers put it, to nail Arafat's colours to the flag of peace, non-violence, and recognition of Israel.

'One can't go on, sitting back and watching the young on both sides in the Middle East die in futile wars,' Mrs Thatcher explained during an interview on the final day of her trip. 'To those who will criticize us for this, I say: look what happened when Anwar Sadat went to Jerusalem.'[23]

Ian Davidson had a personal history which could have been written by any social worker in the depressed north-eastern corner of Mrs Thatcher's Britain. Just 22, unskilled, unemployed, he was one of thousands seeking a future beyond that of the dole queue. In September 1985, three years after he had left his home on Tyneside, he arrived in Cyprus, the same week as Mrs Thatcher visited the Middle East. He had no way of knowing it at the time, but his mission would wreak havoc with the peace process the British government was so keen to nurture.

Davidson aroused no suspicion as he checked in through immigration control at Larnaca Airport off the morning flight from Athens. Much as the Cypriots were aware of the danger of Palestinian terrorism, Davidson carried a British passport; his purpose for visiting the holiday island was noted as tourism. For the next five days, as Mrs Thatcher visited first Egypt, then Jordan, he paid a daily visit to the marina at Larnaca, spending hours reading the British newspapers and taking the sun. He knew which yacht to look for; he was able to match the descriptions of the two men and one woman on board with those he had been given in Athens. At the weekend, after the Prime Minister had flown back to London from Jordan, he called his contact in Athens – a man known to him as Ali Zaibak.*

Zaibak had recruited him for the PLO when Davidson had stopped in Greece two years before, working his way round the world. Zaibak had befriended him first, then slowly explained the plight of the Palestinians. In 1983, Zaibak gave him a ticket to Lebanon and an introduction to Abu Jihad, the military commander of the PLO. The young Englishman had been a member of the organization ever since.

'All my life I have felt the need to do something useful, to help the oppressed,' Davidson wrote to his parents in 1983. 'Don't the Palestinians have a right to a home just like us?'[24]

At the weekend, Davidson informed Zaibak in Athens that the yacht was sitting in the harbour, and that the Israelis were on board. They seemed to spend most days at the marina, he said: they had not set out to sea for days. Davidson was joined by Ali Nassif, whose real name was Salah Nassif, a native of Beirut, and Mahmoud Abdallah, real name Osama Tukan, a Palestinian born in Nablus. They picked up six hand grenades, two pistols with silencers, and a Russian-made AK-47 rifle from a safe house used by the PLO in Larnaca.

---

*Ali Zaibak was the alias for Shafiq Risa'a al-Ansar, who had at various stages of his career been bodyguard to Yassir Arafat and European operations officer for the PLO's elite commando unit, Force 17. A veteran of the Black September squad, the terrorist unit set up by the late Wadi Haddad after the 1970 civil war in Jordan, Ali Zaibak ran the so-called Greek contingent of Force 17 from 1982 onwards, based in Athens. He was killed in the Israeli raid on Tunis on October 1 1985.

At dawn on Wednesday September 25, just five days after Mrs Thatcher had left the Middle East, Davidson and the two Palestinians stormed aboard the yacht at Larnaca marina. The woman became the first victim, her bullet-ridden body left dangling over the yacht rail. When the Cypriot national guard got aboard, they also found the bodies of the two men bound and gagged by the side of the beds in the main bunk. They had been shot through the head. All three had been active agents for Mossad, the Israeli secret service. In 1985 alone, they had tipped off the Israelis to two PLO attempts to land commandos on the coast near Tel Aviv. In both cases, yachts from Cyprus had been intercepted. In the first instance, in April, the Israelis killed 20 Palestinian gunmen.

Little did he know it that Wednesday morning, as he stepped ashore at Larnaca handcuffed to a Cypriot policeman, raising his fingers in a victory salute, but Ian Davidson had helped to spark off the bloodiest period in the Middle East since the invasion of Lebanon in 1982. In the process, the Israelis would bomb PLO headquarters in Tunisia, killing more than 60 people. A renegade faction of Arafat's PLO would hijack an Italian cruise ship, the *Achille Lauro*, carrying hundreds of American tourists. The Reagan administration would force down an Egyptian airliner transporting the Palestinian gunmen responsible for the *Achille Lauro* to freedom.

In the meantime, on the diplomatic front, Mrs Thatcher cancelled the meeting with the PLO in London after Arafat's delegates refused to meet the British preconditions: renunciation of the hijackers' tactics and recognition of Israel. For its part, the White House had ruled out any prospect of a breakthrough in the life of the administration.

In response, King Hussein and Shimon Peres entered into one last, increasingly desperate effort to salvage a compromise that would draw the US back into the region. Their plan, hammered out at a pace that was almost breathtaking given the deadlock of nearly two decades, hinged on the Palestinians of the West Bank.

On Friday October 4 1985, three days after the Israelis retaliated for the killings at Larnaca by bombing the PLO's command post outside Tunis, Shimon Peres flew secretly to Paris to meet King

Hussein. Only the Prime Minister's personal staff knew of the trip. As the *New York Times* later reported, even Israeli diplomats in Washington were unable to track him down with the message that President Reagan wished to speak to him urgently. They were told that Peres, flying on a private Jet Commander to France, was unavailable, even for the President.[25]

During 24 hours of talks, the two leaders made almost as many concessions to each other as their countries had done in all the years since the 1967 war. Peres agreed to an international conference that would include both the US and the Soviet Union, a cardinal demand of Hussein because he sought a forum in which the Arabs would not be left at the mercy of the alliance between Washington and Jerusalem. The two leaders agreed on a 'rolling conference' that could last months, if not years: as long as it took to get an agreement. The superpowers would attend the opening. The agenda would then be taken up by the parties themselves, negotiating directly with each other. In return, Peres obtained the concession he valued above all others. The King said he would avoid the PLO's direct involvement, enlisting Palestinians who could speak for Arafat but still be acceptable to the Israelis. Lastly, they shook hands on an immediate plan for the West Bank. Peres promised to speed up the appointment of Arab Mayors in the major towns: an 'interim solution' which would hold together the agreement reached in Paris. Zafer al-Masri, they agreed, would be the first.

At Saturday lunchtime, the two leaders parted, knowing that both had been compromised by the clandestine session together. Proof of good intent came as Peres was about to leave for Jerusalem. The King gave him a copy of the speech he was to deliver to the UN General Assembly within a few days, soliciting his thoughts. Peres promised to do likewise before his own speech at the UN later that month.

In the last week of October, Peres, speaking before the General Assembly, declared an end to the state of war between Israel and Jordan. He called for talks within 30 days. He said that he was prepared to go to Amman if necessary. He informed the White House of his willingness to accept an international conference. The Reagan administration dismissed the proposal out of hand, saying the inclusion of the Soviets would negate the long-term aims of American policy in the Middle East. King Hussein, who had received an advance copy of the Peres speech secretly from the American envoy Richard Murphy, welcomed it immediately. Peres, he told the *New York Times*, was 'a man of vision, worthy of our applause ... a light in the darkness'. As for the Americans, the King expressed dismay over their refusal to budge. The only viable option, he concluded, lay on the West Bank.

The crowd that waited outside the town hall in Nablus represented a cross-section of the Palestinians who had lived under occupation since 1967. From the host of small villages surrounding the city came peasant farmers, dressed simply in well-worn suits and plain, white *kefiyas*. Well-heeled businessmen, sons of the families that had run Nablus for generations, mingled with workers from their own factories. A group of teenagers, in T-shirts and jeans, stood at the back of the crowd with signs that said 'Nablus first!'

'By coming back to the town hall, I express the wish of the people of Nablus,' said Zafer al-Masri when he emerged from the town hall as the city's new Mayor in December 1985. 'I express the hope as well that others will follow our lead. Together, the Palestinians of the West Bank will march forward to claim our freedom.'[(26)]

Al-Masri had taken his final decision a few weeks before. Visiting Amman, he had seen both King Hussein and Yassir Arafat. Despite the open rift between Jordan and the PLO, created by the wave of killings and counter-killings, the King and Arafat had sanctioned al-Masri's acceptance of the job. The PLO leader had personally assured him that he would come to no harm. 'You have our blessing and protection,' Arafat told him.

Returning home, al-Masri met with Shimon Peres. The Prime Minister had known the al-Masri family for years. Zafer, he felt, had all the makings of true leadership: honest, straightforward, a little naïve maybe, but his own man in the face of the conflicting interests of Israel, Jordan and the PLO. 'I pray your bravery will be rewarded,' Peres said as they parted.

As the people raised their new leader shoulder-high outside the town hall, shouting his name with a passion that made him blush, Zafer al-Masri kept his thoughts to himself. Whether he wanted it or not, he had assumed a key role in what the Middle East defined

Jew and Arab praying at
Abraham's Tomb, Hebron
(Rachamim Israeli)

Kiryat Arba, the first Israeli settlement, 1972

On guard at Hadassah
House, Hebron. 'Did
Abraham live in a
fenced-off Kiryat Arba?
No, he lived in Hebron'
– Miriam Levinger, 1979

Israeli army patrol,
Hebron, 1985

Rabbi Moshe Levinger
and Hanan Porat celebrate
with Gush Emunim
supporters, 1976

The new cities of the West Bank – Maaleh Adumim, Jerusalem

Dhehaishe refugee camp, Bethlehem

Demonstration against confiscation of land near Ramallah, 1985

Riots at Kalandia refugee camp, 1985

Above left: 'We didn't wait 2,000 years to go back to Uganda' – Moshe Arens (*centre*) tours the West Bank
Above right: 'If the PLO accepts Israel, I say great . . . let's talk' – Ezer Weizman, former Defence Minister, 1986

King Hussein and Yassir Arafat, Amman, 1984 (ITN)

Zafer al-Masri, assassinated March 1986

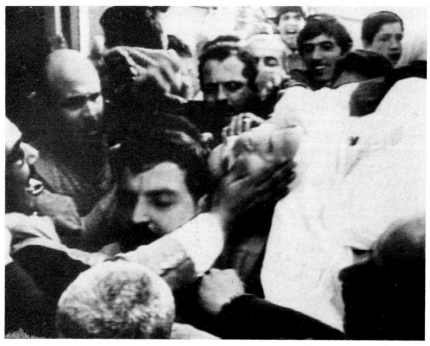

The funeral of Zafer al-Masri (ITN)

Yehuda Etzion, co-leader of the
Jewish underground

Members of the Jewish underground leave court, Jerusalem, May 1985

Palestinian labour market, Gaza Strip, 1985

Waiting for work – Palestinian farm hand, Gaza, 1985

Khalil Utal, born 1913, Breir, Palestine. Resident of Shati refugee camp, Gaza, from 1948

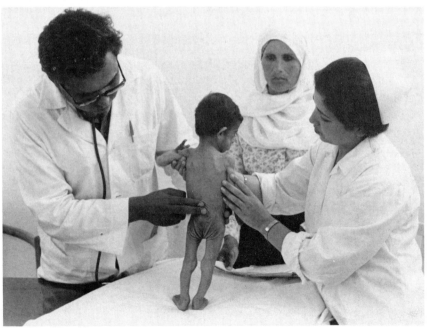

A case of malnutrition and dysentery, Gaza, 1985

Woman demonstrator arrested in east Jerusalem, 1984 (Rachamim Israeli)

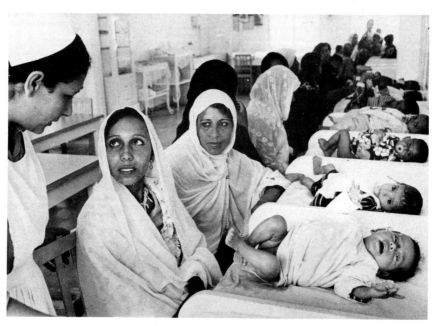

The demographic clock – 'By the year 2020 there will be more Arabs than Israelis'

Morning prayers in the political wing of Ramle prison, 1985 (Rachamim Israeli)

PLO rally at Bir Zeit University, 1987

Student elections, Nablus, 1986

PLO bombing of Israeli bus, 1983

Two Israels – Shimon Peres and Yitzhak Shamir, 1985

'We have never been a conquering nation' – Shimon Peres, 1986

The price of occupation – riots, Gaza, December 1986

The family of Majed Dhra, killed in Nablus, December 1986

Rabbi Meir Kahane: 'Israel can be Jewish or democratic but not both'

'Every day he gets closer to his goal' – Ariel Sharon, 1986

as a peace process. In the words of an aide to Peres, al-Masri was the only cornerstone in place.

Like almost every foray abroad he had made since becoming Prime Minister, the trip to Europe in January 1986 marked yet another success for Shimon Peres. In Holland, in Britain, and finally in West Germany he had been welcomed in a manner that David Ben-Gurion, his mentor, would have enjoyed. His was the voice of compromise and conciliation that the West wanted to hear from Israel. Shimon Peres, remarked Mrs Thatcher during his stop in London, symbolized Israel returning to its principles.

By now, though, Peres was haunted by the prospect of failure. For the first time in 18 months, the Americans, through Ambassador Murphy, were displaying some interest but still no urgency. Murphy saw Peres in The Hague at the beginning of the trip, then went ahead of him to check with Hussein in London, and caught up with Peres again as he arrived at Claridge's hotel. The American shuttle gave the impression of being as intense as anything Kissinger had attempted. Yet Murphy, an able diplomat but not a powerbroker, lacked the political clout Kissinger had always brought to bear on the parties. The US effort, lamented Peres over breakfast one morning in London, was too little, too late.

On the final day of his European tour, the Prime Minister braved biting cold and heavy snow to visit the memorial honouring the tens of thousands of Jews who died in Hitler's concentration camp at Bergen-Belsen. For so many Israelis, the holocaust amounted to both personal experience and the *raison d'être* for the Jewish state. For Shimon Peres that morning, it served as a reminder of his childhood in Poland and the quest for Israel's security in the 1980s. Arriving back in Israel that night, he said: 'Time is running out. We wait for King Hussein. And for a decision.'[27]

Personally, King Hussein once confided, he liked Yassir Arafat. But politically, he explained, they were 'out of sync'. The King's main aim, a solution on the West Bank, conflicted with Arafat's constant juggling of all available options. Hussein's innate honesty never meshed with Arafat's conscious duplicity. The PLO leader was a born optimist, Hussein a life-long pessimist. If the two men who controlled the future of the Palestinians had anything in common, it was caution. That, as much as anything else, explained why their alliance collapsed in early 1986 – and the Middle East peace process died yet again.

For seven days and as many nights, the Jordanians and the PLO haggled over terms that would enable the King to negotiate with the Israelis. The intensity of the negotiations, with daily meetings between Arafat and the Jordanian Prime Minister Zeid al-Rifai, suggested good intent on all sides. But the talks were largely designed to bury the search for peace with decency. The most important decision had already been taken weeks before, in Baghdad, when Arafat had called a meeting of his executive committee to discuss recognition of Israel. The PLO's Foreign Minister, Farouk Kaddoumi, had cut short the discussion by calling for a vote. It was six–five against acceptance. Yet Arafat, the epitome of ambivalence, had abstained without casting a vote. Had he supported the motion, deadlock would have given him the final decision. The King felt betrayed.

As a result, the talks in Jordan assumed a tragic air of unreality. The PLO agreed to veiled recognition of Israel but they sought a clear definition of the Palestinians' right to elect their own leaders. Like Resolution 242 and the issue of terrorism, that question of self-determination became yet another obstacle. Arafat's incentive, to obtain a guarantee that the Palestinians would freely elect the leaders of a future state, became the King's disincentive. The thing that Arafat wanted – PLO control in years to come – was what the King feared more than anything else. The political ballet defied common sense. They were no longer discussing the issue at hand, a way to get talks going with Israel, but rather a future balance of power in a state they had yet to negotiate. Together they stood a chance, however limited, of bargaining for such a state. Separately, neither could challenge Israel to make peace. When they split they knew they had lost the best opportunity since the 1967 war to seek a solution.

The recriminations that followed somehow mocked the high hopes of Palestinians living on the West Bank and Gaza. As always, these people had looked abroad for leadership. As usual, the decision on their future had been taken in a foreign capital by those who had not witnessed their plight for nearly two decades. Arafat accused the King of treachery, Hussein responding with the same charge. 'For every Palestinian it was a nightmare,' said Hana Siniora, the Editor of an east Jerusalem newspaper who was called in as an intermediary. 'We had come such a long way since Beirut, only to fail yet again.'

A week after talks broke up, King Hussein launched a diplomatic offensive aimed at winning the support of Palestinians on the West Bank and in Gaza. 'We are unable,' said Hussein towards the end of a three-hour speech broadcast live to the Arab world and the territories, 'to continue to work with the PLO until such time as their word becomes their bond.' But he had an equally clear message for the Israelis. He would not, he said, go it alone in any negotiations with them.[28]

In Jerusalem, some celebrated. Ariel Sharon called it yet another victory over the PLO. Yitzhak Shamir expressed delight at King Hussein's decision. 'Thank God,' wrote one newspaper columnist sardonically, 'there are still some Arabs who can be relied on not to make peace.'[29]

Of all the country's leaders, only Prime Minister Peres sounded a sombre note. 'The situation has gone back to square one,' he said. 'As always, those who will suffer are the Arabs in the occupied territories.'

Two days after the King's speech, Zafer al-Masri entertained visitors at the Mayor's office in Nablus. He was dividing his time between negotiations with the Israelis for an Arab bank in the city and talks with his fellow Palestinians about how best to respond to the break between Hussein and Arafat.

'The history of the Palestinians is littered with such mistakes,' he remarked at one point. 'The West Bank is learning to trust its own people and no one else. I don't think we can look to the world outside any more for a solution.'

He added: 'It makes me feel even more determined to do my job here. At least there is decency in that.' In the meantime, he proposed to write a letter to the King and Arafat, urging them to reconsider.

For the first time in 20 months, Shimon Peres was said to have stopped work on Saturday, the Jewish Sabbath, and spent a quiet day at home with his wife Sonya, writing letters and reading in the large patio garden of his official residence in Jerusalem. By early evening, he was back at work, devouring proposals from his Finance Minister Yitzhak Modai. The following day, March 2 1986, the cabinet was due to review the economic progress of the past 20 months. Reducing inflation and restoring stability to a country that faced bankruptcy after the Lebanon war represented his major achievements in government.

That evening, in conversation with an aide, Peres had expressed his customary optimism. The peace process had never been anything more than a long shot at a forlorn hope, he remarked. His success on the domestic front made him believe he could win the next election on his record alone.

That Saturday, the first day of the Arab working week, King Hussein received a delegation from the West Bank and Gaza at the Basman Palace in Amman. In long lines, Palestinian notables from towns and villages loyal to the King were ushered into a magnificent reception hall where they bowed in homage.

Under the fierce glare of television lights, the King spoke to each group in turn, defending his decision to break with the PLO, urging Palestinians under Israeli occupation to give him their backing. At one point, he recalled the teaching of his grandfather, King Abdullah, assassinated in Jerusalem with his grandson at his side 34 years before.

'My grandfather always told me: "So much has gone before you, don't be the disappointing link,"' the King reminisced.

'Sirs,' he added, looking down through the body of his audience, 'I will never betray my family's history or the responsibility that goes with it.'[30]

At his headquarters outside Tunis, Yassir Arafat spent much of the day alone, preparing for yet another meeting of his executive committee, this time to discuss the PLO's military build-up in southern Lebanon.

Arafat did not disguise his concern with the King's courtship of West Bankers. Effectively outlawed from Jordan, he had lost access to the very people he represented. The reports from

Amman, of busloads arriving from the occupied territories to see Hussein, presented an open challenge to his monopoly of West Bank support. In the years since 1967, Arafat had done little to encourage local Palestinian leadership in the territories. In isolation once more, he had some reason to fear the emergence of local Palestinian leaders in the town halls of cities such as Nablus and Hebron.

As usual, Zafer al-Masri got up the minute the alarm went off at six, a habit that had become a discipline during his days as a student in Beirut. By 6.30, he was bathed and shaved. By 6.45, he was waking up his two daughters with a cup of tea. That was the only time of the day he could reserve for them. That morning they had teased him about how important he was, how friends at school had mentioned his name, how their uncles talked about him and no one else. The girls remembered his words. The only thing that made him important, he had told them, was the fact that he was their father.

The day before, his wife recalled, Shmuel Goren from the Israeli Defence Ministry had telephoned looking for him. All that her husband would tell her was that Goren wanted him to have bodyguards.* Al-Masri did not elaborate, and he made it clear he did not wish to discuss it any further. Therefore, that Sunday morning over breakfast, they had talked about dinner plans for the evening. He mentioned that two business colleagues would be coming to see him. They had to finish a letter they were planning to send to King Hussein. That reminded him, he said. He had to take the draft of the letter into the office with him that morning.

At 7.45, Zafer al-Masri left for work, one of the joys of his job as Mayor being that it was only a one-minute walk from their apartment to the Nablus town hall.

Raghda al-Masri was getting the children ready for school when she heard the shots ring out. No one would need to come and tell her. She knew what had happened.

---

*General Shmuel Goren was appointed the Defence Ministry's chief co-ordinator for the occupied territories in 1984.

Shimon Peres had never been known as the most punctual of politicians. His appetite for yet another cigarette or that final round of conversation constantly forced his staff to rearrange his schedule at regular intervals during his average 18-hour day. As Prime Minister, though, he was never late for cabinet on Sunday. Just as well, joked one of his Labour Party colleagues. If he had been, Shamir would have taken his seat.

On the stroke of nine that Sunday morning, Prime Minister Peres directed his cabinet secretary, Yossi Beilin, to take note of the Israeli government's condolences to the family of Zafer al-Masri. Israel had lost a partner in peace, he said. The Palestinians had lost a leader of the highest calibre. The Middle East had lost yet another opportunity for compromise.

Afterwards, Ariel Sharon remarked that Peres would have to realize the futility of the search for an Arab ally. Another minister said: 'Whatever hopes Shimon had of progress during his time died this morning in Nablus.'

At the Basman Palace in Amman, King Hussein was said to have been informed shortly after he arrived at his office. The King's reaction, by all accounts, was silent acknowledgement. He ordered that arrangements be made for him to pay his respects at the home of Taher al-Masri, a nephew of Zader's and Foreign Minister in the Jordanian government.

Crown Prince Hassan, heir to the throne, summed up the mood at the palace that morning. The cause of peace, he said, had lost the most valuable of allies. Only the extremists on both sides would derive any satisfaction from the killing of yet another innocent victim.

In Tunis, Yassir Arafat, accustomed to such news, reacted instinctively. His aides recalled that he had dictated a statement of condolence, later issued by the PLO's news agency Wafa. Shortly afterwards he was said to have spoken to Abu Jihad, his deputy, in Jordan. The chairman's order was clear.

No matter that in his life Zafer al-Masri had been more loyal to the King than to the PLO, no matter that he had enjoyed good relations with the Israelis. In death, he would be *shahid*, a martyr for the PLO, a hero of the PLO struggle against both the King and the Israelis. Abu Jihad was to convey that message to every branch of the organization in the West Bank before the funeral.

Shortly before midday, Yacoub Dawani, spokesman for George Habash and the Popular Front for the Liberation of Palestine, released a statement to Western news agencies in the Syrian capital, Damascus. Dawani, who had grown up in Nablus and had known al-Masri as a child, read from a prepared text.

'Today the PFLP commando Che Guevara Gaza, operating in occupied Palestine, carried out the death sentence on Zafer al-Masri in front of the municipal building in Nablus.

'The people's judgement, to execute Zafer al-Masri, was due to his part in the Zionist–Jordanian reactionary project to liquidate the Palestinian cause, against the will of the Palestinian people.'[31]

Weeks later, Dr Habash said in an interview: 'You ask me whether I feel any compunction about such action. Of course I do. But it is not a question of individuals. Individuals can't make peace, behind the back of the people. Only the Palestinian nation can make peace.'

Was Yassir Arafat informed beforehand?

'I do not know,' said Habash. 'But I would expect Arafat to have known what justice demanded.'[32]

Inevitably, Israelis and even some Palestinians pointed the finger of suspicion at the PLO leader. In the Middle East, it is almost customary to weigh the effect before judging the cause.

At dawn on Monday March 3 1986, the Israelis ordered the army to show a presence on the streets of Nablus but no more than that. By mid morning hundreds had started demonstrating in the Balata refugee camp on the outskirts of the city. Coming under attack from rocks and molotov cocktails, one Israeli unit had arrested some 30 masked men building barricades out of burning tyres. Mohammed Abu-Dhra, 57 years old, had grabbed a soldier by the throat. The patrol commander shot him at point-blank range. He died on his way to the hospital, his son Mahmoud with him after being shot and wounded in the pitched battle that followed. Given the fact that the State Department, Downing Street and the Elysée

Palace had told their diplomats to attend Zafer al-Masri's funeral, the Israelis felt they had no option but to withdraw the army.

That afternoon, from the balconies of private homes high on the hill overlooking Nablus, Israeli army officers watched as the funeral procession wound its way down the main street of the city. Thousands of demonstrators, representing universities and schools, trade unions and refugee camps, had occupied the city. They were carrying portraits of both al-Masri and Arafat. They were jubilantly waving the Palestinian flag. They were shouting 'No to Israel! No to Jordan! No to autonomy! Yes, yes, yes to the PLO!'

As they made their way into the casbah, thousands more joined the procession. Many had covered their faces with checked *kefiyas*, their eyes peering out from beneath their masks. Many raised two fingers in a victory salute. Most were clapping, whistling, chanting.

'No to Peres! No to Hussein! No to autonomy!'

'Yes, yes, yes to Arafat!'

Zafer al-Masri's funeral represented, quite simply, the biggest demonstration ever mounted in the West Bank after the 1967 war. The Israelis did not dare intervene. Nablus belonged to the PLO for as long as it took to bury Zafer. After more than two hours the cortege reached its destination: the al-Masri family mosque, built by Zafer's uncle, once himself a Mayor of Nablus.

As the crowd fought among themselves to touch the dead man's face, some to kiss his forehead, the pall-bearers removed the Palestinian flag they had draped over his coffin. Wrapped in a white linen cloth, the blood from the fatal head wound clearly visible, Zafer al-Masri was carried aloft above the heads of the crowd to his tomb.

Throughout the city, it seemed, one cry rang out.

'*Shahid!* Martyr!'

On March 4 1986, two days after al-Masri's murder, Palestinian leaders in the West Bank towns of Ramallah, Hebron and Al-Bireh withdrew their applications to become Mayors.

PART TWO

BETWEEN
TWO TRUTHS

'When truths collide, compromise becomes the first casualty.' – HENRY KISSINGER, THE WHITE HOUSE YEARS

'All government – indeed, every human benefit and enjoyment, every virtue and every prudent act – is founded on compromise.' – EDMUND BURKE

5
THE PALESTINIANS ARE A JEWISH PROBLEM

'History will judge us by the way we treat the Arabs.'
– CHAIM WEIZMANN, PRESIDENT OF ISRAEL, MAY 1948

The eternal rush and ebb of the Mediterranean, the beauty of the white-flecked, green waves and the soft, sandy beach made it Israel's equivalent of a Riviera. Out at sea, a small group of Israelis yachted in calm waters, their sails fluttering gently in the warm breeze. On the beach others sunbathed or played the national game of *matkot*, paddle-ball. They had already built more than 20 settlements. They had plans for holiday villages, windsurfing clubs, even a yachting marina.

Yet the idyllic coastline was marred by one eyesore. A huge refugee camp, teeming with row after row of adobe-like huts built out of cinder block and scrap iron, hugged the same shore. Crowded streets were shrouded by lines of washing. Open sewers emitted the stench of raw sewage. Dozens of children, half-clothed and shoeless, stood in line at a supplementary ration centre. Donkeys and goats fed off piles of rubbish nearby. The narrow alleyways were filled with women, carrying buckets on their heads, padding barefoot towards the sea, where they would dump their garbage alongside the fishing boats.

'I don't want you to be shocked,' said an Israeli army colonel. 'Don't expect to see camps like Sabra and Chatilla in Beirut. Down here they are much worse.'

'Welcome to the Gaza Strip', said the sign that marked the only entrance and exit of this forgotten and unwanted corner of Palestine. An hour from the tree-lined boulevards of Tel Aviv, 20 miles from the busy Israeli city of Ashkelon, a few miles down the road from resorts where tourists paid handsomely for a holiday on the shore, Gaza stood as an indictment of Palestinian history and Israeli occupation. The vast shanty town on the shore was reminiscent of Africa or the Far East, yet representative of the slums that formed so much of Gaza. The majority of its people were refugees: they had lived in camps since 1948. For a generation, until 1967, they suffered the harsh rule of the Egyptians. Since then they had occupied the Soweto of Israel, as critics called it. By 1987, nearly 600,000 Palestinians were living there, crammed into a tiny strip of desert measuring just 29 miles by five. After Hong Kong, the statisticians said, Gaza was the most densely populated spot on earth with 3,560 people to the square mile. With an annual birth rate of 4.7 per cent, three times that of Israel, the population by the year 2000 would rise to the million mark.

'Gaza is Israel's demographic nightmare,' Shimon Peres said in an interview. 'The population explosion has already happened. One cannot imagine what the political fall-out might be.'[1] In 1985, his government had floated the idea of negotiating over Gaza with Egypt separately from the West Bank. Politely but firmly the Egyptians refused. 'Gaza is a time-bomb,' explained one cabinet minister, Ezer Weizman. 'No government in its right mind could possibly want the place. I'd give it back tomorrow if someone would take it.'[2]

'Gaza is proof for anyone who comes to see it,' declared Hatem Abu Ghazala, a Gazan doctor well-known for his outspoken criticism of the Israelis, 'that occupation has become a quicksand for both us and the Israelis. There is no easy way out, either for us or for them.'[3]

At her office, in a maze of newly painted, prefabricated buildings that served as UN headquarters in Gaza city, Mrs Angela

130

Williams offered a newcomer's view of the territory. 'Coming here after working elsewhere in the Middle East,' explained the deputy chief of the United Nations Relief and Works Agency for Palestine Refugees (UNRWA), 'what surprises me is how cowed, how passive the people here are. At times they are pathetic. It is as if they have been beaten into submission, or put to sleep by the system.'[4]

After Jordan, she added, Gaza had more refugees than any other area of the region. Like Lebanon, families of 12 living in one small hut were not uncommon. Like Syria, she said, the local Israeli prisons were full most days with political detainees. With just a trace of disgust in her voice, she listed 840 cells in Gaza jail, 500 more up the road in Ashkelon.

For 4,300 years, Gaza had been the sparring ground for foreign rulers, stretching from the Pharoahs of the Egyptian empire to the Israelis. The first Palestinians, the Philistines who came from the Aegean, were dispatched to the Strip by the Pharoahs as mercenaries against the first Israelis, the Canaanites of the land to the north and west of Gaza. The Romans, the Byzantines, the Arabs and the Ottomans had colonized the territory as the southern gateway to the Holy Land. In his day, Napoleon had coveted Gaza as the ideal military base from which to launch his abortive campaign to control the Middle East. In 1948, Gaza was placed under Egyptian administration, as Palestine was divided between Arabs and Jews. For 19 years, with a three-month interruption when the Israelis invaded the Strip during the Suez crisis of 1956, President Nasser of Egypt had ruled Gaza with a blend of aggression, callousness and inhumanity that the Arab world compared to Nazism.* With the territory bloated by tens of thousands of refugees fleeing south from the newly created Israel, the Egyptians imposed martial law in 1948. They made nightly curfew indefinite; they forcibly conscripted refugees into the Egyptian army. Prohibited by law from purchasing or owning land, facing

---

*Typical of the Arab world's criticism was a broadcast on Radio Mecca in March 1962: 'Imagine, Arabs, how Nasser treats the starving people of Gaza ... The methods are the ones which the dictator Hitler used on the countries he occupied.'

the kind of restrictions the blacks of South Africa have endured for generations, the Palestinians turned the camps into permanent homes which came to resemble South African's bantustans. With little Egyptian support for housing, health care, farming or industry, Gaza became a human wasteland.

President Nasser had specific use for the people of Gaza. The strip was, he said after Suez, a dagger at the heart of Israel and a base from which to send Palestinian *fedayeen,* guerrillas, on a campaign of sabotage and murder. As for the unremitting squalor and degradation of the refugee camps, a British relief worker of the day, Alexander Galloway, had defined the tactics of the Arab states. Galloway resigned from UNRWA in the late 1950s with this bitter denunciation of Arab leaders such as Nasser: 'They don't want to solve the refugee problem. They want to keep it as an open sore, as a weapon against Israel. Arab leaders don't give a damn whether the refugees live or die.'[5]

When the Six-Day War began, the Egyptians armed the civilian population and ordered them to support the Palestinian units which Nasser's field commanders had been recruiting since 1948. They fought street by street, one refugee camp to another, house by house for the towns of the strip – Khan Younis, Rafah, Gaza city. Furious hand-to-hand combat claimed scores of lives in the final hours. Early on June 7 1967, the third day of the war, Gaza fell. With the exceptions of Jerusalem and Nablus, Gaza Palestinians mounted the only serious resistance to the Israelis – as Israel's retribution reflected.[6]

The Israeli army destroyed thousands of homes in the camps, relentlessly hunting down those fighters who had got away, opening fire on anyone who dared to break curfew. When the army gave PLO suspects a straight choice – prison or exile – hundreds chose deportation. Refugees were told to submit names of family members working abroad in the Arab countries. Many of those who did so were dumped at the Jordan River and ordered to cross.[7]

'There was no way to contain the situation in Gaza,' recalled Motta Gur, whose triumph at Temple Mount had been rewarded with appointment as Gaza's first Military Governor. 'The size of the refugee camps, the way they had been built, and the people themselves. It was like a wall of hatred, standing in front of us.'[8]

When the Israelis captured Gaza, they discovered that the

132

population had, since 1948, almost doubled to more than 350,000. In the months that followed, the fledgling PLO distributed arms caches that had been stored underground in a secret network of tunnels and sewers. By day, the Israelis controlled Gaza. By night, the *fedayeen* guerrillas of the PLO patrolled, executing 'collaborators' and conscripting young recruits to the cause. The *fedayeen* fed off the hatred Motta Gur felt among these people: by 1970, they had converted hatred into open rebellion. In stark contrast to the relative calm on the West Bank, Gaza had become a battleground representing the PLO's first challenge to Israeli occupation.

Moshe Dayan's initial instinct was to abandon Gaza. 'Let them turn their lives into hell,' he said in 1969. But by the end of 1970, with the situation deteriorating into street warfare, he opted to crush the Palestinians. Dayan sent in Ariel Sharon with the elite commando unit Sharon had created in the 1950s to fight insurgency from the Jordanian-controlled West Bank. Sharon was said to have told his men: 'The only good terrorist is a dead one.'[9] Dressing as Arabs and posing as refugees, Sharon's brigade combed every corner of Gaza, hacking down orchards to clear a line of fire, bulldozing hundreds of refugee homes to enable them to drive through the camps, dressing as Arabs and living as refugees. According to Israeli estimates, they destroyed 6,300 homes. They evicted more than 20,000 Palestinians, imprisoned 1200. Sharon's men killed 742 'terrorists'.

'What we achieved in Gaza,' said Sharon in 1986, 'was something the Americans couldn't in Vietnam – total pacification.'[10]

In Gaza, the Israelis had no religious motivation for occupation. The territory had never been the Biblical land of the Jews. Unlike the West Bank, Gaza represented neither a national aspiration nor a political objective. Jews did settle there, but in small numbers and, initially at least, for defence purposes. Furthermore, the Palestinians of the territory expressed no firm allegiance to Israel's neighbours. The Egyptians had alienated opinion through a policy of intimidation and coercion. King Hussein and Jordan had never ruled there. Once Ariel Sharon had flushed the PLO out of the refugee camps, Gaza presented little immediate threat to Israel on either the military or political front. Indeed, the territory offered a human resource that Israel could exploit.

What Israel was short of – cheap manual labour – Gaza had in abundance. A vast Palestinian labour force, under-employed for generations, found a natural outlet in an Israeli society enjoying an economic boom after the Six-Day War. The Palestinians served Israel's purpose, manning a growth economy at a price that facilitated ever speedier development and improved the quality of life for the average Israeli. To the Palestinians, a job in Israel offered a short-term panacea for the poverty and desperation of the refugee camps. The relationship started as a marriage of convenience; it quickly became an economic necessity for both. Some Israelis saw the danger that such integration and interdependency posed. They argued that the exploitation of Arab labour raised a moral issue for which Israel had no easy answer.

'I must say that it's very sweet building Zionism with Arab labour, to build cities of the economy and enjoy it,' the trade-union leader Yitzhak Ben-Aharon said in 1973. 'We shall soon hear that anyone who says he doesn't want to get rich on the work of the Arabs from the territories questions the realization of Zionism and holds back redemption and development.'[11]

Successive Israeli governments voiced euphemistic concern about the impact Palestinian workers would have on Israeli society. The late Yigal Allon, deputy premier under Golda Meir, cited the 'undesirable social, human and moral distortions' their employment created. Yet for years Israeli leaders chose to ignore the trap their dependency on Palestinian labour presented. They believed that, in providing employment, they could solve the economic crisis Gaza faced and meet the needs of their own people. Throughout the 1970s and the early 1980s, as the number of workers from the territories increased dramatically, they did little to control the flow. By 1986, Israel employed more than 100,000 workers from the West Bank and Gaza. Approximately half of them were registered with the Israeli authorities: they paid regular income tax but received few of the benefits an Israeli could claim. The rest formed a large, illegal work-force: vulnerable prey for the Jewish farmers, builders and contractors who paid them less than the minimum rate for the job and who demanded a 12-hour day.

'It is a vicious circle, a symbiotic relationship between the haves and have-nots,' said Michael Shaleev, a sociologist who conducted a 1985 survey on workers from the territories. 'Like South Africa,

Israel has become dependent on black labour, in this case provided by the Palestinians. We need them as much as they need us.'[12]

The Israeli government did not deny it, nor did Israeli leaders doubt the long-term implications. For every Jewish settler who had moved to the West Bank or Gaza, two Palestinians migrated to Israel each day in search of jobs. The conditions under which they worked compromised the principles of justice and equality that modern Zionism claimed to espouse. Their presence alone suggested that Israel was no longer a Jewish state, but rather a bi-national country divided between Arab and Jew. In exploiting the spoils of victory after 1967, Israel had set a trap in which it would itself be caught.

At five a.m. the exodus of workers from Gaza to Israel began. Hundreds, then thousands gathered in Palestine Square, at the bus station that straddled Omar al-Muktar street. To the visitor, it could have looked more like a fiesta as the street sellers marched up and down, pushing small carts that served as mobile kitchens. They had soft, round bread rolls topped with sesame seeds or pita bread filled to overflowing with humous, a chick-pea sauce. They sold coffee or the refreshing *sahlab*, an aromatic beverage made of crushed almonds, milk and mastic. Shortly after five the *ra'isin*, the labour contractors, arrived. The men for hire flagged them down as they drew up in their cars and trucks. Some of the contractors did not bother to get out; they negotiated a deal through the driver's window. The *ra'isin* assumed the indifferent air of those who could afford to wait. The Palestinians in the crowd – asking, answering, accepting or rejecting – revealed the anxiety of those who did not dare to do so. It was the same most mornings in the winter of 1986. Invariably there were too many Palestinians chasing too few jobs in Israel.

Forty years old, the stooped figure of 'Khalil' hinted at years of work on the farms and kibbutzim of Israel. His hang-dog expression belied acceptance of the law of supply and demand that brought him to the labour market. That morning he was not looking for work, merely waiting for a ride to a farm just north of Ashkelon. He had been working there for the previous month, picking apples and oranges on a 50-acre plot owned by an Israeli whose name he did not know. He was grateful because the

135

guaranteed job avoided the bartering over a daily wage that so many others had to endure in Palestine Square. For a day that began at six and ended at four in the afternoon, he would earn 12 shekels, eight dollars, less than half the rate for the lowest-paid Israeli doing a similar job. He was thankful because, as dawn came to Gaza and the Palestinian working-day in Israel started, those left behind in Palestine Square would be forced to accept less than the 80 cents an hour he was getting.

At 5.30 the truck arrived, Khalil and three other labourers clambering on board with deceptive enthusiasm. By all accounts, being late at the farm cost an hour's pay. The talk that morning was of a *ra'isin* back in the square who had opened the bidding at the lowest rate heard for several weeks: nine shekels a day for a 10-hour shift at a bakery in Tel Aviv.

'He was offering a place to sleep, though,' said Wahid, a young, unshaven man with the kind of good looks that set him apart from the rest. 'That makes a big difference.'

'Not if you don't have papers,' added Fayez, a middle-aged man wrapped in a blanket at the back of the truck.

'In Tel Aviv one job usually leads to another.' The voice belonged to Ahmed, a friend of Wahid's, about the same age. His face was half-covered by a *kefiya* so well-worn that the colours were fading. 'And the money usually gets better as it goes along.'

Khalil, sitting close to Fayez at the rear, kept his thoughts to himself. Being and oldest and most experienced, he would wait his moment to lead the conversation, receiving rapt attention when he did so. As we left Gaza, being waved through the Israeli army checkpoint with none of the usual body-searches, he spread a blanket out beneath him and settled down to talk.

He remembered Tel Aviv well. For two years, he said, he had worked as a waiter at a restaurant in King George Street. On some days he waited on tables, on others he washed dishes. There had been six of them in all from Gaza. For a while, he had travelled back and forth every day, two hours there and two hours back. *'Min al-farshe al-warshe, min al-warshe 'al al-farshe,'* he said. 'From the mattress to the workplace, and back to the mattress.' After three months, he had joined the others and slept in a small room at the back of the restaurant. The manager would lock them in when he closed up so the police would not find them. All of them would travel back to Gaza on Friday afternoon, shortly before the

Jewish Sabbath began, and return at first light Sunday morning.

'After nearly two years,' he explained, 'the job finished. The manager didn't give me a reason.' He nodded knowingly, as if passing on wisdom to a younger generation. 'They never do give reasons.'

What followed, Khalil said as the truck headed north along the narrow, two-lane highway that led to Ashkelon, was the best job he had ever had. He had been gardener and cleaner for a Jewish family in Herzliyya Pituach, a wealthy, fashionable suburb on the coast just north of Tel Aviv. The money had been better, as had the food. They had given him a bed in the garden shed. He worked five and a half days a week for $45, paid in American currency, he added. He talked affectionately about the man of the house, a well-known Israeli businessman who spoke enough Arabic to hold a conversation with him.

'He would always say hello to me. He always made me feel I had a place there.' He stopped, wiping away the remains of breakfast with his cuff to reveal the faintest trace of a smile. 'I learned to like him. Somehow there was respect in that man.'

He gave no reason for the way that job ended. When the others resumed talking about Tel Aviv, he fell silent. When the younger ones suggested the bakery could have been a better prospect than their farm, he spat on the floor. As the truck approached Ashkelon, a traffic jam built up. Dozens of cars and buses, their headlights glaring in the early-morning mist, jockeyed for position as they reached the motorway that began just south of the town. There was not an Israeli to be seen. Yet thousands of Arabs had taken their place; the highway leading north belonged to them.

In 1948, they had been driven south to Gaza, forced to flee their homes and farms in villages that lay on either side of this road. For an hour or so this land was theirs once again in all but name. The dawn-to-dusk invasion of Palestinians from Gaza might have been inevitable, but they personified Israel's dilemma, both moral and political. Tens of thousands made this journey every day. Some paid taxes and received nothing in return. Many earned half the Israeli rate for the job. A few slept in Israel, illegally because they had no permits to do so. As for peace, such dependency on Arab labour raised serious doubts about whether Israel could ever afford to relinquish a territory that provided so much manpower for its farms, factories and building sites.

At six o'clock the truck pulled into the farm, a medium-sized Jewish homestead comprising about 50 acres of apple orchards and greenhouse nurseries growing tomatoes. As Khalil scrambled out of the back, he pointed across the fields to what looked like another kibbutz: his village, he said. Khalil was just one of many who returned most mornings to work on the land where they had been born.

For nearly 20 years, Rashad Shawa had given Gaza the kind of practical, hard-nosed leadership that the West Bank lacked. The last of the Palestinian aristocrats, Shawa had been the first of a new breed of politicians who defied both the Israelis and the PLO. In the process, he had expressed the despair of his people with a conviction that demanded respect. His refusal to compromise had won him the grudging admiration of all parties to the Middle East conflict. 'Much as we disagreed with him,' Yassir Arafat once remarked, 'we could never ignore him.'

Shawa was born to rule. His family had once owned vast tracts of Palestine. His youth was spent as a renowned sportsman and notorious playboy in the cities of Beirut, Cairo and Amman. He enjoyed expense-account living, complete with his own tailor and an old Cadillac. If he had undergone a conversion, he said, it had probably occurred in the unlikely surroundings of a ballroom in Haifa 50 years before.

A British friend had introduced the young, well-spoken, fastidiously dressed Rashad Shawa to a pretty Jewish girl. As they danced, she had asked him where he was from.

'From here,' he replied. 'From Palestine.'

'Where in Palestine?' she had inquired.

'From Gaza.'

'You mean you are not Jewish?'

'No, I am an Arab.'

Shawa, well into his 70s but still the tall, lean, impeccably dressed figure of his youth, grinned wryly as he recalled that night in Haifa.

'The minute I said that, she let her arms drop and left me stranded on the dance floor,' he said. 'It made a profound impression on me. Basically, I think I learned the Jews didn't want us here.'[13]

138

For nearly 40 years, since his return to Gaza in 1949, he had applied that lesson as he built a political career. Under the Egyptians, he acquired power by acquiescing in their use of the Strip as a springboard for guerrilla attacks on Israel. After the 1967 war, he flexed that political muscle to make himself indispensable to all parties in the conflict. Appointed Mayor of Gaza by the Israelis in 1972, then deposed in 1981, he kept an open line to King Hussein, his natural ally, and the PLO. Independent of all of them, he was the one they all listened to; pessimistic about Gaza's plight, he remained optimistic about a regional settlement; an advocate of conciliation, he managed to talk the PLO out of numerous plots to kill him. For almost 20 years, Shawa had proved to be the best barometer of political thinking in the occupied territories. Time and again he had set the pace for the direction taken by his fellow Palestinians, both in Gaza and the West Bank. The fact that he had always thrown his weight behind the PLO had been a decisive element in the support Yassir Arafat retained there.

'People are desperate, all they have left is the PLO,' he explained during an interview in 1985. 'Poverty and deprivation breeds politics and religion in a place like this. The PLO is like a religion for these people.'

Yet, in the summer of 1986, Shawa underwent a second conversion of sorts. The cue this time was the collapse of the alliance between King Hussein and Yassir Arafat a few weeks before. The PLO, he said, no longer understood what was happening in the territories. While they argued about whether to recognize UN resolutions and so legitimize Israel, the Jews were colonizing the territories, building settlements, assimilating workers; every time the PLO launched an attack or refused to negotiate, they gave Israel more time to destroy what was left of the Palestinian identity. As a consequence, the Israelis were enforcing a solution in the Middle East entirely on their own terms. The solution was the maintenance of the status quo. In July, he launched a devastating personal attack on Arafat and the PLO leadership he had done so much to create. He produced a damning litany of accusations to make his case for new leaders who would negotiate with Israel. For the first time, a Palestinian politician of substance offered an alternative to the PLO.

'The PLO is leading us blindly towards disaster,' Shawa said in a broadcast from Amman, seen and heard throughout the West

139

Bank and Gaza. 'They don't understand what we are suffering under Israeli occupation ... They hear but they don't listen ... instead they retire to their summer villas and forget ... They should serve us ... instead we serve them.'[14]

Shawa had always been his own best spokesman. Returning to Gaza, to face death threats and a chorus of criticism from all but the Israelis, he displayed a patriarch's disgust for those he considered lesser men.

'Can you imagine what 20 more years of occupation will do to Gaza?' he asked. 'We can't sit back any more and tell ourselves that time is on our side,' he declared. 'We have to challenge the Israelis, give them an alternative to the PLO.'

He concluded: 'The Palestinian problem is a Jewish problem. The Palestinians must save the Jews from themselves.'[15]

By eight o'clock Sama, who at the age of 12 was the eldest of Khalil's daughters, had started work in the orange groves of Beit Hanun on the outskirts of Gaza city.

Ever since her parents took her out of school a few months before, she had joined her mother in a 10-strong work gang, picking fruit for the Schurab family, one of Gaza's largest citrus producers. Tall for her age, and with her mother's strong, handsome features and eyes, Sama appeared to be built for the job. With a wicker basket over her shoulder, her hair and her forehead covered against the dirt, she worked faster than most through a lush, dense orange grove nearing the end of another harvest season. Methodically she paced the orchard, snatching fruit still on the leaf, stacking one basket after another at the end of each row of trees. A pleasant, happy girl, she stood out from the rest because she alone had the delight of an innocent in such exhausting work.

'She has to start some time,' said her mother. 'I started when I was much younger.'

'We don't have any choice,' remarked Ahmed Schurab, one of two brothers running the family's citrus corporation. 'Business is bad enough without worrying about who is going to get the fruit in before it rots.'

Under Israeli law, Sama was an illegal child labourer. Under Egyptian law, which was still applied in the Strip, she qualified at the age of 12, although not for the six hours a day, six days a week she worked for the Schurabs. In Gaza, the Israelis intervened only when they found cases of serious abuse; by that they meant child workers under eight years old. Such indifference was ironic – because her livelihood and that of thousands who worked in Gaza's citrus industry was threatened by Israel's rule of law in the occupied territories.

After 1967, the Israeli Military Government in Gaza and the West Bank passed more than 1,000 special decrees. Taken together, these formed a labyrinthine body of military 'legislation' to cover not just security matters but most aspects of day-to-day civilian life. The decrees ranged from how many eggplants a peasant farmer could grow, to how much money an individual could bring in from Jordan or Egypt, to the myriad rules governing the confiscation of land for Jewish settlement. Palestinians had little say. One West Bank lawyer, Jonathan Kuttab, recalled complaining to Israeli officers that a new tax form required information not justified by any military decree.

'Maybe that is so,' an Israeli replied. When Kuttab responded that he would appeal to the Israeli high court, he was told: 'Why bother? If you were to win, we'd just issue a new military order tomorrow justifying the tax form.'

In Gaza, the Israelis issued a series of military rules aimed specifically at stunting the growth and development of the territory's citrus industry. Their thinking was easy to understand. Until 1967, Gaza had been a major supplier of oranges and lemons to the world outside. The land, 'sweet and delicious' as the Roman traveller Antonius once called it, was virtually the only natural resource. It produced the *shemouti*, the soft eating orange limited to the orchards of Palestine and Cyprus. The markets of Arabia and Europe, started under the Ottomans and nurtured under the British, had made the leading families of Gaza millionaires in their time. In turn, the industry employed nearly 50 per cent of the Strip's work-force – men, women and children. For the Israelis, however, that productivity presented a serious threat to their own citrus industry. In the 1950s, Ben-Gurion's policy of rural settlement had been based on an economic plan that would make Israel not merely self-sufficient but also an exporter of its produce, paying its way in the world economically. The threat of competition from the territories of the West Bank and Gaza had been an important factor behind Ben-Gurion's thinking in the early 1960s,

141

when he had opposed plans to capture the territories. Israel, he said then, was not equipped to handle the economic challenge occupation would create. After 1967, his successors tackled the threat by effectively throttling the competition with special military laws that closed markets, reduced water supplies, even limited the number of new trees the Palestinians could plant.

As early as 1968, the Israelis issued a military order banning Palestinian exports to any country importing Israeli produce. In Gaza's case, this shut the door on the lucrative markets of Western Europe, specifically Britain and Norway, unless it first sold its citrus to the Israeli Marketing Board, at less than competitive prices. In 1976, a second ordinance banned the digging of new wells and prescribed the amount of water any Palestinian farmer could use, fixing it at subsistence level. In 1984, Military Order No. 1015 prevented all non-Jews from planting new trees without a permit from the military government. As a result, thousands of acres of citrus groves, in urgent need of tree renewal, yielded less and less each subsequent harvest season.

Typically, the plot where Khalil's daughter Sama worked was 60 years old by the winter of 1986. The owners had applied for permission to replant, even though that meant a five-year wait for a harvest. That year the Israelis had given their permission for re-cultivation of a portion of the land; but they had denied the Schurabs a permit to plant the *shemouti* trees they wanted. Instead, the military authorities had told them they would allow only new trees growing the *valencia*, a hard, watery orange designed for juice. In 1986, as in previous years, the Schurabs left 50 per cent of the *valencia* crop to waste because the profit margin on the fruit was so low. The net result was a 50 per cent drop in citrus exports from an all-time high of 256,000 tons in 1976.[16]

The Israelis defended the policy as a necessary evil, forced on them by the economic recession of the late 1970s and early 1980s. They maintained that Gazans had access to all markets abroad as long as they worked through the Israeli citrus board. This did not satisfy Israel's allies. Throughout the 1980s, the European countries of the Common Market pressed the Israelis to allow Gaza to export direct to them. The US urged the same concession, arguing that it would improve the quality of life in the Strip. But the Israelis resisted the idea. The loss of revenue and jobs could be measured – the effect such discrimination had on the people of Gaza could not be gauged with any precision.

Yet Israeli policies helped to explain why, even after Rashad Shawa's bitter denunciation of Yassir Arafat, Gaza remained loyal to the PLO. So loyal that, in 1986, the Israeli Military Governor said Arafat would win an overwhelming majority if an election were ever held in the territory.

Raja Sourani was one of the most dangerous Arabs in Gaza, according to the Military Governor. In late 1986, the Governor told Sourani he had him under constant surveillance. He was waiting only for a good enough reason to arrest him. Sourani did indeed present an extraordinary dilemma for the Israelis – because he was a self-styled leader of the PLO in Gaza and the source of political inspiration for the youngest generation of refugees. Yet, barring a mistake on his part, there was little the Israelis could do to stop him giving leadership to the people of the camps.

Like Rashad Shawa, Sourani had been born a scion of the land-owning aristocracy that was here before 1948. Like Shawa, he had gone abroad for his education, to Beirut and Alexandria. Unlike Shawa, though, Sourani had not spent his youth on the playing fields and in the night clubs of the Arab world. Raja Sourani had lived more than half his life under Israeli occupation. He had experienced years in and out of Gaza prison as a result. A lawyer by profession, Sourani returned to Gaza in 1977 as a member of George Habash's Popular Front for the Liberation of Palestine (PFLP), which had recruited him during his student days at Alexandria University. What the PFLP wanted, Sourani said, was a lawyer to work with the second generation of *fedayeen* in the Strip. A Marxist by belief, a nationalist by instinct, Sourani did just that.

'The Israelis tend to believe that people like me were somehow converted to the cause, brainwashed or blackmailed into doing it,' he said in an interview at his family's villa in the most fashionable district of Gaza city. 'I became a member of the PLO the day the Israelis took Gaza in 1967.'[17]

In the years that followed the war, the Israelis had shown no compunction about jailing or deporting Palestinians who joined the PLO's military cadres in the territories. At that stage, the PLO had been committed to armed resistance; its campaign against the

143

Israeli army had required little, if any, soul-searching as the Israelis retaliated. Yet, by the late 1970s, with the PLO increasingly isolated from its natural constituency on the West Bank and Gaza, Dayan's successors had adopted a more tolerant policy. The thinking of Shimon Peres, Ezer Weizman, even the hawkish Moshe Arens, was that Israel had to wean Palestinians away from the PLO: the heavy-handed approach, they argued, had only served the purpose of Yassir Arafat, recruiting volunteers for the cause every time a PLO activist was imprisoned or exiled. Raja Sourani was a typical example of the problem Israeli governments had created for themselves.

In 1977, Sourani opened an office giving legal aid to those arrested for membership of the PLO. Financed by the PLO, his family's land and the few clients who could pay, he quickly became a permanent fixture in the military courts. The squalor and deprivation of the refugee camps had spawned a new generation that regularly attacked Israeli patrols; the recession symbolized by the decline in the citrus industry, the backbone of the local economy, exacerbated the climate of hatred and hostility. In 1979, the Israelis arrested Sourani and charged him with membership of George Habash's PFLP. On the 12th day of an interrogation that lasted 12 weeks, he confessed. Sentencing him to two and a half years – harsh by 1979 standards, but lenient when compared to a decade before – an Israeli military judge said: 'I have no choice because we cannot tolerate a lawyer working the system from within for the benefit of the PLO. Sourani is dangerous because of what he has done and because of the influence he has on those around him.'[18]

In Gaza jail, a heavily-fortified compound in Omar al-Muktar Street close to the city centre, Sourani became a leader of the political wing. More than 400 prisoners lived there, usually six to a cell, refusing to work, spending most days in study or debate. Sourani built an in-house library that contained everything from the works of Marx and Engels to Carlos Marighella's mini-manual for urban guerrillas, provided by the PLO courtesy of Arab guards who had been bribed.*

---

*Marighella, a Brazilian communist and close friend of Cuba's Fidel Castro, wrote his handbook for urban guerrillas in 1969. Since then it has become something of a standard reference book for guerrilla groups the world over.

144

'Inside Gaza prison, we created another generation of *fedayeen*. It was hardly difficult,' he said. 'Every time a prisoner was released, he was replaced by a new detainee. The place was always full with people from the camps.'

Sourani was released in 1982 and then shuffled in and out of prison for the next two years. In 1985, however, the Israelis changed tactics by placing him under administrative detention, limiting him to Gaza by day and his family's home by night. In 1986, they barred him from defending Palestinians in military courts. The Israelis kept him under surveillance and the army normally interrogated him once a month. They offered him a permit to leave Gaza and move abroad, with a promise that he could return after three years. But he refused, becoming ever more outspoken in support of his radical wing of the PLO.

The apparent stalemate left him weighing Israel's options rather like a young professional might evaluate career possibilities. 'I have the impression they don't know what to do with me any more,' he said at a final meeting. 'They have exhausted the legal process. They could expel me but I'm a lawyer and Israel is sensitive to criticism from lawyers abroad,' he contended. 'They could jail me again for membership, but they probably know I'm more dangerous, as they themselves say, inside prison than outside.' He concluded: 'It is Israel's problem not mine.'

After 1967, Israel displayed extreme sensitivity about health care for Palestinians on the West Bank and Gaza Strip. In the years since 1948, Israel had built one of the finest public-health systems in the world, offering cradle-to-grave welfare for the Jewish people and pioneering research to the world at large.

But in 1967, Israel inherited the responsibility that the Jordanians and the Egyptians had shirked during their rule. Conditions in the territories were scandalous, Moshe Dayan commented when touring hospitals after the war. The government's dilemma was whether to invest taxpayers' money in an occupation supposed to be temporary or to offer the bare minimum, so reinforcing Dayan's concept of a short-term commitment. Health quickly became the litmus test of both Israel's intentions and conscience. It raised a question of principle that dismayed many Israelis in the years that followed. It also highlighted how Israel could make a financial profit out of military occupation.

'Do we judge ourselves by our own standards or by those of the Arab world?' remarked Motta Gur, Health Minister in the Peres government between 1984 and 1986. 'The problem for us is that there is an obvious yardstick. The Israeli one.' Like many of his predecessors, Gur claimed that health care in the territories had improved dramatically since 1967. 'But still the question is always whether that is enough,' he said.[19]

Every six weeks, Khalil and his youngest son 'Walid' visited an Israeli hospital in Gaza city. Walid was diagnosed with anaemia when he was only three months. Ever since he had required blood transfusions from the Shifa hospital, the largest in the Strip and the only one with a blood bank. In 1984, the hospital had run short of blood and Walid had gone much longer without than he should have. By 1986, a friend of the family was providing the blood the child needed. For Walid, a weak, pale boy who showed few of the emotions and little of the co-ordination normal in a four-year-old, the arrangement amounted to a guarantee of life.

On a sultry, oppressive evening in 1986, the child and his father paid one of their regular visits to the hospital. The one Palestinian doctor on duty recognized Walid almost immediately. In a matter of minutes he produced the friend's blood and attached Walid to a drip-feed. The doctor smiled. Not only did the patient live with the illness, he said, but his family had to find the blood. He called it do-it-yourself medicine. Holding his father's hand, the child quickly fell asleep and Khalil explained how the health system worked. Like most people he knew, he said, he paid Israeli health insurance to cover the cost of treatment. At $20 a month, it represented more than a tenth of his income but it was worth the peace of mind. Apart from the problem of blood, the system worked. At that point, the doctor interceded. Did Khalil know, he asked, that the Israelis took more out of Gaza than they put back in? Khalil did not; indeed, he looked totally bemused.

A few weeks before, in May 1986, Meron Benvenisti's research unit had conducted its first survey of Gaza since it started monitoring the territories. Benvenisti had concluded that Israel was indeed spending less on the Strip than it raised in taxes and health insurance. The government had reported total expenditure for the Strip that year as totalling $52.5 million. The study estimated the government's revenue from Gaza, including all taxes and social security payments, at more than $60 million.[20] 'The people of Gaza,' Benvenisti claimed, 'are not only suffering occupation. They are paying for it.' The government denied the report but refused to produce figures to support its argument.

Benvenisti's survey had focused on health, the Shifa hospital in particular. Built by the Egyptians in the 1950s, it bore comparison to many in the Third World but not to any facilities in Israel. Doctors suggested there was severe lack of equipment, ranging from basics such as X-ray machines to comparative medical luxuries such as cardiac monitors. The wards were seriously short of specialist nurses. One Palestinian, a general surgeon, explained how he had to send emergency cases to Israel, which tightly limited the number accepted. Gaza's budget had to pay for every case referred; that, he said, only reduced the revenue available for improvements at hospitals such as his.

Shifa showed years of neglect. Almost every room was crowded; doctors claimed that two patients slept in one bed on occasions. Stray cats roamed the kitchens, eating food patients described as inedible. The overworked and undermanned intensive-care unit bordered on the chaotic. That day a young mother died there after a routine operation for an ectopic pregnancy, outside the womb. The hospital's initial inquiry revealed that she had been left unattended for hours, having been moved there in a critical condition.

'Shifa is a disgrace,' said Dr Eli Lasch, the Israeli Director of Health in Gaza for 12 years until he resigned in self-proclaimed disgust in 1985. 'The excuse has always been that we are doing a better job than the Egyptians did. I ask you: when did Israel ever compare itself to Egypt on a matter like health care?'

The experience of working in Gaza had made him question whether he should stay in Israel. 'I left Gaza because I could no longer be party to fraud,' he said in a phone interview from Scotland, where he was on extended vacation, considering whether to return. 'I left Gaza with a bad conscience, both as an Israeli and as a doctor.'[21]

At his office in Jerusalem, Dr Ted Tulscinski, the civil servant in

147

charge of health in the occupied territories, produced an impressive array of statistical evidence highlighting the improvements Israel had made. The figures suggested more beds, more doctors, a dramatic reduction in the diseases once endemic to Gaza refugee camps, such as dysentery and tuberculosis, eradication of the malnutrition that was rife in children after the 1967 war. He cited reports from the World Health Organization, which has chronicled Gaza's progress since 1967.

'Still, there's no denying it,' said Dr Tulscinski, as if he had produced the figures in mitigation. 'Gaza is nowhere near Israel when it comes to health. But should it be? It is not Israel, it is occupied territory. Should it be compared to us or to the Arab world? I can't decide that. If you think about it, only Israel can.'[22]

Eight Israeli soldiers, backed by an armoured unit in half-track vehicles, had blocked off the entrance to the largest refugee camp in Gaza city. By all accounts, the unit had come under grenade attack an hour or so before. The teenagers responsible for the attack escaped so the soldiers were resorting to the tactic the British first taught the Palestinians and the Israelis: collective punishment.

On this occasion, retribution was far less costly than usual but somehow more brutal. No houses were blown up. Few arrests were made. And there was no curfew until later in the day. Instead, the menfolk of Gaza, returning home to the refugee camp, were made to dance. Some danced in the sand; others did it on tables. Some were allowed to keep their clothes on, others were not. Some were told to bark like dogs while their friends had to bray like donkeys. Palestinians were being press-ganged into degrading antics to get back their identity cards, which had been seized by the Israelis at the road-block. The only purpose appeared to be the humiliation of those unlucky enough to fall victim to a soldier's mood. The incident encapsulated the common tragedy of both the Palestinians and the Israelis, symbolizing the degradation both suffered under occupation. Yet it no longer shocked either party to the conflict – only the world outside that looked in on their demise.

Later, Captain Eli Hurewitz, spokesman for the Governor of

Gaza, dismissed such incidents as isolated and distorted.* It was true, he said, that such things were happening, but it was not officially sanctioned or condoned. He suggested that it was a consequence of the war in Lebanon. By September 1985, many men serving in Gaza were veterans of the Lebanon campaign. Some apparently forgot they were working in the very different climate of the occupied territories.[23]

Joel Weinberg was 26. He had served in Lebanon and had been assigned regularly to the Gaza Strip as sergeant of a paratroop unit that did frequent tours of duty in the occupied territories.

His men represented a cross-section of Israeli life. Under his command he had Sabras, native Israelis, Ashkenazim, Jews of European descent, and Sephardim, Oriental Jews. For every university graduate, he had a factory worker. For every hawk, he had a liberal. Weinberg had moved to Israel from the United States with his family when he was a child. Like 99 per cent of Israelis, he never questioned the call to military service. Like a majority of his generation, the war in Lebanon made him think twice. Accepted into the elite Paratroop Regiment, he had risen quickly through the ranks. A lively, good-humoured young man, he had also proved to be a dedicated soldier. But Lebanon, he acknowledged, had changed him. As Ariel Sharon's invasion of 1982 became an occupation, and the occupation became a war of attrition with the Lebanese, soldiers like Weinberg grew to doubt their leadership. In time, they started to doubt themselves.

'The army is the truest gauge of the state of mind of Israel that I know,' he said in an interview in 1986. 'Before Lebanon there were few doubts in anyone's mind about our purpose as soldiers. After Lebanon, there was barely a soldier in my unit who didn't question what he was doing and why. All of us grew up in Lebanon. And many of us returned home recognizing that occupation can be self-defeating. In Lebanon, it didn't solve the crisis, it made it worse.'[24]

By then a university student, Weinberg still served in the occupied territories as a reservist, called up twice a year for duty.

---

*The Governor of Gaza, Colonel Shaike Erez, refused repeated requests to see the author regarding this chapter. In the year spent researching this book, Colonel Erez was the only Israeli to refuse in principle the author's request for an interview.

Hebron, Nablus, Ramallah, the cities of the West Bank, Gaza, Khan Younis, Rafah, the towns of the Strip, they all conjured up memories of seven years in the army. Like most conscripts, he had spent most of his time in the territories, the training-ground for all young Israeli soldiers. Gaza, he said, was a personal nightmare. In 1981, his unit came under grenade attack outside Khan Younis. He recalled how some of his men felt revulsion at the subsequent killing. Yet others were buoyant after shooting young *fedayeen* their own age. When told of the humiliation inflicted on civilians at the refugee camp a few months before, he said he understood why soldiers resorted to such action. His own men had felt that way.

'By anyone's standards, Gaza is the bottom of the heap,' he submitted. 'Just being there, living there for a month at a time, being with people who are living like semi-human beings. It affects the way you react. Your moral standards can so easily change.' He contended that Israel was not responsible for the plight of refugees in Gaza. Conditions in the camps would be just as appalling, if not worse, if the Egyptians were there. 'But our presence creates a hatred. It's the barrier between those who have plenty, and those who have nothing. Us being there is degrading. For them and for us.'

Every time he went back to Gaza, Sergeant Weinberg experienced the futility he once felt in Lebanon. The Israeli army used twice as many men in the territories as they did seven years before, when he was a new recruit. Fewer and fewer Palestinians were willing to help. The Palestinians might have looked pacified, he remarked, but they stifled a hatred that he defined as manic.

'When I first went to Gaza, we used to fear grenades and revolvers,' he confided. 'Today, it's the prospect of someone cutting your throat with a kitchen knife.' He concluded: 'We can't win in a place like Gaza. It's just like Lebanon. The more men we send, the longer we stay, the worse it becomes for all of us.'

6
ALIENATED ISLANDS

'You can take the Jew out of the ghetto, but not the ghetto out of a Jew.' – EZER WEIZMAN, ISRAELI CABINET MINISTER

To visit Jerusalem on any weekday afternoon was to witness a miracle of sorts.

At around three o'clock, tens of thousands of Arabs and Jews would stop work and head for home. Seen from a high building, the exodus looked like the peaceful disengagement of two rival ant colonies: down on the streets below it seemed as if two powerful magnets were drawing people back to their separate halves of Jerusalem. The Arabs went east and the Jews west. Ever since the 1967 war they had lived together yet apart, defying the rule of co-existence imposed then, seeking shelter in two distinct sectors of a city that remained as divided as ever.

Most Jews had never visited an Arab home and vice versa. Joint ventures were rare, except in the criminal underworld. Often Arabs went months, even years, without crossing into the Jewish sector of the city. Jews would avoid making the journey the other way unless they wanted their cars washed or their teeth fixed at half the price they paid in west Jerusalem. By morning they came together as they headed for work, in many instances working side

151

by side in factories, offices and stores. In the afternoon, they retreated to their respective quarters. Some Israelis called it cultural ballet. The Palestinians feared they had entered into an arrangement that could last for ever. Both agreed the system was a miracle because their unspoken conflict so rarely erupted into violence. Neither dared to consider the consequences of the system breaking down. Yet the result was a city polarized by two identities.

In 1986, a young Jewish journalist, who spoke fluent, dialectic Arabic, experienced first-hand the gulf that separated Arabs from Jews. Wearing a tatty, dirty jacket and a chequered Palestinian headscarf, his chin bristling with a week-long growth, he masqueraded as a stereotypical Palestinian living and working in the Jewish sector of the city. His findings amounted to a devastating indictment of the attempts to bring harmony, integration and co-existence to the holy city after 1967. In the cafes lining the fashionable pedestrian mall of Ben-Yehuda Street, for example, he received anxious looks from even the waitresses.

'They stared at me as if I was a walking bomb,' wrote Yoram Binur. 'My feeling was that the Jews were as much afraid of the Arab as he is of them.' On a Jewish bus, he made eyes at a pretty blonde. 'Soldiers glared at me, patting their rifle butts. Nothing needed to be said,' he reported. At a singles bar in a middle-class suburb of the city, the men ogled his attractive and obviously Jewish girlfriend, a fellow journalist who was in on the secret. Binur recalled: 'They kept away from me as if I was infectious. Wherever I went, a vacuum was created.' When he tried to chat to a single woman, she called the manager and complained that Arabs were being allowed in. The manager said he had no choice but assured her it would not happen again. Attempting to rent an apartment, he and his girlfriend were told it was available. When they called back to confirm the deal, the landlady said it had been let. Hours later a colleague checked with the landlady. The flat was still available.

In summing up his weeks as an Arab in Jewish Jerusalem, he commented: 'Stepping into an Arab's shoes brought home to me very powerfully the unbridgeable gap between the two sides. The Arab will never know the fear he creates in the Israeli. And the Israelis are not aware of the feelings of humiliation, alienation and fear that lie in the heart of the Arab he sees every day.'[1]

Located south of the old walled city, the Arab village of Abou Tor ranged along one of Jerusalem's most splendid heights. At its lower end, the neighbourhood merged into another Palestinian community, Silwan, and then rose up on to Gai Ben Hinom, the cliff where, in ancient times, the Canaanites hurled children down to their deaths in sacrifice to Baal. Moving westward up the hill, the view became even more dramatic: the lookout peered eastward to the hills over the Dead Sea while, to the north, Temple Mount with its golden dome stood out majestically. In a city that prided itself on its beauty, Abou Tor offered one of the most prized panoramas.

Until 1967, Abou Tor was the front line between Israel and Jordan. Israelis, who had moved into abandoned Arab homes after the war of 1948, and Palestinians lived on opposite sides of the barbed wire that separated the armies of the two countries. After the Six-Day War, the two halves came together to form one of only two mixed communities in the holy city. In two streets they lived side by side, in some cases next door to one another. 'Ruth', a middle-aged Jewish housewife who had lived all her life in Jerusalem, lived six doors down from 'Yussa', a slightly younger Palestinian woman. They met in the street, shopped in the same Arab grocery, their children played in the same park. Yet in almost 20 years they had never had a conversation.

'Things don't get better or worse,' said Ruth in an interview in 1986. 'There's a set of rules and most people observe them. I know there's no point in trying my hand and starting a relationship. We get along by avoiding each other.'

Yussa, a talkative mother of three children, cast her mind back to the 1973 war. 'I will never forget that. For days and days our people were at war and we were living here,' she recalled. 'All of us acted as though nothing was happening. It's the same with the occupation. All the time it's hanging over you, stopping you from trying.'

Ruth compared relations with the Arabs to marriage. 'When you start out, you have such hopes. Then you realize that your partner isn't necessarily going to change because you want him to. But at least in marriage the individual decides that. Here politics makes the decision for you.'

'My husband,' remarked Yussa, 'says you have to be deaf,

dumb and blind to survive here. That's the way most Arabs feel about it.'[2]

Given Jerusalem's history, it was hardly surprising that the physical barriers came down but the psychological barriers stayed up. For almost 2,000 years, Jerusalem had endowed religious conflict with a sanctity of purpose. After 1967, this enabled Jew and Arab almost to cite God's will in their refusal to co-exist with each other. In keeping with its history, the holy city defied a solution.

'What we are learning in Jerusalem is neighbourhood relationships,' said the city's Jewish Mayor, the indefatigable Teddy Kollek. 'What we hope to learn is tolerance.'

Kollek had been in charge of Jewish Jerusalem since 1965. After the war of 1967, he became Mayor of the united city. Ever since he had coaxed, bullied and forced Jews and Arabs into living together, even though they could not find any justification for doing so. At times, typically in the aftermath of Palestinian terrorism and Jewish reprisals, he was the object of abuse from all sides, a political go-between caught in the crossfire of suspicion and hatred. But Kollek, the supreme realist in an age when most politicians had become dogmatic, always recognized the limitations of the relationship between Arabs and Jews. He believed that two peoples thrown together by fate were not supposed to love each other, merely to learn how to live with each other. His vision was not intermarriage, but rather interaction. 'What I am after is small steps, not tremendous concepts,' he said in 1985. 'The mistake made by many people is to look for integration. We are not looking for it. We do not want it.'[3]

As Jews and Arabs went their separate ways at the end of another working day, creating an indelible image of simmering conflict, the modern-day prophets argued that Jerusalem would forever thwart any attempt at a settlement. Only a minority maintained that the process of enforced co-existence, initiated in 1967, kindled the hope of future conciliation between Arab and Jew. Yet the minority view highlighted the sense of loss so many Israelis and Palestinians felt in the years after 1967. It recognized the failure of both sides to convert the opportunities created by war into lasting peace, and it urged both to bury the past as a way of salvaging the future. Rabbi David Hartman, the most dynamic and arguably the most controversial Jewish philosopher of modern

Israel, voiced that hope with a passion few others dared to show. The 1967 war prompted him to leave the United States and move to Jerusalem. Much as the years since had led him to question the chances of peaceful co-existence, he still nurtured the belief that Israelis and Palestinians could build a new Jerusalem together.

What had happened in the holy city these past 20 years, he believed, was healthy. It filled him with hope. Until 1967, Arabs and Jews lived apart, stubbornly denying each other's existence. But the Six-Day War made it a head-on clash. He conceded that Jews and Arabs fought over the holy city, be it Temple Mount, the Western Wall or the Lion's Gate. But we drink the same water, he declared, we eat the same fruit, we watch the same movies. After 20 years, no Israeli could deny that the Palestinians existed nor could the Palestinians refute the reality of Israel. 'We Jews are here.' At this point his voice rose in anger. 'Here to stay.' He paused to weigh his words, seeking the philosopher's deduction. 'Now the two peoples have stopped denying the existence of each other,' he explained. 'Now therapy can begin.'

He pointed to the Bible. He referred to the land of milk and honey. Until 1967, he said, it was the land of milk or honey. The Arabs of the West Bank had the land of milk, the empty desert of Judaea in which they tended their herds. The Jews down on the coast had the orchards and citrus groves of the Mediterranean, the land of honey. But since 1967? Since 1967, there had been no front lines, no national boundaries, no barbed wire separating Jew and Arab. The only barriers were in our minds. He rose from his seat, bringing the Bible down from the shelf.

'But,' he asked rhetorically, 'what about the Bible?' Didn't the Bible teach us how the extremists usually win out in the end? Couldn't we all cite God's teaching to drive the Arabs out of the land? Did the Bible encourage co-existence? He halted in the middle of the room. 'Hardly,' he said. The Bible offered the most intolerant view of history, the history of one triumph after another. At the mention of the Christian ethic of 'Love thy neighbour', drawn from the same text, he laughed. 'Go tell that to the Arabs,' he said. 'Or to the Jews for that matter,' he added.

He walked to the window, looking out on a suburb of Jewish Jerusalem. For 2,000 years, he remarked, Jerusalem had been haunted by the belief that there was only one truth, one vision, one way for all mankind. The question had always been who was the carrier of that truth? Was it Jesus and Christianity? Was it the Prophet Mohammed and Islam? Could it be Judaism? Rabbi Hartman sat down.

'What we have to learn is to bury whole sections of the Bible, the notion that one religion has a monopoly on truth and wisdom,' he insisted. 'We have to break the mould of history that has one religion, one people, one philosophy triumphing over another. That is the potential for us and the Palestinians. And it can only happen here, in Jerusalem and the West Bank.'[4]

Like any minority, the Jewish settlers of the West Bank might have been expected to cherish the idea of co-existence with the Arabs. The peaceful integration of those two communities would have ensured the security of the Jews living there and effectively legitimized everything they had created since the 1967 war. Co-existence and co-operation between Arab and Jew would have proved that settlement was a means to the end of solving the Arab–Israeli conflict.

'Co-existence is the best possible guarantee of our survival here,' insisted Israel Harel, leader of the Council of Jewish Settlements on the West Bank. 'Co-existence means peace. And, if there's peace, then why should any politician negotiate a settlement that returns the West Bank to the Arabs?'[5]

Such thinking, and the fear of failure, undoubtedly explained the need so many Jewish settlers felt to stress the co-existence they enjoyed. In almost every settlement, they offered evidence of their burgeoning relationship with the Arab communities living around them. A young Israeli businessman, newly arrived in the Samarian settlement of Sheve Shomron, spoke with pride about playing soccer in a team made up of settlers and Arabs from the nearby village of Deir Sharaf. An ultra-Orthodox couple from the religious settlement of Shiloh took delight in producing pictures of the Arab wedding they had attended in the Palestinian hamlet of Sinjul. In Kiryat Arba, outside Hebron, one settler talked with disarming candour of an Arab carpenter who had an affair with an Orthodox Jewish housewife employing him. Co-existence, said the settler, was a fact of life neither side could deny.

Yet the Jewish leadership on the West Bank acknowledged that co-existence remained a dream based on their logic rather than any genuine desire of their followers. The thinkers of the settlers' movement, notably Elyakim Haetzni in Hebron, could be brutally honest with themselves. They recognized that discrimination between Jew and Arab, the exploitation of the Palestinians and inequality between the two races, had created new barriers instead of dismantling the age-old points of conflict. Much as they might chastise themselves, though, the settlers rested content in their belief that the Palestinians were primarily responsible for the failure to integrate their two communities since 1967. 'If the PLO didn't have a knife at their throats and a gun at their backs,' claimed Haetzni, 'then most Arabs would accept the reality of living together with Jews. Don't blame the Jews, blame the PLO.'[6]

In the 1980s, the Palestinian leadership did undoubtedly view the concept of co-existence as a threat comparable to settlement a decade before. For them integration signalled assimilation into the state of Israel and the destruction of the Palestinian identity that had emerged after 1967. They harboured few illusions about the outcome of such co-operation between the two peoples. They foresaw only that working harmony on the West Bank would allow the Israelis to set the terms of any agreement, and to impose the minority will on the Palestinian majority. 'I see co-existence as the final stage of the battle for the West Bank,' said Bassam Shaka'a, the former Arab Mayor of Nablus and a die-hard supporter of the radical wing of the PLO. 'It is the last Palestinian card, the only card we hold. We cannot give it up because that would present the Israelis with an instant solution. They would present it as a final settlement.'[7]

Such leadership explained why many Palestinians, especially the educated middle class, refused to live and work alongside the Israelis as a matter of principle. For the average Palestinian, however, the dilemma did not afford room for political philosophy. Often obliged to work for the Israelis, invariably dealing with them every day of their lives, always vulnerable to the pressure of occupation, the Palestinians of the occupied territories had little choice but to accept de facto integration with Israel after 1967. The law of survival and the common wish to improve the standard of living seemed to dictate that the barriers of race, religion, language and nationalism would eventually disappear.

Among Palestinians of the occupied territories, Elias Freij, the Mayor of Bethlehem and the most celebrated of Arab moderates,

157

had pursued a policy closest to Teddy Kollek's vision of limited co-existence. A wily, cunning figure, far more astute than his many critics believed, Freij made Bethlehem the only Arab town which Jews visited out of choice rather than necessity. On an average Saturday night, hundreds of Israelis descended on the town of Christ's birth to eat, drink and shop. The square that housed the Church of the Nativity became a thoroughfare of Jews and Arabs, a cross-current of two peoples who rarely mixed elsewhere. Each wore a uniform, the Arabs in glistening white or chequered *keffiyas*, the Jews in colourful shirts and slacks. But they both spoke the same language, usually Hebrew; and they ate in the same restaurants, from menus boasting Jewish or Arabic cooking, Israeli beer or the sweet wines from the local Arab vineyard.

'Co-existence isn't forbidden fruit,' commented Mayor Freij, a Christian Arab like most of his constituents. 'It is a necessity if we are both to survive. The Palestinians will come around to recognizing that eventually.'[8]

Freij drew the contrast between Bethlehem and other Arab communities of the West Bank. Co-existence had brought economic prosperity and tranquillity. Elsewhere, he argued, segregation had created poverty and hostility. Far from swimming against the political tide of the 1980s, he felt his town was setting the pace for Palestinians of the West Bank. Come back in 20 years' time, he remarked, and Bethlehem will be one of many Palestinian communities enjoying the fruits of a working relationship with the Israelis.

After the 1967 war, the expectation of successive Israeli governments had been that economic progress would lead to greater co-operation between Arab and Jew in the territories. Based on the figures alone, Israel made an impressive case for its perennial claim that the standard of living on the West Bank had improved dramatically under occupation. The welter of statistics the government produced did not merely salve an uneasy conscience: they also convinced many Israeli politicians that the Palestinian equation could be solved by tackling the economic ills of the average Arab.

In the years after the war, income from agriculture on the West Bank rose 700 per cent, exports to Israel increased by nearly 1,000 per cent. In measuring the quality of life, Israel pointed to household appliances: in 1968, less than two per cent of Palestinian homes had a television, only five per cent had a refrigerator, just 24 per cent had a cooker of some sort. By the 1980s, almost three-quarters of households on the West Bank had all three, and one in three families boasted a motor car. The average wage increased tenfold after the June war, giving the Palestinians more disposable income than their counterparts in Jordan and twice as much as the average Egyptian or Syrian.[9] Even though the West Bank suffered from the economic woes of Israel – rampant inflation, low productivity, a worsening balance of trade – the Israelis still fostered the belief that personal advancement would bring a measure of peace and integration.

'Nothing dictates thinking in any community, especially an Arab one, like bigger and better incomes,' said Yitzhak Modai, then Israel's Finance Minister, in July 1985. 'Every Palestinian may think of himself as a nationalist. But the economics dictate that he can't afford to be.'[10]

Until the 1980s, politicians on the Israeli right, like Modai, could produce the figures to back their claim that co-existence was inevitable because of the benefits occupation brought to an under-developed population. This was, however, to ignore whatever political aspirations the Arabs might have nurtured. By the 1980s, moreover, the much-vaunted economic boom on the West Bank was a fading memory for most of the people living under Israeli rule. Until 1981, for example, the peasant farmers of the territory exploited Israeli expertise in irrigation, cultivation and mechanization to produce more field and cash crops than ever before. But subsequently, there was a steady decline in both production and revenue – a by-product of the strict quotas the Israelis introduced to protect their own farmers from competition. Equally important was the recession within the Israeli economy. With the country experiencing serious unemployment for the first time in its history, the job market for Palestinians from the territories shrank. Inflation ate away at the quality of life Palestinians had come to appreciate as one of the few blessings of occupation. A government freeze on wages undercut their ability to bargain for anything more than the going rate dictated by an Israeli employer. For an Arab community wholly dependent on Israel for its economic survival, the 1980s brought an abrupt halt to the expansion of the 1970s. For the Israelis, it marked the end of an era in which self-interest offered the best prospect of integration and co-existence.

'In a business sense,' explained the Palestinian industrialist Victor Nasser, a textile manufacturer based in Beit Jala near Bethlehem, 'there was a honeymoon in the first few years after the war. We expanded our markets, the Israelis found a cheap supply of produce and labour. But the honeymoon ended.'

'Business has traditionally been the starting-point for dialogue between Jew and Arab,' said Yaacov Raizman, the manager of one of the few large Israeli factories on the West Bank. 'It's difficult to see how we can improve relations if we don't do business.'[11]

Over the years, Raizman and Nasser had become friends and business partners. Raizman, a plain-speaking, affable figure, ran the Aderet carpet factory in the industrial zone attached to the Qarnei Shomron settlement in Samaria. The plant represented a model for the Israeli future on the West Bank. Jews and Arabs worked alongside each other, the Jews providing management and the Palestinians the shop-floor labour. Instead of the Arabs commuting to Israel, the Israelis commuted to the West Bank. Economics and the political philosophy of the company's founder, Ernst Vollek, dictated that the plant be moved from its original base in Herzliyya, on the coast near Tel Aviv. The company received generous grants, covering the cost of both the land and construction, when they relocated; by doing so, it cut the cost of transportation for its predominantly Palestinian work-force, drawn mainly from the West Bank towns of Qalqilia and Tulkarem. The economic attractions for both company and workers made such industrial developments far more viable than settlement. There was little friction between Jew and Arab on the factory floor: both earned the same wages for the same job and they ate together in the canteen. Given the isolation of so many Jewish settlements, such integration was rare. Yet of the $2,000 million spent on West Bank homes for Israelis since 1967, the government had allocated less than $100 million for factories such as the Aderet plant. In Raizman's view, the policy had proved a serious mistake: an example, as he put it, of the way in which government had misread the situation in the territory.

'Jewish settlement on the West Bank puts me in mind of a heart transplant,' he said as he toured the factory, stopping to talk to his Arab workers with an ease that approached friendship. 'The new

160

heart can function, but so often the body doesn't respond. In contrast, we're trying to graft ourselves on to the West Bank in a far less dramatic way. To live together you have to work together first.'

Victor Nasser had dealt with the Israelis ever since 1967. In that time, his output and turn-over had doubled, largely because of trade with Israel. When it came to business, he said, the chemistry worked but the relationship foundered on the personal level.

'When I look at the Israelis, I see their hearts leading their minds,' Nasser emphasized. 'Their minds tell them that integration is the best way out for all of us. Their hearts resist. So they hold back. It's almost as if they're frightened of getting too close to the Palestinians.'

The Jewish settlers of Hebron had called the meeting, in 1984, in an attempt to ease tension between Jews and Arabs. On a cold, frosty night, more than a hundred Arabs attended, outnumbering the Jews by two to one at the main hall of the municipality in the heart of the city. They came from most walks of Arab life: businessmen, farmers, even students from the local Islamic college. Surprised by the Arab response to the call for a public debate on co-existence, Rabbi Moshe Levinger was left speechless by the poignant remarks of one young Arab who took the floor early on.

'Rabbi Levinger,' he said, addressing the man who had led Jews back to Hebron from 1968 onwards, 'I don't know you and you do not know me. But often I see you in Hebron, at the fruit market or the casbah, and I feel I want to say hello to you, to stop and talk. I always stop myself because I do not want people to misinterpret me. They will think I want something from you, or that I am trying to flatter you.' The Arab paused for a second, casting an eye over his shoulder at the ranks of Palestinians behind him. 'Rabbi Levinger, why don't you greet me first?' he asked. 'It is easier for you than me to break the ice. A simple greeting would mean so much to all of us. But it has to come from you.' For once the political and spiritual guru of Jewish settlement on the West Bank seemed intimidated, somewhat cowed in the presence of an Arab. He had no answer, he admitted. But he said that, as a Jew, he understood the emotion of any man seeking equal recognition.

That encounter became folklore in the narrow, closed worlds

inhabited by the Jews and Arabs of Hebron. Some of the settlers would interpret the Arab's plea as an expression of the fear Palestinians felt about dealing with the Israelis. The Arabs cited it as evidence of the Jewish sense of superiority. Levinger's inability to start a conversation in the street was proof of the Jews' refusal to treat them as equal partners to their common future. 'On one thing we could agree,' commented Levinger's friend, Elyakim Haetzni, recalling the meeting at the municipality. 'If we can't even say hello to each other, then co-existence is a myth.'[(12)]

In Hebron, where Jews and Arabs lived on the same street, in some cases next door to each other, the absence of integration defied any conventional logic. Throughout the 1980s, settlers and Palestinians lived there in greater proximity and numbers than anywhere else in the region. Business, be it the employment of Arabs as labourers or Jews shopping in Hebron market, had initiated a relationship. Some settlers, usually the less religious, worked assiduously at creating closer ties. They spent time with the Palestinians, buying or selling, looking for labourers, taking coffee together. But to find an Arab in a Jewish house, doing anything other than working, was rare. The relationship had assumed a pattern, an unwritten code to which everyone adhered. An Israeli could accept an invitation from a Palestinian but he felt no obligation to reciprocate. When the settlers wanted something, the Arabs usually provided it. An Israeli could go into business with a Palestinian as long as he had the controlling interest. The Israelis gave the orders, the Arabs carried them out. Israeli sociologists, surveying Hebron in 1985, compared the relationship to that of a horse and its rider.

Yitzhak Shimon, a well-known figure in the settlement of Kiryat Arba, viewed relations with genuine sadness. In the early 1970s, he lived in the Arab quarter of Hebron, doubling up as a businessman and a self-confessed spy for the Israeli army. He learned the value of co-existence with the Palestinians. They accepted him, they respected him; together with an Arab metalsmith, he opened a highly successful workshop close to the casbah. At moments of tension, the Arabs even made use of his connections with the army, asking him to intervene on their behalf, to arrange a *sulha* or truce. But Kiryat Arba changed his philosophy. Attracted by government help, he left Hebron and built an all-Jewish factory in the settlement's industrial zone. He had stayed there ever since.

'At the time, living with Jews seemed the most natural thing to do,' he recalled, expressing the kind of regret few settlers ever admitted. 'But I realize now that we were retreating. Kiryat Arba is like an armed camp. It's the same with the settlements down in Hebron,' he insisted. 'Just as we were segregated from the Poles in the Warsaw ghetto, and the Russians in Minsk, so we segregated ourselves from the Arabs on the West Bank.'

He concluded: 'There is a fundamental flaw in the Jew. It's the mentality of the ghetto. It is a state of mind that has been passed from generation to generation. The people of Kiryat Arba live the way they do because they have built the perfect ghetto.'

Ayyoub Chroulmay, Shimon's erstwhile business partner in Arab Hebron, voiced similar regret but offered a different interpretation. Their years together, he said, made them recognize their differences first-hand. Professionally, they disagreed about working for both Arabs and Jews. Shimon wanted only Jewish clients; Chroulmay sought both. Socially, Chroulmay entertained; Shimon always visited. Politically, the Arab accepted the Jew's commitment to the policies of Begin and Sharon; but Shimon was loath to acknowledge Chroulmay's allegiance to the PLO. 'Jewish discrimination is so strong that sometimes they forget it's there,' he submitted. 'But that doesn't mean we're not friends. I don't blame him at all. I blame the system.' In Kiryat Arba, Yitzhak Shimon was characteristically blunt. 'How can we live together when there is one law for the Jews and another for the Arabs?' he asked. 'We can't. We can't have co-existence at the point of a gun.'[13]

'In Jewish history you find the Jews of the ghetto or the pogrom forced to make deals with whomever they can bribe or subvert, usually criminals,' remarked Dedi Zucker, secretary-general of Israel's left-wing Citizens' Rights Movement. 'The same is true of the West Bank. The settlers co-exist better with Palestinian criminals than any other sector of society.'[14]

In the autumn of 1985, Zucker's party issued a report that unmasked a secret network formed by Jews and Arabs on the West Bank. The report revealed the complicity of both in a fraudulent plot to buy Arab land for Jewish settlers. The West Bank land scandal, as it became known, highlighted close co-operation between Israelis and Palestinians and the greed of both when it came to exploiting the opportunities presented by occupation. Had the operation been legal, it would have represented unprecedented co-ordination between the two. Instead it showed how the Jewish drive to settle the territory brought together criminals on both sides in common cause. After years of occupation, the Israelis had been unable to enlist honest Arabs to the cause of integration on the West Bank, so they turned to those Palestinians willing to defraud their own people. The land scandal marked a nadir in the attempt to build a working relationship based on trust, good faith and mutual interest. The fact that the government was implicated exacerbated the sense of dismay among ordinary people on both sides. 'Such co-existence corrupts both Arabs and Jews,' commented Yossi Sarid, a left-wing Member of Parliament and co-author with Zucker of the report. 'It makes a mockery of the pious hopes we express about living together with Arabs.'

In 1979, Menachem Begin's government had passed legislation enabling Jews to buy land on the West Bank for private development. The government sought to expand Jewish settlement but to ease the massive burden on public expenditure that settlement involved. It believed that, in opening the way for Israeli entrepreneurs, middle-class Jews both at home and abroad would build on the promised land with their own resources. Building magnates quickly moved in, setting up consortia and development companies, offering dream homes on new settlements that would have everything from country clubs to tennis centres and riding stables. Land, however, presented a problem.

Much as many Palestinians might have been willing to sell, they faced the death sentence for doing so, under a law passed by the Jordanians in 1975. The threat of PLO reprisals was also to be taken seriously. So, to obtain the land, Israeli businessmen enlisted the only Palestinians willing to do business: middlemen who would secretly arrange deals with Arab farmers and not even tell them that the land was being sold to the Jews. In many instances, the go-betweens were gangsters. As a result, hired thugs forced Arab landowners to sign away their property at gunpoint; Israeli lawyers used forged powers of attorney to sell land owned by Palestinians living abroad; Israeli officials processed phony deeds in a matter of days to meet the clamour for parcels of land that were being sold for as little as $6,000. In the process, hundreds of

Arabs were cheated out of their land – and thousands of would-be settlers bought property to which they had no legal claim. Yet the government defended what amounted to fraud on the grounds that the Jews were fulfilling Biblical duty. 'Don't touch the redemption of the Land of Israel!' shouted Likud leader Yitzhak Shamir at a public meeting in 1985. 'Sometimes tricks and schemes and unconventional means were used to purchase land,' he argued. 'It is intolerable that a witch hunt should try to block this patriotic mission.'[14] One of Shamir's leading acolytes, the former deputy Minister of Agriculture Michael Dekel, offered another rationale. 'Zionism is a political movement,' said Dekel, who was directly implicated in the scandal. 'It isn't a boy scouts' movement for good citizens and neighbours.'[15] Under such patronage, co-existence on the West Bank flourished – between dogmatic Jews and pliable, often unscrupulous Arabs. It highlighted the limited common ground between the two communities; it revealed a meeting of minds based on the principle of Jewish domination and Arab subservience; it bore investigation because it produced Israelis who tried to shed the ghetto mentality and Palestinians who compromised on almost every count.

Moshe Zaar, an electrician by day and a land agent by night, made his fortune out of land deals between Arabs and Jews on the West Bank. After 1979 and the government's decision to open the territory to private developers, Zaar became a key figure in the secret purchase of land from the Arabs by the Jews. His home, a splendid, hilltop mansion in the lush, green mountains of Samaria, stood as testament to his success.

'Co-existence is something I practise every day of my life,' he claimed over coffee in the huge basement of his home that served as his office and study. 'You never hear about it because the Arabs are too frightened to talk about the way they deal with the Jews.'[16]

A diminutive, rather suspicious man in his early 50s, Zaar was a disciple of Rabbi Levinger at Moshav Nahalim, the religious co-operative near Petah Tikva where they both lived until the 1967 war. In 1980, he founded an Orthodox settlement a few miles outside Qalqilia, the Arab town closest to Tel Aviv. Within a few months, he became disenchanted with settlement life.

165

'They didn't go about it the right way,' he recalled. 'They were living just like they did in the ghettos of Europe. They put up electric fences, they built a cage for themselves. Nobody went out to the Arabs, the Arabs never came in. There was no integration.'

Zaar's response was to buy the plot of land where his house stood and move out of the settlement. His first acquisition, four acres of Samaria for $10,000, taught him a lesson that had guided him ever since. The 1967 war, he maintained, broke the mythical bond that tied the Palestinians to their land. Given the choice of a hand-to-mouth existence as a peasant farmer, or hard cash and a job with the Israelis, the Arabs of the West Bank would usually take the money and the work.

'The secret is never to lie to them,' Zaar claimed, citing the thousands of acres he had since bought from Arabs and sold to Jews. 'The Arabs do not trust most Jews because we have tried to trick them. We have stolen land without paying for it. I always make them a fair offer. I do not cheat them even though I could. They respect me for that and they usually go out and buy a new home, or a car, or another wife. They are satisfied. So am I.'

Despite such expressions of altruism, Zaar was under investigation in 1986 for complicity in the West Bank land scandal – and in 1985 he had been convicted of membership in the Jewish underground. Years before, he acted as a driver for the Jewish terrorists who planted the car bomb that crippled Bassam Shaka'a, then the Arab Mayor of Nablus. He admitted the fact with a sense of impunity, pointing to the lenient sentence of four months he received at his trial. He justified the actions of the underground, claiming that Jewish reprisals for Palestinian attacks improved the chances of co-existence.

'The average Palestinian wants nothing to do with the PLO and people like Shaka'a,' he submitted, recalling that one Arab *mukhtar* from a nearby village brought him a sack of sugar as a gift the day he was released. 'They took their hats off to me afterwards. The Arabs respect force and honesty.'

A morning with Moshe Zaar made Arab–Israeli integration on the West Bank sound ridiculously simple; all it required was cash, truth and intimidation. If that were the case, why did the psychological barriers remain in the minds of so many Palestinians? Why, for example, had Arabs from a nearby village attacked and seriously wounded him in 1983? Typically, this outspoken

166

maverick of a man defied conventional Jewish logic.

'It's the Jews who keep the barriers up,' he replied. 'For so long we have lived in the ghetto that we can't break out. So now we have moved the ghetto to the West Bank. We want co-existence but on the terms we had elsewhere: the Arabs can live in the valley, we will live on the hill. Together but separate.'

Depending on whom one listened to in the West Bank, Ahmed Odeh was either the scum of the earth or a symbol of the new breed of Palestinian. A *fellah* (peasant farmer) by birth, Odeh taught himself to read and write in Hebrew, then found himself a job as a clerk in the Israeli military court in Nablus. When Begin's government passed that landmark legislation on private development, Odeh presented himself to the Israelis as a middleman. The years in court gave him the expertise; he knew every legal device the Israelis used to get round Jordanian and Ottoman land laws for the first Jewish settlements. In the 1980s, he arranged for the Jews to purchase thousands of small farming plots from his fellow Arabs, taking a personal commission of up to 30 per cent. In the process, Odeh played a major role in the creation of the middle-class Jewish homesteads that surrounded his village. He became friends with leading members of Begin's Likud Party. He made himself a dollar millionaire. Meanwhile, the Jordanian government sentenced him to death.

Like Moshe Zaar, whom he knew well, Odeh referred back to the 1967 war in explaining his thinking. The war, he felt, isolated the Palestinians of the West Bank from the Arab world for the first time. The Arabs had to look after themselves and they had to face the reality of Israel. Their vulnerability made them easy prey. 'The Palestinians are cowards,' he remarked at one point, chain-smoking as he ate lunch at his Mexican-style hacienda in the Arab village of Habla. 'They haven't got the guts to challenge the Israelis. So they sell their land secretly to people like me. When they find out that it's going to the Jews, they get frightened. By then it's too late to back out.' As for the Jews, he expressed a strong admiration.

The Israelis, he explained, had learned how to bully the Arabs into submission. By using force, just as every Arab regime did, they had won grudging respect. 'The Jews will not get anywhere by playing the game by the rules,' Odeh declared, telling his body-guards to get ready to leave. 'Once the Jews make it clear that they will get the land, come what may, the Arabs will understand. And they will cash in.' To that end, he added, he had made donations totalling $70,000 to the Likud Party of Begin, Shamir and Sharon. He defined Sharon, whom he claimed to know personally, as his kind of politician: tough, uncompromising, ruthless. Sharon, he said, was like an Arab ruler. The Palestinians could do business with him.

Leaving his lunch, Odeh insisted on making a tour of what he called 'his settlements'. Loading his Mercedes with rifles, bought with a permit from the Israelis, he drove north to the new settlement of Oranit. He offered the neat rows of pretty, two-storey villas, many of them still under construction, as proof of his 'contribution to co-existence'. Settlement, he judged, was building a quick route towards peace. The more Jews who lived on the West Bank, the faster the Arabs would recognize the futility of resis-tance. If it were left to the Arabs, peace would prove impossible. 'Ninety per cent of the Arabs who live here want a PLO state on the West Bank,' he says, driving on to the Arab village of Sanniriya. 'There's only a small minority of us who believe in the idea of living together. So I say to the Jews: get the land any way you can. That would do us all a favour. Then we would have to live together, whether some of us liked it or not.'

A few days after the meeting, in June 1986, Ahmed Odeh was arrested and charged with involvement in the land scandal. Specifi-cally, he was accused of coercing Arabs into selling property to the Jews. Later that year, as he awaited trial, Odeh said in an interview from his prison cell: 'You can forget co-existence. No Arab is going to stick his neck out and do business with the Jews after what has happened to me.'[17]

Taleb Ghraith and Yona Chaiken had never met, and the chances were they never would. Yet they lived within a few hundred yards of each other. They shopped in the same market. They read avidly in the same public library. They prayed within a few hours of each other under the same roof at Abraham's tomb in Hebron.

Chaiken was 37, a native of Springfield, Massachussets, a computer engineer and a devout Jew.

Ghraith was four years older, a native of Jerusalem, a building contractor and part-time manager of his family's butchery. He was a dedicated Moslem.

Chaiken lived with his wife and five children at Beit Romano, a Jewish settlement and school in Hebron, close to the ancient Jewish quarter of the city. He brought his family here in 1984, citing anti-Semitism in the United States as a major factor in his decision. America, he claimed, masqueraded as a haven for world Jewry; in his experience, the white, Protestant communities of New England hounded the Jews wherever they lived. He compared life there to the *shtetl,* the closed, segregated communities the Jews of Eastern Europe built to protect themselves from persecution. In moving to the West Bank, he gave up a successful career and a salary of more than $100,000 a year. 'America could never be a home for the true Jew,' he contended. 'Even though we had every material possession we could ever want, we still felt we were the outsiders, the object of hatred and abuse. In no way were we integrated.'

Taleb Ghraith's family lived on the edge of Hebron, close to the butcher's shop his father started when the family fled from Jerusalem in 1948. Until 1974, Ghraith ran a building company responsible for the construction of the first homes in Kiryat Arba. By day, he worked for the settlers; Rabbi Levinger was his boss. By night, Ghraith acted as the guerrilla leader of Yassir Arafat's PLO on the West Bank, taking orders directly from Arafat and the PLO's military commander, Abu Jihad, in Beirut. Sentenced to life on 16 counts of murder and bombing in 1975, the Israelis released him in May 1985 as part of a prisoner exchange for the freeing of three Israeli soldiers captured by the Palestinians during the Lebanon war.

'Hebron can never be home for the Jews,' submitted Ghraith. 'I felt that when I worked at Kiryat Arba. I feel it now even more. Religion, culture, politics, they make Jews and Arabs simply incompatible.'

To talk to the two of them was to sense, nevertheless, the symmetry that existed between the majority of Jews and Arabs on the West Bank after 20 years of enforced co-existence but de facto segregation. Both acknowledged the aims and aspirations of the other. They respected each other's religious beliefs yet they recognized the gulf that separated them. Both diagnosed only one

169

solution: the removal of one or other from the territory. Neither believed in the concept of co-existence. Neither sought it.

'In the 1970s, there was a time when I believed co-existence was not just possible, but probable,' said Ghraith, a moody introspective character who did not conceal his contempt for the Israelis. 'But during my years in prison that dream died. When I came home, I found Hebron had divided in two,' he explained. 'There is a Jewish colony in a Palestinian city. Our paths cross even less than they did at the beginning.'

Chaiken, a garrulous, absent-minded figure who expressed loathing for the Arabs, nurtured few hopes that relations between the two peoples would improve in the foreseeable future.

'I didn't live in harmony with the Protestants or the Catholics in Massachussets,' he argued, 'so there's little prospect of making out with the Arabs on the West Bank. I came here to live with Jews, to bring my kids up as proper Jews. I didn't come here to live with Arabs,' he admitted. 'Why would anyone try to co-exist with people who want to kill you?'

Like many Jews and Arabs on the West Bank, these two dismissed the prognosis of those politicians, both Palestinian and Israeli, who believed integration would be the inevitable consequence of Jewish settlement and occupation.

'Hebron is a heavy dose of reality,' remarked Chaiken, 'for all those Jews who claim the war is over, and that now is the time for getting Arabs to accept us. That's pious nonsense.'

'We have come to know the Jews,' commented Ghraith, 'in a way no Arabs have ever done before. Hebron proves we can't live on the same land and hope that the hatred and animosity will disappear. That's naïve.'

As for the future, they foresaw a religious and racial conflict that would outlive them.

'If we can't live together,' declared the Palestinian, 'then there will be more bloodshed. As a religious man, I don't see that as a disaster. I see it more as God's design.'

'The only viable alternative,' concluded the Israeli, 'is the removal of the Palestinians. We have to get them out. That's what the Bible tells us to do. Remember, Judaism is not the religion of turning the other cheek. That's Christianity.'[18]

7
THE CONSPIRACY
OF CONFLICT

'The West Bank is becoming Israel's wild west.'
– GIDEON SAMET, ISRAELI COLUMNIST – DECEMBER 1986

To prevent demonstrations, the Israeli army ordered the family of Majed Abu Dhra to bury him in the dark hours of early morning. On the instructions of the Military Governor, only the boy's father and the local sheikh were allowed to attend. Dozens of Israeli troops stood guard as the two Palestinians carried the simple, birchwood coffin from the family's home to the cemetery on the edge of Balata refugee camp outside Nablus. When the soldiers offered to help, they turned them away. Abdullah Dhra lowered the corpse, shrouded in a white linen sheet, into a makeshift grave. Behind him the sheikh whispered the Moslem prayer of *'Allahu Akhbar!* God is great!' Arm in arm, praying together, the two Palestinians refused to leave without a decent period of vigil. But at two o'clock, on a bitterly cold night, the army ordered them back home. As they walked through the backstreets of Balata camp, the boy's father hummed a ballad that dated back to the first Arab revolt against the British and the Jews in 1929.

171

'The revolt started in Jerusalem
    It echoed up to heaven
The Arabs attacked the Zionists with daggers
    And Zionist blood flowed on the ground

'O, Arab men, pick up your rifles,
    Pick up your daggers
To protect our country.'[1]

According to his family, Majed Dhra was a fairly typical adolescent: headstrong, somewhat defiant, keen to leave school and start work, more interested in soccer than books. In the eyes of the Israeli army, he was just one of many young Palestinians responsible for violent incidents in Balata camp: in the words of one Israeli officer, 'he was probably PLO'.

On December 5 1986 Dhra joined a crowd demonstrating in the main street of the camp. The day before, two Arab students had been killed by the Israelis at a university on the West Bank. As word of their deaths reached Balata, PLO supporters in the camp had issued a leaflet calling for a demonstration. With his face covered to prevent identification, a stone in his hand, Dhra had waited for the army to arrive. Some of his friends had built a barricade of old car tyres. When the troops reached the scene, the demonstrators set them alight. Tall for his age, and known to be pluckier than most, Dhra had been among the first to throw stones as the soldiers took up position. The Israeli commander said he could be seen on the front line of the barricade, urging others to stand their ground. In accordance with army regulations, the soldiers fired tear-gas grenades. Then rubber bullets. Many of the young Palestinians pulled back. Majed Dhra did not. More stones were thrown.

Moments later, the commander gave the order to open fire with live ammunition. Dhra, standing on the front line of the barricade, was struck by a single bullet. He died in the street before the ambulance arrived. At 14 he was too young to be classified a 'terrorist', but old enough to know his own mind. Dhra was just one of hundreds killed in the ritual of conflict that followed the 1967 war – and his death, like that of so many before him, became the reason for others to die.

'Israeli rule today is no more acceptable to the Arabs of the

172

administered territories than it was in 1967,' commented Israel's leading newspaper *Ha'aretz* after the boy's death. 'The root of the problem – and here we must not delude ourselves – is the fact of the occupation.'[2]

Israel's occupation did indeed produce extraordinary resistance among Palestinians. Bloodshed might have been the inevitable consequence of a military regime running the lives of more than a million people. But the fierce opposition of people under occupation for so long, and so divorced from the world outside, was less explicable. Far from healing the wounds of the past, time served instead to aggravate them. The longer the Israelis stayed, the more bloody and brutal occupation became. Some argued that violence on the West Bank was less serious a problem than it might have been. 'In terms of lives lost, and casualties suffered, the cost has been surprisingly low,' said Shlomo Gazit, a former head of Israeli military intelligence. 'The policy of containment has worked.'[3]

Such thinking tended to ignore the increasingly heavy-handed tactics to which Israel resorted. Within a few months of the 1967 war, Moshe Dayan quickly discovered that his plan for 'an invisible occupation', which would have kept the army off the streets and in barracks, was untenable. The insecurity and suspicions of soldiers surrounded by such a large population of Arabs led the government to sanction draconian measures: the demolition of suspects' homes, detention without trial, deportation and the use of both psychological and physical torture. Yet the so-called iron-fist policy did not curb the cycle of violence nor stamp out resistance among ordinary Palestinians. Instead, it fuelled defiance. The figures showed the extent of the conflict.

By the mid 1980s, nearly 200,000 Palestinians, one in six of the total population under occupation, had been arrested at one time or another since 1967. Still the number of Palestinian attacks on Israelis rose steadily each year. In 1985, the government reported an average of three terrorist incidents every day on the West Bank, all of them involving the use of guns, explosives or fire bombs. In Samaria, the region attracting most new Jewish settlers, armed assaults on Israelis almost doubled that year.[4] The Palestinians used home-made bombs, molotov cocktails, even knives. The army said the most drastic increase was in random attacks carried out by those who had no previous record or any links to the PLO. They pointed to cases such as that of Mahmoud Amer, an 18-year-old

Palestinian from the village of Dura, south of Hebron. In February 1986, Amer stabbed and seriously wounded a rabbi on a bus in east Jerusalem. When he was arrested, he told the police: 'I simply couldn't bear the sight of a Jew any more. I could understand what the rabbi was saying to other Jews on the bus. He was insulting the Arabs. I really meant to kill him.'[5]

That confession could have been an epitaph for the generation of Palestinians who had grown up under Israeli rule. They felt a growing sense of frustration, humiliation and hatred. They showed increasing indifference to the consequences of rebellion. Mahmoud Amer stabbed a rabbi with a pocket knife in the presence of dozens of Israelis, one of them the soldier who arrested him. Majed Dhra threw stones at an Israeli riot squad knowing he could be killed just as his uncle had been shot dead in similar circumstances a few months before. 'There is blind despair among many of our young people,' explained Hana Siniora, the Editor of the Palestinian newspaper *al-Fajr*. 'I understand it but I have no idea how you control it.'[6] Thomas Friedman of the *New York Times* wrote: 'They [young Palestinians] no longer seem to view violence as a means towards a particular political objective; most say that they have given up hope for any solutions. Theirs is simply a politics of revenge.'[7]

For many Israelis, the spectre of such indiscriminate, manic violence aroused a fear as old as the 1967 war: that Israel's occupation would spawn civil war between Arab and Jew, first on the West Bank and then inside Israel. Some drew a comparison with South Africa's racial conflict. 'By staying on the West Bank,' remarked a former Israeli Ambassador to Pretoria, Yitzhak Unna, 'we are heaping on our society the same nightmare South Africa is experiencing.'[8]

In the Middle East, Anwar Sadat once remarked, neither side ever took anything at face value; to them, nothing ever seemed what it was. Accordingly, Israelis and moderate Palestinians looked for the hidden motives and reasons which they felt lay behind the conflict. Occupation alone, they believed, could not explain the enduring nature of Palestinian resistance. It was a sign of how intractable the struggle had become that some saw conflict on the West Bank as a machiavellian conspiracy. Israeli governments, they argued, had deliberately manipulated the PLO to provide the pretext for permanent occupation. They maintained that the PLO had been allowed to function under occupation to furnish the excuse for rapid Jewish settlement. In the ritual of daily conflict, they saw a mutual interest for the PLO and those Israelis who sought to populate the territories with Jewish settlers.

'As long as there is a PLO,' said a long-time deputy chief of Israeli military intelligence, 'Israel will stay on the West Bank. Work it out for yourself. Those who don't want to give back the territories need the PLO. As long as they have the PLO, they don't have to make peace. I'd call it an old-fashioned conspiracy.'[9]

'I always think of the PLO and the Israeli right-wing as a trade union,' remarked veteran Labour Party politician Abba Eban. 'They feed off each other, they nurture each other. It's the perfect conspiracy.'[10]

To a limited extent, the PLO had indeed served the purposes of some Israelis in the years since the 1967 war. As the drive to establish Jewish settlement in Hebron showed, PLO terrorism proved a powerful weapon in the hands of settlers' leaders such as Rabbi Levinger. By operating above ground as well – in the trade unions, the universities, the press – the organization had provided the Israeli army with an enemy which it felt it could identify and control.

At the same time, however, the PLO exploited every opportunity to establish a network of political cadres, supporters and even institutions throughout the West Bank. In doing so, they used a strategy the Zionists first applied during the days of the British mandate: of working the system from within. That political insurgency, as much as occupation, explained the PLO's overwhelming support among Palestinians of the West Bank. Much as the Israelis questioned its validity, an opinion poll taken in 1986 reported that nearly 80 per cent supported Yassir Arafat.

The result was a conflict as unique as the occupation. As so often in the Middle East, conspiracy theories tended to obscure the fact that the wounds were self-inflicted – and the consequences detrimental to the chances of future peace.

Every year, some 4,000 students turned the Arab University of an-Najah outside Nablus into what the Israeli press called 'a small Palestinian state'. They hung red, green and black Palestinian flags

175

from almost every window of the largest faculty buildings. They handed out insignia and leaflets bearing the stamp of the different factions under the PLO umbrella. Many wore lapel badges carrying a portrait of Yassir Arafat. Young women, dressed in olive-green fatigues and black berets, marched through the crowds rather like PLO fighters on parade. In one corner of the main courtyard, a tall, lantern-jawed student named Hamdan Saifan harangued a large group of students seated in front of him.

'Are we Jordanians?' he shouted over the public-address system that relayed his message to every part of the university. 'No! No! No!' chanted the crowd in reply. 'Do we want the Americans?' he asked, a broad smile creasing his face. 'No! No! No!' was the answer. 'So what about the Israelis?' he cried. 'Down with the Israelis! Down with the Jordanians! Down with the Americans!'

Saifan, who had been released a few months before after nine years in prison for a bomb attack on the Israeli army, waited for the crowd to settle. 'We are the sons of Arafat,' he declared. 'We are the daughters of the PLO,' he added, pointing to women students in the audience. 'And ours is the future.'

The students at an-Najah staged such demonstrations annually with the full knowledge of the Israeli authorities. The following day, they elected a new student council. Similar elections were held on every campus in the territories. In 1967, only 1,000 students had attended universities on the West Bank and Gaza; by the mid-1980s, there were 22,000 students at colleges which had opened under Israeli occupation. Ever since an-Najah had been converted from a polytechnic into a university in 1977, a group representing Yassir Arafat's branch of the PLO had controlled the campus even as it dominated much of student politics elsewhere on the West Bank. July 1986 proved no exception. The PLO won nearly 50 per cent of the votes and a majority of seats on the council.

Publicly, the PLO activists at an-Najah supported the causes that any student body in the Western world advocated – lower tuition fees, greater student involvement in curricula, better food in the university cafeteria. Privately, they formed the command centre of pro-PLO activities in the city. From here well-known student leaders such as Hamdan Saifan, Khalil Ashour and Ghassan Boorsin ran a network of youth movements, known as A-Shabiba or Youth, in almost every town and village in the district. Much of their work was humanitarian: virtually every community on the West Bank had a youth club or a kindergarten affiliated to the movement; it was common to see groups of teenagers organized by A-Shabiba collecting garbage or carrying out street repairs in rural villages.

In the process hundreds of young volunteers were recruited for an organization which openly identified with the PLO. 'There's no point in fighting the Israeli system on a military level any more,' said one student leader in a 1986 interview. 'The only answer is to work within it. By staying within the law, we turn democracy to our advantage.' Like 70 per cent of students at an-Najah, he had been imprisoned by the Israelis. In his case, he served nearly 10 years for an abortive attack on an Israeli military base on the coast in the early 1970s. Born near Nablus, and trained by the PLO in Lebanon as a young man, he reflected the change in PLO thinking in the territories. As he put it, 'I cannot be punished for what I think, only what I do ... I am no longer involved in the military side of the PLO. The Israelis know that. Whatever I do is legal.'[11]

According to PLO sources and the Israelis, Yassir Arafat spent more than $1,000 million in the occupied territories between 1977 and 1986 to establish a quasi-legitimate political machine under Israeli rule. A portion of the investment came in legally, via the joint Palestinian-Jordanian committee set up after the Arab summit in Baghdad in 1979 to aid Palestinians living under occupation. But much of the money came from the PLO's enormous war chest, funded by the oil-rich sheikhdoms of the Gulf and a tax levied on the two million Palestinians living and working abroad. With assets running into billions of dollars, with investments world-wide in property, industry and blue-chip stock, the PLO was able to maintain a regular flow of cash to its supporters on the West Bank: *mal a-samud*, money for the struggle, as it was known. The sources said the cash was paid directly to a dozen or so key figures in the territories, a select band of academics, lawyers, journalists and businessmen responsible for maintaining Arafat's control over the largest single Palestinian community in the world. While there may have been allegations of corruption, the PLO's wealth created an empire of sorts for the leadership in exile.

By the 1980s, Arafat's Fatah organization controlled the universities, the leading trade unions, the major refugee camps. It boasted the largest morning newspapers, all printed in Arab east Jerusalem. It had started women's associations, private health-care schemes, schools for the illiterate and the mentally retarded. The PLO even had its own poets, playwrights and artists. The greater their loyalty to Arafat, the more money they were said to receive. Democracy, observed Colonel Ephraim Sneh at Israeli army headquarters on the West Bank, had no simple method for dealing with the fighter who carried a cheque-book instead of a gun.

Typically, in the event of imprisonment, a supporter of Fatah on the West Bank could expect financial help from the Prisoners' Friends Association, created in 1979 and run by Nazareth lawyer Walid Fahoum. The group paid monthly allowances to Palestinians in jail, small salaries to dependants on the outside. It provided interest-free loans on a prisoner's release and a grant if his home had been destroyed following his arrest. Fahoum had a budget of nearly a million dollars a year raised by a Geneva-based charity, Atamoun. Israeli intelligence said the funds came from PLO offices in Europe. A witty, erudite character, Fahoum did not deny that. 'Every time we visit a prisoner and give him, say, a carton of cigarettes or a food parcel, he knows where it's come from,' Fahoum explained, carefully avoiding any mention of the PLO. 'When he leaves jail, he remembers who looked after him ... It's perfectly legal. Someone has to do it.'[12] Such organizations were common on the West Bank by the 1980s, forging a direct link between the leadership abroad and Palestinians under Israeli rule.

'I wouldn't say the PLO has flourished under occupation,' remarked Shehadeh Minawi, the head of the PLO's trade union federation on the West Bank, 'but it operates despite occupation. We have 30,000 members and I would say 90 per cent consider themselves supporters of the PLO.' Minawi, who reported directly to Arafat's adviser on labour affairs, Haider Ibrahim, added: 'I consider us a unique trade union. We rarely fight wage battles with Arab employers. Our main concern is uniting workers behind the banner of nationalism.'[13]

Much as the Israelis could claim that the general standard of living had risen since 1967, the poverty and deprivation endemic to many Palestinian communities enabled the PLO to provide much-needed support on a mundane, day-to-day level. Even critics of Arafat, such as Bethlehem's Mayor Elias Freij, acknowledged the role PLO investment had played. 'Without it,' he said in 1985, 'we have to go cap in hand to the Israelis.'[14] At her office in Jerusalem, Zahera Kamal, the founder of a women's movement which identified with the radical wing of the PLO, outlined plans to supply teachers and doctors for the 130 branches her organization had built in the West Bank and Gaza. 'What we have found is a huge void in the lives of ordinary Palestinian women,' she explained. 'Many can't read or write. Often they can't afford a doctor. Some want to learn the simplest thing, like how to sew. The Israelis don't fill the void and the Jordanians can't.' Her organization used a simple slogan, 'The PLO can, the PLO does.'[15]

Yet perhaps the PLO's most important 'ally' was Israel. Not only did occupation create widespread opposition but democracy imposed some restrictions on what the military government could sanction in response to non-violent political insurgency. For example, Zahera Kamal was placed under town arrest, limiting her to Jerusalem. Yet the army did not dare to take action against her organization because it stayed within the law and met the genuine social needs of Palestinian women. More important was the strategy of the military establishment. What the military wanted was exactly what the British had once sought in Malaysia, the French in Algeria, the Americans in Vietnam: an identifiable enemy, a known address for political subversion and terrorism. It believed the best guarantee of limited peace lay in having the PLO show its hand in the universities, identify its support among workers, demonstrate its thinking in the Palestinian press.

'The thinking is that we are better off allowing the PLO to function above ground,' said Aryeh Shalev, Israeli Military Governor in the mid 1970s. 'We know who they are, how they work, what they are planning and we can deal with them accordingly. It means you can allow people to let off steam without being threatened by it.'

'Better the enemy you know and can locate,' explained former intelligence chief Amos Gilboa, 'than a Palestinian underground capable of surprising you.'[16]

Ironically and tragically, it was the Israeli settlers who adopted the tactics of the underground.

In the summer of 1986, Yehuda Etzion, one of the leading pioneers of the Jewish settlement movement on the West Bank, was allowed home on weekend leave from his prison in Jerusalem. At the end of the Jewish Sabbath, which he had spent in isolation with his wife

179

and five children, Etzion spoke to a foreign journalist for the first time since his arrest in 1984 as co-leader of the Jewish underground.

Courteous, agreeable, at times self-deprecating, Etzion revealed how Israeli government policy in the occupied territories had led him to plan murder, sabotage and the destruction of the holiest Moslem shrine in Jerusalem, the Dome of the Rock. Far from expressing misgivings, he defended the killings and bombings of the early 1980s. He spoke openly of another Jewish underground emerging in the future. 'I don't see that anything has changed. We still have the PLO living in our land ... settlers still feel dismay and despair about the way the government handles the territories.'[17]

Until his arrest Etzion had been the epitome of Jewish settlement. Devoted to his family and zealously committed to his cause, he reflected the kind of phenomenal, individual achievement that enabled Israelis to settle on the West Bank. His past exemplified how a group of extremists blackmailed a democratic government into giving them virtually free rein.

At 24 Etzion had organized a group of settlers who camped out in a derelict Jordanian army base in Samaria for months on end, masquerading as labourers employed to clear the site for development. Through sheer persistence, they had bullied the government to grant them permission to stay and build the settlement of Ofra, a few miles from Ramallah. His guiding principles represented a mixture of religious and secular Zionism. The 1967 war and the capture of the West Bank, he believed, heralded the age of the Messiah; settlement pre-empted any future possibility of the genocide his parents' generation had known in Europe under the Nazis. The Bible justified Ofra. At the same time, he advocated the socialist thinking of a kibbutz and he planned communal enterprises such as the settlement's chicken farm and cherry orchard. However isolated he appeared to be after his arrest, Yehuda Etzion remained a classic example of post-1967 Israel.

The dream which he personified, however, turned sour in the 1980s. The religious settlers had achieved almost every target in creating Jewish homesteads on the West Bank but there were fewer and fewer volunteers for their cause. Secular communities grew, particularly in areas close to Jerusalem and Tel Aviv. The religious settlements did not. The reservoir of pioneers, drawn mainly from Orthodox seminaries, had been exhausted. 'Building settlements is no longer the problem, we have more than enough housing already,' said Daniella Weiss, a leader of the Gush Emunim movement. 'The task is to find people and bring them here.'[18] In other words, the battle to redeem the land of Israel had stalled at a critical juncture.

Increasingly, the settlers realized that time could work against them. Their ranks were expanding slowly, while the Arab population grew. The Hebron settlement of Kiryat Arba, for example, had existed since 1972, yet its population remained static at just over 4,000 Israelis. During the same period, the city's Arab population rose from 80,000 to nearly 100,000, as a consequence of a high birth rate and the return of many Hebronites from the Gulf states because of the economic recession in the mid 1980s. Despite the government's investment of more than $2,000 million, the settlers formed barely three per cent of the people living in the territory and seemed destined to remain as such – a tiny minority. Few talked any more of a million Jews on the West Bank by the 21st century. 'Numerically speaking,' remarked another settlers' leader, Israel Harel, 'we don't stand a chance. What can you do with a million and a half Arabs?'[19]

In the circumstances, the settlers became paranoid about the political activities of the Palestinians. They demanded that the government take action against the network of PLO organizations occupation had spawned: close the universities, shut down the Arab press, deport Palestinian leaders, introduce the death penalty for attacks on Jews. When the government balked, they took the law into their own hands, as they had done in the past. They formed new squads of vigilantes, a 'civil guard' designed to protect their interests. In cities such as Hebron it became acceptable practice for armed settlers to harass, intimidate and punish those Palestinians suspected of supporting the PLO. The Jewish underground was not necessarily an isolated phenomenon, as Israel had claimed. Many settlers felt they had every right to take unilateral action in so-called self-defence. They were an inevitable by-product of a system that had rewarded extremism for years. As Rabbi Levinger was fond of telling his followers, 'Act first, argue later.'

Yehuda Etzion saw it as a question of survival. 'At best we stay the way we are. That means a few thousand Jews surrounded by Arabs getting more confident, more thirsty for blood all the time,' he said as he sat playing with his eldest son in the living-room of his home. 'At worst we give up Judaea and Samaria to the PLO. Whichever way you look, it is a recipe for the annihilation of the Jews.' Etzion put his child down, focusing his attention on his argument. 'What Israel needs is a shock to the system.' He paused, trying to translate his Hebrew into simple English. 'More than that. It needs a political earthquake...Something that would put an end to the chaos...Something so big that it would renew the commitment to redemption and close the book for always.'[20]

Etzion had argued that way once before, shortly after Israel made peace with Egypt in 1978 and agreed in principle to autonomy for the Palestinians on the West Bank. His response was to organize a group of settlers who planned to blow up Temple Mount: an act of such magnitude that it would have destroyed the chances of peace, arguably for generations. In Etzion's world, there was no time to wait for another miracle such as the 1967 war. All the conditions for the redemption of the Jewish people existed; he had merely to act, to save the Jews from themselves. In purging Temple Mount of the Arabs, he would create a modern theocracy fit for the Messiah. 'For the Gentiles,' he wrote, 'life is mainly a life of existence, while ours is a life of destiny, the life of a kingdom of priests and a holy people, the kingdom of David. We Jews exist in the world in order to make our Messianic destiny a reality.'[21]

Those Israelis who dismissed such thinking as marginal lunacy ignored Etzion's background and the highly practical nature of the plot. The years since 1967 had taught him to take matters into his own hands, to act rather than wait for a government to move. For Temple Mount, Etzion mobilized the resources of a settlers' movement which enjoyed extraordinary freedom from the constraints of the law. He stole more than a thousand pounds of explosive from an Israeli army base in the Golan Heights; he and Menahem Livni, co-leader of the Jewish underground and an explosives expert, manufactured 28 precision bombs to destroy the Dome of the Rock without causing damage to the surroundings. They purchased Uzi sub-machine-guns with silencers to kill the Moslem guards if necessary. They recruited more than 20 settlers, many of them respectable members of the West Bank movement, to take part in the operation.

'Had we not been distracted by Arab terrorism,' said settler Dan Be'eri, a co-conspirator who subsequently denounced the plot, 'I think we would have destroyed Temple Mount. There was such dismay about what was happening on the West Bank that it made Temple Mount a legitimate target.'[22]

In the end, the underground's preoccupation with day-to-day violence between Arab and Jew proved its undoing. In response to Arab attacks on Israelis in Jerusalem, especially a PLO bomb which killed Jewish commuters in December 1983, the underground planted explosives under the fuel tanks of Arab buses in the holy city. Every detail was taken care of. In his confession Livni stressed the need to cause maximum damage and loss of life while avoiding Jewish casualties. 'We eliminated the risk of harming Jews,' he told his interrogators.[23] At the last minute, the Israeli secret service uncovered the plot. The members of the underground were arrested in April 1984. 'History will be our judge,' said Etzion as he was sentenced to seven years' imprisonment in 1985. 'No Jewish government can abandon its children to murderers in the name of political expediency.'

By 1986, most members of the Jewish underground had been pardoned or granted early parole. Senior right-wing figures within the government, notably Prime Minister Yitzhak Shamir and Ariel Sharon, had campaigned for their release. 'These boys are heroes,' Shamir claimed at one point. 'PLO terror was responsible for such vigilantism.'

Yet the government and the military bore the ultimate responsibility. For years they had turned a blind eye to the underground operations of the settlers while providing the wherewithal for private Israeli armies in the territories. By encouraging the PLO to come out into the open, as a means of enabling the military to control the day-to-day situation, the establishment had created the climate for lasting conflict. 'I blame the government as much as Yassir Arafat,' declared one of the underground's leading figures, Natan Nathanson, in an interview after his release in 1986. 'I don't regret what I did. I would do it again if necessary.' He added ominously: 'Little has changed in Judaea and Samaria. It seems the government still believes in tolerating the PLO.'[24]

On his weekend furlough from prison, granted after incessant pressure from the Israeli right, Yehuda Etzion expressed anything but remorse for the plot to blow up Temple Mount. 'I stand by the operation,' he said, hinting openly at the creation of another Jewish underground after serving his sentence. 'I shall have to switch from planning the actual deed and first build up a solid body of Jews who understand. But the plan has not been dropped. You don't just bury the cause of Jewish redemption.'

Much as he had been criticized and derided – some of his fellow settlers called him 'Israel's Ayatollah Khomeini' – Etzion remained sublimely confident of future support. 'Every time you hear of a settler shooting an Arab, or going out into the streets to put down a riot, ask yourself why,' he suggested. 'It's because they see their government playing games with the Arabs. The settlers know you can't mess around with an enemy like the PLO,' he maintained. 'You can't keep things the way they are. It is no solution to have Arabs killing Jews and Jews killing Arabs.' Etzion concluded: 'There was much talk about an Islamic holy war if we had blown up Temple Mount. Would that have been so terrible? The alternative is civil war. And that could last for ever.'[25]

While 99 per cent of settlers would have disagreed with the strategy, many shared the same sentiment. That explained why they formed themselves into de facto militias and devoted their time to building up a network of committees, councils and support groups which worked independently of the government. They could not attract enough Israelis to join the crusade but they could create a mini-state capable of thwarting any attempt to give back land for peace.

As Dani Rubinstein, an Israeli journalist who had reported the territories since 1967, wrote: 'The organization the settlers have built in the territories is like a knife at the country's throat, making hostages of us all . . . if we seek compromise with the Arabs we will face the threat of internal destruction and civil war.'[26]

At five o'clock on a crisp, clear morning in November 1986, four heavily armed officers of the Israeli security service Shin Beth woke up Akram Hanniye at his home in Ramallah and gave him 15 minutes to get ready. One of the Israelis, who used the undercover alias of Abu Janoun, spoke to Hanniye on first-name terms. 'Akram,' he said, 'you're being deported.'

Eight weeks later, after a futile battle in the Israeli courts, Hanniye was driven from Ramle prison to Ben-Gurion airport and handed over to a French official representing the Red Cross. Every page of his identity papers, which defined him as 'stateless', was stamped with the word 'deported'. After a brief call to his parents, he was forcibly put on an early-morning flight to Zürich. 'I keep imagining I am going to wake up and discover it's all been a nightmare and nothing more,' Hanniye said the following day in a telephone interview from Europe. 'To me exile seems like a living death.'[27] By the beginning of 1987 Akram Hanniye, newspaper editor, novelist and unabashed opponent of Israeli occupation, had linked up with the PLO leadership in exile. 'This young man is an inspiration for Palestinians the world over,' Yassir Arafat was reported as saying, 'and a symbol of the attempts by Jordan and Israel to crush the Palestinian revolution.'

The governments of Europe, led by the Foreign Office in London, denounced the action as a breach of international law. In Washington, the State Department cautiously expressed 'concern'. At the United Nations, the PLO delegation mobilized Arab and Third World support for a Security Council motion attacking the policies of 'the aggressor Israel'. The proposal was dropped when it became clear the Reagan administration would use its veto. In the circumstances, the Israelis did not disguise their sense of righteous-ness. 'Akram Hanniye was one of the most senior PLO activists in the administered territories,' said an army spokesman. 'He was involved day and night in placing PLO people in every labour union, youth group, university and newspaper.'[28]

Leaving aside the hyperbole, the Israeli claim was by and large correct. Hanniye had indeed worked actively in support of the PLO for many years. He had provided both leadership and guidance for the host of pro-PLO organizations on the West Bank. He had selected and nurtured young protégées in the unions, the media and the universities. Specifically, he co-ordinated demon-strations at the Bir Zeit campus and he advised leaders of the A-Shabiba youth movement throughout the West Bank.

Yet the Israelis had known for years that he was playing that role and, apart from one brief spell in prison in 1981, they had not stopped him. Through censorship, they had seen virtually every word he had ever written before it was published. By constant surveillance, they had tracked almost every move he had made among PLO supporters on the West Bank. With regular interroga-tion, they knew he was not a guerrilla, but a dedicated nationalist who believed passionately in co-existence and a Palestinian state alongside Israel, not in place of it. Yet, by the end of 1986, the

Israeli establishment had no further use for Akram Hanniye. His deportation represented an act of supreme cynicism, born out of a policy aimed at neutralizing the PLO and strengthening the hand of King Hussein.

That year the King and the Israelis had secretly agreed on concerted action in the occupied territories. During talks in Amman with Avraham Tamir, director-general of the Israeli Prime Minister's office, the King's advisers formulated a joint assault on the hearts and minds of Palestinians living under Israeli rule. In theory, the plan was designed to boost the King's support in the territories and undermine that of the PLO. Notionally, the scheme prepared the way for Jordan to enter negotiations with Israel along with moderate Palestinians from the West Bank.

The Israelis subsequently appointed pro-Jordanian Mayors in West Bank towns and approved the creation of the first Arab bank in the territory since the 1967 war. For his part, the King launched a billion-dollar aid programme to improve schools, hospitals and social services in the territory. 'The status quo can only bring disaster,' the King told Western correspondents over lunch at the Royal Palace. 'We have to present the Palestinians of the West Bank with a viable alternative.'

Almost immediately the Israelis, with apparent Jordanian compliance, sought to dismantle the PLO network they had sanctioned for so many years. They began with the Palestinian press based in east Jerusalem, much of it financed and directed by Arafat's mini-empire. Despite censorship, the morning newspapers and magazines that the authorities tolerated had been able to propagate PLO policy for more than a decade. Journalists such as Akram Hanniye were classic examples of a system that gave the PLO a voice on the West Bank which the Israelis believed they could control for their own ends. In July, the government closed two pro-PLO organs; in August, the Jordanians launched a new daily edition of the only newspaper loyal to them, *an-Nahar*; in September and October, the papers run by Hana Siniora and Hanniye were repeatedly banned from distributing in the West Bank.

In the 20th year of occupation, then, the PLO apparatus on the West Bank was under siege. More than 30 of Arafat's most important supporters had been deported, scores arrested and imprisoned under a law that allowed detention without formal charges for up to six months. Dozens of private Palestinian homes were destroyed or sealed up as families were punished for the alleged political activities of a child, parent or a close relative. As in the 1970s, there were persistent allegations of torture inside West Bank jails. Prisoners reported physical abuse: it was common practice for young offenders to be beaten, blindfolded and subjected to days of interrogation at a time. Equally serious was the use of psychological torture. Prisoners were told they would be deported unless they confessed to membership of the PLO, they were ordered to write farewell letters to their families and sign over power of attorney so that their assets could be sold by their relatives. Most convictions were based on the 'confessions' that resulted.

The Israelis claimed they had the 'address' for the PLO in their midst and hundreds of special military ordinances, passed by the government since 1967, gave them virtually free rein to act with little or no reference to international law. Typically, Akram Hanniye was never told of the allegations against him and no charges were filed before he was put on a plane to exile. Yet, as the *Jerusalem Post* noted afterwards, 'For every Akram Hanniye there will be another Palestinian, less moderate, more extreme, to take his place.'

To the world outside, the protests and killings on the West Bank so often appeared to be just another stage in the perennial conflict between Israelis and Arabs. By the standards of the Middle East, the human toll was usually low. Given the bloodshed elsewhere, notably Lebanon, the conflict on the West Bank received limited attention in a Western press preoccupied with arms control, or South Africa, or hostages in Beirut. Yet the violence of the 1980s in the occupied territories marked the end of an era in relations between Jews and Arabs – and it suggested an even bloodier future.

For years, both sides had relied on a working arrangement that kept bloodshed to a minimum. Both adhered to the unwritten rules of the fray. Knowing a protest was being planned, for example, the Israelis would set up roadblocks to prevent Palestinians reaching the site. The Arabs would waste half a morning waiting by the side of the road for identity checks and body-searches. The Israelis would pre-empt the latest attempt at insurrection. Increasingly, however, the arrangement collapsed, the pact was broken off by both sides. One incident, in December 1984, showed how and why.

The Israeli army moved into place at dawn, sealing off the narrow, winding roads that led to the two halves of Bir Zeit University in anticipation of a pro-PLO demonstration. Palestinian students and teachers squatted before an Israeli checkpoint. The soldiers singled out one Arab professor; he was kicked, beaten and dragged away to an army jeep. By that time, PLO activists on campus had called for students to march from the university down to the roadblock. As they approached, the students unleashed a hail of rocks and molotov cocktails. Some ransacked a nearby building site for iron bars to be used as clubs. The working arrangement, enacted dozens of times in the past, dictated that the demonstrators retreat when the soldiers opened fire with tear gas or rubber bullets.

But the difference this time was that the Israeli troops were being led by officers who lived in West Bank settlements. These were men who made little secret of the hostility they felt towards the young men and women of Bir Zeit; they were soldiers who believed that their homes and families would be threatened if they did not stamp out the first sign of Palestinian resistance. Some of the men serving with them said they panicked. Army commanders maintained the officers had no option but to kill. The outcome represented one of the most tragic incidents on the West Bank since the 1967 war. Two students died, 12 were wounded.

'We were in an impossible situation,' the Israeli officer in charge said later. 'They kept coming at us with rocks and iron bars.' He concluded: 'When you have to choose between your life or his, you choose your own.'[(29)]

The officer, a major in the army based at military headquarters in Ramallah, lived in the Jewish settlement which the underground leader Yehuda Etzion founded, Ofra. He defined himself as a religious Jew and a dedicated settler; politically, he said, he identified with Israel's radical right wing. His action, he argued, had been dictated by the fear that the students would occupy the main road that linked nearby Jewish settlements to Ramallah and Jerusalem. Retreat from the campus, he submitted, would have threatened the safety of family and friends.

The following day, the West Bank erupted with the worst riots for years. In Bethlehem, Jenin, Tulkarem and Ramallah hundreds demonstrated amid running battles with army units firing tear gas and live rounds over the heads of the protesters. In Balata camp outside Nablus, Majed Abu Dhra was shot dead as he led other teenagers to the barricades. Two days later, another child, 12-year-old Ramadan Zeitan, was shot during a demonstration on the same site where Dhra had died. The army denied responsibility but admitted that Jewish settlers had been on the scene as well, in plain-clothes and wielding M-16 rifles. That night they were seen on national television, among soldiers shooting at the crowds. The image of the Jewish vigilante fighting the Palestinian mob offered a chilling reminder of the warnings issued by those Israelis who had dealt first-hand with the West Bank and who read the long-term implications of such confrontation. 'I see the fury building up on both sides,' said former Military Governor Binyamin Ben-Eliezer in an interview in 1986. 'I see the Arabs in the camps with petrol bombs and rocks, the Jews in the settlements with rifles and machine-guns,' he explained. 'I see us heading for civil war.'[30]

Government ministers chose to draw other conclusions. They argued that the numbers of dead and wounded were minimal when compared to the situation elsewhere, typically in Lebanon. They insisted that the Israeli strategy was working, making ordinary Palestinians defect from the PLO and support Hussein.

'The PLO felt it was about to lose control,' said Defence Minister Yitzhak Rabin in a speech to parliament at the height of the crisis. 'So it adopted what Lenin once said: "The worse it is for the people, the better it is for us." ' He added: 'I call out from this dais to the Arab residents of the territories and I say: If you want a solution, unite with Jordan and enter into negotiations with us.'[31]

Yet while the PLO was undoubtedly threatened by the unbridled assault on its supporters, its leaders remained confident of ultimate survival. 'The Israelis believe they have us where they want us,' said Faisal Husseini, widely acknowledged as the co-ordinator of pro-PLO activities on the West Bank. 'But they don't recognize just how deeply embedded the PLO is. The organization has made itself the only voice for Palestinians who live here.' Husseini, who was restricted to Jerusalem by day and his home by night, added: 'If we have played an Israeli game, than I can't see how we can lose. We are in a position to stop whatever kind of deal the Israelis want to make.'[32]

Some Israelis agreed. 'I think we became victims of our own

strategy,' said a former West Bank Governor, Aryeh Shalev. 'With the PLO in the territories there can be no real movement towards a solution... Yet without the PLO representing the Palestinians, there won't be any serious negotiations. We're caught in a trap.'

As for those theories of conspiracy, many saw a much simpler explanation. 'The only way to understand what's happened in the past 20 years,' said former intelligence chief Shlomo Gazit, 'is to appreciate that the policy has always been to maintain the status quo. It worked.'[33]

8
THE GENERATION GAP

'The years teach much which the days never know.'
– RALPH WALDO EMERSON

'The first thing I feel when I hear the word "Arab" is deep nausea and great anger,' wrote a pupil described by his teacher as 'a sensitive boy'.

A 14-year-old girl whom teachers called an 'excellent student' described at length her feelings of hatred and bitterness. 'The Palestinians are murderers,' she explained. 'I very much want to kill all the Arabs.'

One of her classmates concluded: 'We don't like the Arabs because they're not our race, and their race is frightening ... Palestinians are garbage.'[1]

Those selections, from essays written at a Tel Aviv high school in the summer of 1985, reflected the way in which the new children of Zion were heading in a vastly different direction from their parents and grandparents. The men and women who founded Israel as a utopian haven for world Jewry had been succeeded by a generation which espoused few of their values and cherished little of their hope for peaceful co-existence. Throughout the 1980s, surveys of Israeli youngsters showed them to be increasingly conservative, hawkish, zenophobic and suspicious of the merits of democracy.

191

One study, published by an Israeli pollster, Mina Zemach, found that 25 per cent of 18-year-olds held what she called 'consistently anti-democratic views'; 44 per cent said they favoured a comprehensive ban on any media criticism of government policy towards the Arabs; a clear majority insisted that no Palestinians were entitled to the same rights as Jews. As for politicians, the younger generation consistently named Ariel Sharon as the man they wanted to lead the country.

'When I listen to our youngsters, I sometimes wonder whether this is my own country,' said Shmuel Toledano, a left-wing Israeli who frequently lectured in schools and army bases. 'They march to a different drummer than what we used to.'[(2)]

Educators and political leaders cited the dramatic and painful progress of the decades since independence. The founding fathers, they argued, fought their way to Palestine from the ruins of the holocaust; they were united in their vision of a sanctuary where Jews could live in peace. Yet, in the 1980s, the new generation lived in a country deeply divided by factions. Judaism, once the common tie that bound them, had split into rival camps, Orthodox and secular, each deeply suspicious of the other. In spite of Sadat's peace with Begin and the Camp David Agreement, the gulf between Israel and its Arab neighbours seemed as wide as ever. Genuine fear remained the strongest undercurrent of Israeli society, be it of terrorism or the possibility of facing Arab troops in another war. Almost every high school had a monument of some sort to the former pupils who had died in Israel's wars. In some cases, the walls of the school library were covered with the photographs of those killed only a few years before in Lebanon. Students leaving school for the army cracked black jokes about holding class reunions at the local cemetery; at one high school outside Tel Aviv, they called the graveyard 'Youth City'. Fear of future conflict undoubtedly helped to explain the swing to the right so evident in the nation's classrooms. Yet their parents and grandparents had lived with similar anxiety all their lives without becoming radical reactionaries. What separated the new generation from the old was the occupation of the West Bank and Gaza Strip. For many, the promise of a country born to be 'a light unto the nations' clashed with the harsh reality of Israeli rule over more than a million Palestinians. The treatment meted out to West Bank Arabs – arbitrary arrest, long detention without trial, the demolition of private homes – could not easily be reconciled with their parents' image of a land dedicated to peace. Teachers and sociologists diagnosed a widespread feeling that democracy was not consistent with military rule. In time, they maintained, Israeli youth become anaesthetized to the issue of equal rights and indifferent to the values of previous generations.

'Put yourself in the mind of a 20-year-old,' remarked the country's former President, Yitzhak Navon, in a 1986 interview. 'He cannot recall a time when we didn't control the territories. He serves in the army on the West Bank. He has to carry out orders that are not necessarily democratic, he is often obliged to be firm because of an Arab attack or demonstration.' Navon, who was Education Minister in the 1980s, commented: 'I can understand why so many youngsters could be confused about their democracy. I suspect the West Bank is a conundrum for them.'[3]

The result was a generation both disenchanted with the past and deeply troubled concerning the future. According to surveys, more than 40 per cent regarded democracy as too weak to deal with all the dangers facing the country: inflation, terrorism, the threat of the Arab armies. They felt that Western values had failed and that their elected government offered no solution. The sense of supreme self-confidence enjoyed by their parents after 1967 had been replaced by self-doubt in the wake of the 1982 Lebanon invasion. 'We have a new breed of Israeli growing up,' commented Rabbi David Hartman, 'who can't stand the heat any more. He cries out for simple answers and quick solutions.'[4]

The extreme right benefited most. Where the parents once embraced Western liberalism, an increasing number of sons and daughters turned to right-wing parties, such as Tehiya, which demanded the immediate annexation of the occupied territories and the expulsion of up to half a million Palestinians. In the election of 1984, Tehiya became the third largest party in the Israeli parliament. Its leader, a nuclear physicist, Yuval Ne'eman, subsequently made the removal of Arabs a cardinal principle of the party's manifesto. Yet at least he supported the concept of democracy. Others, such as Rabbi Meir Kahane, who was elected to the Knesset for the first time in 1984, did no such thing.

For many years, Kahane, an American-born Jew who emigrated to Israel in 1971, was dismissed as a fascist and bigot whose constituency was limited to street hooligans and criminals. His outrageous declarations of racist intent, and the way in which he craved media exposure, made him appear more of a public nuisance than a serious politician. 'There is no place for even one Arab in the land of Israel,' he declared at almost every rally in 1984. 'I want the Arabs – out, out out!' Conversation with Kahane, however, hinted at a demagogue who saw fertile ground in the uncertainty of Israeli youth. 'Talk to kids in this country and you'll see the Israel of tomorrow,' he said in an interview in 1985. 'They're running scared of the future. They see themselves surrounded by millions of Arabs who want to take Jewish land, sleep with Jewish women and kill every Jewish male they can lay their hands on. That's not Meir Kahane speaking. That's the way they speak.'[5]

Kahane's solution might have seemed like the lunatic ranting of a maverick desperate for votes. Yet a 1985 study of high schools showed that 42 per cent of Israeli students supported his 'final solution'. Kahane's manifesto amounted to a crafty combination of religious Orthodoxy and political expediency, cleverly tailored for the generation growing up in the 1980s. In Kahane's world, the Arabs became the cancer requiring surgery: the survival of the Jewish nation demanded sacrificing Israeli democracy. The state of Israel could be democratic or Jewish but not both; and since it was bound to be Jewish, the sooner the Arabs were expelled, the better. 'I'm not a democrat, I'm a Jew,' he explained. He turned to the Bible for his justification. He compared the Palestinians of the West Bank to their forefathers, the Canaanites conquered by the Israelites under Joshua. 'Let us make the same offer to the Arabs today as Joshua made to the people of Canaan,' he submitted. 'They can leave the land, they can fight for it or they can accept our rule and stay as our guests! If I have my way, we'll simply put them on buses and move every single one of them out of here.' When the Arabs were evicted, he claimed, the Messiah would come to redeem his chosen people, the Jews.[6]

Much as his fellow parliamentarians looked upon Kahane as a pariah, the rabbi built a following among Israeli youth during the 1980s. To them, Kahane's programme looked like a simple way out of the crisis with which they had come to feel so frustrated. Dressed in yellow T-shirts, emblazoned with a clenched fist, hundreds of young toughs followed Kahane as he tried to visit Arab communities on the West Bank and in Israel. The incongruous outcome had the Israeli army protecting Palestinians from Jewish extremists. The rabbi's supporters stalked the streets of Jerusalem, threatening physical violence against Israelis who shopped in Arab stores; they became 'Jewish honour guards' whose task was to identify Jewish girls dating Arabs and threaten them. In both spirit and deed, Kahane's shock-troops displayed a militancy that invited ominous comparisons with the anti-Semites of the Hitler Youth. Yet they seemed oblivious to the painful analogies in Jewish history.

'The Nazis regarded themselves as superior and wanted to destroy the Jews for racist reasons,' said 16-year-old Nati Ozeri, one of Kahane's 400 youth leaders, in an interview with *Newsweek* magazine in 1986. 'We want to get rid of the Arabs not because of their race, but because they're dangerous. Kach [Kahane's party] is not fascist; Kach is the truth.'[7]

In many respects, Kahane's emergence was a natural corollary to the rise of the Jewish settlers in the years after 1967. Like them, he used Messianic philosophy as the basis for political belief. Even as they legitimized settlement by reading the Bible as historical fact, so he made racism sound like God's teaching. Such fusion, of religion and politics, provided both a moral defence and a rationale for attack. What made it so disturbing was that young Palestinians were seeking a similar way out.

A whitewashed concrete wall separated men from women at the Islamic University of Gaza. Female and male students studied separately, used the library at different hours and elected representatives to student councils independently of each other. Even outside class, the sexes never mingled. Segregation, reinforced by that high wall, was complete. On one side, women students, wearing long-sleeved gowns and demure headscarves, crowded around examination results posted on classroom windows. On the other, male students, many with luxuriant beards, strolled arm in arm through the courtyard to midday prayers. The wall was plastered with slogans and posters. 'Islam is the only truth,' declared one freshly painted sign. A colourful mural showed an Islamic sword slashing through American and Israeli flags. 'God is great,' read the inscription. Another poster depicted a fist holding a map of Palestine, with blood running down and tracing the letters 'Allah'. Almost 5,000 students were enrolled at Gaza University, the largest in the territories. In the 1986 elections, nearly 75 per cent voted for an extreme religious organization known as Al-Mujaama, the Community, otherwise called the Moslem Brother-hood. Ideologically, the movement represented the tidal wave of Islamic fundamentalism which had swept through the Arab world in the 1980s. On Israel's doorstep, it represented an explosive, new threat to occupation.

'The population of Gaza is undergoing a revolution,' reported the Israeli newspaper *Ma'ariv* in July 1986 with a combination of concern and fascination. 'You see it in the streets. Young men and women are decked out in conservative dress. Men wear white, knitted skullcaps and long, flowing tunics. Women wrap themselves in grey scarves or black veils that cover their faces. Their bodies are hidden under full-length, wide robes.' The newspaper summed up: 'Religion has penetrated and permeated the younger generation at a dizzying rate.'[8]

By the mid 1980s, a staggering 65 per cent of Palestinians living in the occupied territories were under the age of 20 – too young, in other words, to remember anything other than Israeli rule. In contrast to their parents, they no longer espoused compromise as a means to the end of survival. While their parents had expressed the hope of a negotiated settlement, many of their children felt that the search for peace was an exercise in futility. More educated, more politicized, less intimidated and inhibited by Israeli rule, they sought release from a bleak future that promised only the hand-to-mouth existence their parents had known. In a closely knit society, bound by respect for family, honour and tradition, such disaffection signalled a dramatic upheaval. 'For the first time we have a younger generation that rejects the values of its elders,' explained the West Bank historian Abdul Lattif Barghouti. 'It's hard to imagine what goes through the mind of an 18-year-old living on the West Bank or Gaza. But I know he doesn't see a future for himself, he sees only more of the same. So he looks to the PLO. If not, he looks to God.'[9] One result was a dramatic increase in the number of young Palestinians observing daily worship. By 1986, the Supreme Moslem Council of Jerusalem reported an 80 per cent rise in those attending mosque throughout the territories; the number of students at Moslem colleges rose by 30 per cent that year. 'God is the last resort for many of our children,' explained the Mufti of Jerusalem, Sheikh Saad al-Din al-Alami. 'They feel lost, they believe their politicians let them down. God cannot fail them as their leaders on earth have done.'[10]

Moslems, who formed 90 per cent of the Palestinian population in the territories, were predominantly Sunni, the mainstream of Islam. Historically they had been conservative but not extremist. Typically, a city such as Hebron had never permitted the sale of alcohol or a cinema, yet Hebronites tolerated the presence of a Jewish community for centuries. During the final years of the British Mandate, religious leaders, such as Haj Amin el-Husseini, Mufti of Jerusalem and the leader of Arab resistance to the Zionists, built an army from the ranks of the faithful. But his defeat and exile in 1948 shattered the alliance that had welded Palestinian nationalism to Islam. Both before and immediately after the 1967 war there was little evidence of religious militancy; indeed, the Western influence of Israel seriously undermined the precepts of Islam. The 1980s marked a decisive change in both devotion and direction, the 1979 revolution of Ayatollah Ruhollah Khomeini in Iran providing one factor. Khomeini proved how Islamic fundamentalism could inspire mass opposition to a dictatorial regime. The Lebanon war then proved to be of even greater importance to the fledgling Islamic movement.

As the Israeli army retreated from southern Lebanon in 1984 and 1985, young Palestinians learned a lesson from the radical Shi'ite Moslem groups who led the Lebanese resistance to that Israeli occupation. For the first time in the history of the Arab–Israeli conflict, the Arabs could claim a victory in southern Lebanon. A holy war of attrition, of suicide missions and popular resistance, had forced the Israelis back towards their northern border. 'Our people draw inspiration from what has happened in Lebanon,' explained Gaza's Mayor, Rashad Shawa, in 1985. 'They see that Islam worked to end the occupation in Lebanon. Weapons, it seems, are not as important as faith in God.' Shawa warned: 'For too long the Palestinians have suppressed their despair. Islamic fundamentalism thrives on misery ... I see the time coming when there will be suicide attacks from Gaza.'[11]

In Gaza itself, Islamic fundamentalists made no secret of their intentions. 'The mosque is the fortress which protects us,' Ayatollah Khomeini had said during his years of opposition to the Shah of Iran. The mosques of Gaza provided a perfect cover for those who sought to instill the faithful with Khomeini-style

197

fanaticism. As early as 1979, the year of the Iranian revolution, a group calling itself the Moslem Brotherhood of Gaza filed for legal recognition from the Israeli Military Government; given Israel's respect for freedom of worship, the request was granted. 'The mosque is both the medium and the message,' observed an Israeli officer serving in Gaza. 'It's just about the only area of Palestinian life we dare not enter.' The territory's Islamic University became the headquarters for an organization that used the Koran as the basis for political and military ends. As in Egypt, Lebanon and the Gulf states, the Brotherhood had begun at grass-roots level, enlisting recruits in the schools and refugee camps of Gaza. 'Islam is not just an expression of faith in God,' said Ahmed Yassin, a self-styled cleric who founded the movement, 'it is a code of conduct for life itself. It is an identity.'

As early as 1983, the Israelis uncovered a stockpile of weapons, including rifles and rocket-propelled grenades, which had been bought by the Brotherhood with funds allegedly supplied by the Iranians. Yassin and 27 other leaders of the Islamic movement were jailed. When they were released, as part of a huge prisoner exchange in May 1985, they returned to Gaza and rebuilt the organization within a matter of weeks. 'In the name of God the Merciful, the Compassionate,' began a document issued by the Moslem Brothers later that year, 'the first priority is to cleanse ourselves of the evils which surround us.' What followed was an increasingly violent campaign aimed at destroying all traces of Western influence. Just as Rabbi Kahane's thugs harassed secular Jews, so the young fundamentalists of Gaza attacked Moslems in street cafes that sold hard liquor; they broke up marriage cere- monies at which bands played dance music or where the bride's dress wasn't modest enough; they stabbed those whom they accused of 'collaboration with the Zionist enemy'.

Elsewhere, on the West Bank, the Moslem Brothers gained increasing support as the PLO's fortunes declined. In refugee camps, such as Kalandia, on the main road from Jerusalem to Ramallah, Palestinian teenagers talked openly of their commit- ment to an Islamic *Jihad*, or Holy War, the name Jihad coming to be used by pro-Iranian groups in Beirut and elsewhere in the Arab world. They revealed how they had been 'initiated' into the movement by radical religious leaders such as Ahmed Yassin. The task allotted to them had been an attack on an Israeli patrol outside the camp. In April 1986, they had hurled hand-grenades and petrol bombs at two armoured vehicles parked at the entrance to Kalandia. Behind the evident bravado lay young men whose thinking was comparable to that of the generation of Lebanese Shi'ites which had matured so quickly under Israeli occupation just a few years earlier. Their language and reasoning bore an uncanny resemblance to that of the street fighter in Beirut or Sidon. 'I believe our future can only be resolved by bloodshed,' said 19-year-old Ziad, who was once convicted of PLO membership. 'The Koran tells us to fight for equality for all. That is what I am doing.' Khaled, a burly, intimidating figure, much admired by fellow teenagers at Kalandia, explained: 'Alone I am not important. As a member of Jihad, I have a role in this life. God gives me that role. God tells me what to do. I would die for God, willingly.' As for the Israelis, they expressed a surprising degree of respect. 'It is a battle of equals,' said Mustafa, at 16 the youngest of the group. 'They have their Tora [Bible]. We have the Koran. The last holy war will be fought between us.'[12]

In the autumn of 1986, the Brotherhood carried out a series of attacks in Gaza, the West Bank and Jerusalem. At first they chose easy targets: Israeli civilians shopping and doing business in the territories. Two had their throats cut, another was seriously wounded. But, in October that year, the fundamentalists staged their most audacious raid, hurling Soviet-made grenades into a crowd of soldiers who had just been sworn into the Israeli army at a glittering ceremony close to Jerusalem's Western Wall. One died, 69 were wounded. Despite initial claims of responsibility from the PLO, Islamic Jihad was behind the attack and had worked in tandem with Arafat's Fatah organization to carry it out. At the end of the year, the Israelis rounded up dozens belonging to the Islamic movement, including Ahmed Yassin. Among those arrested were four youths from Kalandia refugee camp.

'The more Islam spreads, the more it will become a weapon against Israel,' predicted Shulamit Aloni, a left-wing member of the Israeli parliament. 'Yet what came first? Jewish Khomeneism or Islamic fundamentalism? To me they are symptoms of the same illness which is affecting the youth of both our societies.'[13]

'No one, not even the Israelis, will be able to control the new generation of Jews and Arabs,' concluded Ibrahim Dakkak, a veteran leader of Palestinian opposition in the territories. 'The

Israelis were able to buy some peace from my generation. But our children don't listen any more – neither to their parents nor to authority.'[14]

Anwar Nusseibeh's house stood on the old border between Jordan and Israel in Jerusalem, just a few metres from what had once been no man's land. During his life, this suave, urbane diplomat tried to cross many such frontiers. As a young lawyer, educated at Cambridge in the 1930s, he had supported the Mufti's holy war against the Jews in 1948. In middle age, he switched allegiance to the Jordanians, becoming King Hussein's Defence Minister in the 1950s. After 1967, he tried vainly to mediate between Jordan and Israel, delivering messages back and forth, making friends of politicians such as Moshe Dayan. Before he died, in November 1986, he reluctantly backed the PLO while condemning its terrorism. A man for all seasons, his life acted as a mirror to the Palestinian experience in the 20th century.

The Nusseibehs, one of Jerusalem's oldest Arab clans with a history in the city that dated back 1400 years, had always been a major influence on Palestinian thinking. Since the seventh century, the Nusseibehs had been the guardians of the Holy Sepulchre, the site acknowledged by most Christian denominations as the tomb of Christ. They had been teachers, civil servants, government ministers. Anwar Nusseibeh was apt to call his forefathers 'lazy'. They lacked the initiative, he remarked sardonically, to move on elsewhere. Yet, by staying in Jerusalem, as others fled the colonial rule of successive foreign powers, they had given countless generations of Palestinians leadership and inspiration. One of the tragedies of Anwar Nusseibeh's life was that his children had broken with family tradition and emigrated abroad to work in the years after 1967. Only one, his son Sari, had stayed to perpetuate the family's political dynasty. Father and son were close, spending most afternoons together at the family home. Both were politically active: Anwar as head of the Jerusalem Electricity Company, one of the few Arab industries to resist an Israeli take-over; Sari as a professor at Bir Zeit University and a leading advocate of the PLO. Yet they openly disagreed on the past, present and future; the gap between two generations produced a lively debate most afternoons.

To listen to Anwar Nusseibeh was to hear the political philo-sophy of the older breed of Palestinians: highly self-critical, tolerant towards the Israelis, disarmingly confident that justice would ultimately prevail. He saw the defeat of 1967 as a disaster for the Palestinians. He blamed the Arabs for the failure then and the consequences with which the Palestinians had lived ever since. 'We lost everything in 1967. It was the end of Palestine because all our land had been taken,' he said in an interview in the summer of 1986. 'It was always my belief that we should have recognized Israel, accepted the return of the territories and settled for a homeland with Jordan. Instead of that, we said no to everything. What was the point?'

He viewed the years after the war as a monumental blunder. 'Every day we lost, yet all the time the Arabs and the PLO maintained this fiction of war against Israel. What the hell for?' he asked despairingly. 'Why did we make it so difficult when the only option was to accept the reality of Israel?'

His son had returned to Jerusalem from Oxford after the Six-Day War, not out of duty but out of choice. Sari Nusseibeh was representative of the new generation of Palestinian: defiant, uncompromising, convinced that 1967 had marked a new beginning for the Palestinians. 'In some respects, I look upon 1967 as a blessing in disguise,' he explained. 'Palestine wasn't destroyed. It was reunited, albeit under Israeli rule. The two halves of Palestine and two groups of Palestinians were brought together again. My father sees it as a matter of land. I don't see that Palestine was taken by the Israelis or given to them. For me, the people are more important than land – and people are not for another country to take or give.'

The years since, he argued, had been fruitful for the Pales-tinians, despite the cost of occupation. 'What we have created is a new identity,' he remarked. 'The PLO has been largely responsible for that. It has given us a sense of nationhood we never had before. Whatever the price, the Palestinians are no longer a people the world can ignore. To my mind, that is a crucial development.'

Like most of his generation, his father remained committed to the concept of Arab unity. The ideals of Egypt's President Nasser, the dream of one Arab nation, had dominated the thinking of his contemporaries. Even after the disaster of 1967, he still cherished the hope that the Palestinians could unite with Jordan and the

Arab world beyond. 'I see the Palestinians not so much as an independent people as a part of the Arab entity,' he submitted. 'Philosophically, culturally, spiritually, we are Arabs first. I don't believe we can ever separate ourselves from the rest of the Arab world and build a viable state on our own. United, we are strong. Alone, the Palestinians will always be weak.'

Sari Nusseibeh expressed indifference bordering on contempt to such Arab unity. Like most of the younger generation, the experience since 1967 had made him disillusioned about future ties with Jordan. 'To me there's nothing magic about being an Arab. If it helps the cause of the Palestinians, all well and good. But the Arabs have done so little for the Palestinians in the past few years that I wonder what the point of Arab unity is.' He paused, glancing at his father, half-expecting a rebuke. 'I ask myself as well what kind of home we would have alongside another Arab state,' he added. 'Do the Arabs provide liberty, or human rights, or progress for their own people? I don't believe they do. I don't sense we would be better off under an Arab regime.'

In 1986, Sari had made an extraordinary appeal for his fellow Palestinians to challenge Israeli rule on the West Bank and Gaza. In a series of speeches, and interviews with a somewhat bemused Israeli press, the younger Nusseibeh had urged Palestinians to launch a campaign of civil disobedience. The Arabs under occupation, he contended, should seek Israeli citizenship en masse and demand the formal annexation of the territories. Apart from its propaganda value, the proposal highlighted the belief of his generation that it had to take the battle to Israel and so make the Palestinian problem an internal Israeli issue. 'Our greatest strength is our ability to divide Israel,' he said. 'What would Israel do with more than a million Palestinians seeking the right to vote and demanding representation?' he maintained. 'We all know the crisis is coming. So let's induce it.' He added: 'Israel has always had a nightmare about what to do with the Arabs. I want them to live with that nightmare all their lives.'

Anwar Nusseibeh was amused yet horrified. 'The idea is anarchic,' he retorted. 'We are Arabs. We wish to govern ourselves. I may not want to live under occupation, but I surely don't wish to be a second-class citizen in Israel.' He turned to his son, a look of dismay creasing his face. 'That's the difference between us. My generation still looks to the Arabs for a solution. The young generation believes they have it within their own power.'

In contrast to Sari, Anwar Nusseibeh was optimistic about the future. All his life, he insisted, he had lived with the Jews; he had faith in their common sense. 'Israel cannot live for ever as an island in the Middle East. Its future depends on recognizing that justice must prevail.'

The younger Nusseibeh had no such illusions. 'My father's generation knew what it was to have a relationship with the Jews,' he concluded. 'To me the idea of co-existence is as radical as a Palestinian state.'[15]

The drive from the farming kibbutz of Massuot Itzchak outside Ashkelon to the Gaza Strip and the small Jewish settlement of Azmona took about 40 minutes. Yet, almost every time Eliezer Bashan travelled to see his son Gidon, he felt the same tension – between father and son, religion and politics, the Israel of the past and the Israel of the 1980s. The experience of the Bashan family acted as a microcosm to a national debate that often pitted one generation of Israeli against another.

'I disagree with what my son is doing,' said Eliezer Bashan, a professor of Jewish history at Bar-Ilan University near Tel Aviv, in an interview in 1986. 'To me, Jewish settlement in the territories is a betrayal of the values I grew up with ... It saddens me to see what we are doing with our past and our future.'

At his home, a small prefabricated house close to the settlement school at which he taught Bible study, Gidon Bashan remarked, 'It's more than just a question of generations. It's an entirely different approach to Judaism and the responsibility of being a Jew.'

The life of Eliezer Bashan spanned the 20th-century exodus of the Jewish people. Born in Budapest in 1925, he had with his family fled Nazi persecution in Europe to seek a new beginning in Palestine. After several years in the mixed city of Haifa, they moved to the West Bank in 1945 at the end of World War Two. They set up home in the Jewish settlements of Gush Etzion, between Bethlehem and Hebron. When the Etzion block was attacked by the Arabs, at the beginning of the war of independence in 1948, the 23-year-old Eliezer was taken prisoner by the Jordanians and transferred to a prison camp in the kingdom of Iraq. For nine months he was held in the desert town of Umm el-Jamal, finally being released in March 1949 as part of the armistice between Jordan and Israel. Returning to Israel, he married a childhood friend from Gush Etzion. In 1952, Gidon, their second son, was born in the newly established kibbutz of Massuot Itzchak, south of Tel Aviv. In both spirit and membership, the kibbutz was a replica of the Etzion settlement destroyed by the Arabs in 1948.

'I always taught my children that the main priority for the Jews was to become part of the Middle East,' he recalled. 'My generation had built Israel with one purpose, namely, to provide a home for the survivors of the holocaust. The task of the next generation was to take it on, and make us neighbours with the Arabs.' Like many of his contemporaries, he viewed victory in 1967 as a military triumph and a political risk. 'We didn't need the land. The last thing we wanted was more Palestinians. I feared only one thing after 1967 – that the momentum towards peace would stop.'

In the early 1970s, Gidon, the most devout of the Bashan children, enrolled as a student in the Biblical academy of Rabbi Zvi Yehuda Kook, the spiritual guru of the settlers' movement. In keeping with other Jewish settlers, he was taught to view 1967 as the dawn of redemption. 'My father thought only in day-to-day terms. He missed the true meaning of the war. I saw it as God's intervention,' he explained. 'God was telling us to go forth and settle all the Biblical Land of Israel. He was reuniting the land and the people for the purpose. The destiny of my generation was to fulfil God's plan and hasten the coming of the Messiah.' Intense, introspective, constantly using Biblical language, Gidon insisted that settlement was a duty not a choice. 'There are moments when I feel almost overwhelmed by the sheer magnitude of what we are doing. I was created by God to establish a new holy kingdom. I honestly believe that ... to my generation has fallen the burden of making the Jews the leaders of the world ... Not just a light unto other nations, but the heart of all other peoples.' At the mention of the Palestinians, he retorted: 'They may call it racism, but that is only because they have never read the Bible.'

Yet, for his father, settlements such as Azmona represented racist thinking and intent. His generation had been brought up to consider the Arabs as equals; as a child in Haifa, he had known Arabs as friends. 'My mother always taught me that the Jews had the brains,' he recalled at one point, 'and the Arabs had the money and the skills. Together we would make irresistible partners.' Modern-day settlement in the occupied territories made him despair because of the lack of contact between Jew and Arab and the ensuing bitterness. 'My generation knew the value of Arabs. My son sees them only as servants. By anyone's standards, it can't be called progress when you go back to having masters and slaves. To my mind, that's what we've got in Gaza and the West Bank.'

The younger generation of Israelis expressed indifference to such parental judgement. Gidon decried his father's concern for the Arabs as naïve and misplaced. 'The Jews of my father's generation always feel they have to apologize for themselves. It's a legacy of the holocaust. They feel they have to win acceptance from the people around ... They crave it because, as children, they were treated like filth.' He paused for a moment, pointing to a picture of his own son. 'My child will never have to say sorry to anyone. He is made in the image of God, to serve God's purpose. He is answerable to no one except God.'

Unlike the Nusseibehs and the Palestinians in general, Gidon's generation expressed hope for the future while his father voiced a deep foreboding about the years ahead. As a Jewish historian, Eliezer Bashan turned instinctively to the siege of Massada in the first century AD when the Jews had made their last stand against the Romans, choosing mass suicide rather than slavery. For centuries, Massada had symbolized a Jewish complex; ever since 1967, it had become a potent symbol for those who argued that the Jewish people were forever besieged and encircled, with the whole world against them, fighting for national freedom and social justice.

'There are two Israels,' concluded Eliezer Bashan. 'It's not just a question of old and young ... it's a matter of mentality and identity. My generation instinctively looks for peace and a way out. Younger Israelis have the Massada complex. They see themselves living permanently in a bunker, facing extermination in a war with the world around them.'

His son scoffed at the idea. 'My father believes we are creating the scenario for disaster. I see that we are building an entirely new identity,' he insisted. 'My generation recognizes the call of God and we are already the majority. So where he sees despair, I see hope. I see the day when we will be one nation capable of dominating the world around us.'[16]

Back in 1967, no Israeli had epitomized the strength and self-confidence of a victorious nation more than Ezer Weizman, commander of the air force. His pilots had destroyed 80 per cent of the Egyptian squadrons on the first morning of the war and given Israel the decisive advantage within a matter of hours. 'We have a plan for everything – even for capturing the North Pole,' said Weizman in a moment of typical bravura at the height of the fighting. Explaining Israel's phenomenal success in those first few hours, he remarked: 'We don't go in for preconceived and therefore inflexible master plans.'[17]

Ezer Weizman had been improvising all his life. Born in Tel Aviv in 1924, the nephew of Israeli's first President had talked his way into the British air force as a young Zionist who matched ambition with determination. Trained as fighter pilot by the British in Rhodesia in 1942, he returned to Palestine to lead the embryonic Israeli air force in the war of 1948. Dashing, good-looking, as reckless as he was imaginative, Weizman carried out the first air raids of the Arab–Israeli conflict when he bombed the Egyptians from an ageing Spitfire in May 1948. His spirit of daring made him a hero. As a brash advocate of war in 1967, and a major architect of victory, Weizman established himself as a natural leader of the second generation blooded by the June conflict. As a native Israeli, not inhibited by personal experience of the holocaust, his life was an expression of the new Jewish identity.

'For 2,000 years, Jews always woke up always asking themselves: "Who's going to attack me this morning?"' he remarked in a series of candid interviews in 1986. 'I grew up with the attitude "Who am I going to attack?"'[18]

That self-confidence had led him actively to encourage his political masters in the war of 1967. Far from being concerned about the political implications, Weizman had urged the seizure of Jerusalem and the West Bank so as to conquer all of Palestine and the Land of Israel. By no means a religious Jew, he was nevertheless an ardent Zionist. For Brigadier-General Weizman, Hebron was as much a part of Israel as his home town, Haifa. He saw and sought no accommodation with the Arabs.

Yet, in the aftermath of the 1967 war, he underwent a dramatic metamorphosis. Ezer Weizman, the supreme hawk of 1967, became the most dedicated dove of the 1980s; the politician who once craved war became a standard-bearer of peace. His conversion mirrored that of many Israelis who recognized the shortcomings of their most glorious, military victory. His fate – increasing isolation from the mainstream of national life – reflected that of countless Jews who found themselves out of step with post-1967 Israel. Matured by war, they were unable to make peace alone.

The changes in Ezer Weizman's attitude began immediately after the war. Touring the West Bank, he was struck not so much by Israel's conquest as by the tragedy of the Palestinians. Like Anwar Nusseibeh, he had always seen the conflict in terms of land. In June 1967, he recognized the human cost. With Dayan, he visited the Arab town of Qalqilia on the West Bank, close to Tel Aviv. The Israeli army had forcibly evacuated everyone, apparently believing there would be a repeat of the Palestinian exodus in 1948. Weizman arrived in a town already deserted. 'What we found was one of the saddest images of war imaginable,' he later wrote poignantly. 'Qalqilia was virtually untouched, yet abandoned by thousands of people. All the shops had been broken into, most had been looted. I saw only one old man, carrying the burden of age and despair, wandering glassy-eyed, numbed by the experience we had inflicted ... The refugees of our war have festered like a malignant wound. To ignore their plight was a fatal mistake.'[19]

Years later, Weizman put it like this: 'In the eyes of the world, we were magicians, the all-bestriding colossus which had crushed so many Arab enemies. But the reality was that we had captured hundreds of thousands of Palestinians as well,' he explained. 'In that moment I saw the truth of what every general tells his men: military victory is the seed of the next defeat.'

In 1970, Weizman, fresh out of the armed forces and embarking on a political career, suffered a personal tragedy. His son Shaul, a paratrooper, was seriously wounded by sniper fire during the war of attrition with the Egyptians on the Suez Canal. He had a bullet lodged in his skull. Weizman spent days at his bedside, paralysed by the fear of losing a child. His son lived, but never fully recovered, and Weizman experienced a grief he had not known before. 'I made a vow to myself that the next generation of Israelis, my grandchildren, would never have to suffer what Shaul did ... It took his injury to make me wake up to the consequences of what we'd been doing all our lives.'

During the 1970s, Weizman emerged as the most popular politician of the day. Outspoken and unconventional, he followed Menachem Begin into government as a maverick preaching peace born out of strength. When Anwar Sadat made his dramatic visit to Jerusalem in 1977, Weizman became his closest friend in the Israeli hierarchy. Sadat's flamboyance and ambition was matched by Weizman's flair and boldness. The subsequent negotiations, culminating in the Camp David Agreement, completed Weizman's conversion. 'In Sadat I recognized greatness,' he recalled. 'He was capable of defying history. Why? Because he had a crisis at home and a big enough ego to tell everyone else where to get off ... Sadat made me see the light. We had a crisis as big as his. Did we have the guts he had? For me that was the question.'

In the years that followed, Weizman fought a frustrating battle in government, trying to maintain momentum towards peace despite Begin's policy of settlement on the West Bank. Committed to compromise, he could not abide by plans that pre-empted a negotiated solution. 'Never let me hear that only the Arabs were responsible for the stalemate,' he declared. 'We blew it. We did so much damage with Jewish settlement. Israel may have needed 100 new fighter plans to protect itself. But it didn't need 100 settlements for defence. The whole thing was bullshit.'

In 1980, Weizman resigned in disgust. Tempestuous, arrogant, at times petulant, he proved his own worst enemy. 'Every time Ezer Weizman opens his mouth,' gloated a right-wing colleague in cabinet, 'he shoots himself in the foot.' The result was exile into the political wilderness.

When he returned to government in 1984, as a member of the coalition formed by Shimon Peres, Weizman cut a lonely figure in a government preoccupied with its internal divisions. There were others who recognized Israel's failure to face the tragedy of the Palestinian refugees; who acknowledged the human price Israel paid for a permanent state of conflict. Most of them lamented the inability to convert peace with Egypt into a comprehensive solution, yet it was Weizman, the eternal improviser, who remained the only minister who was prepared to take the gamble that peace entailed: negotiations with the PLO.

'I'm still a hawk, but now I'm belligerent about peace,' he remarked. 'In 1967, I always argued that we should tackle our strongest enemy, Egypt, first. I believe nowadays we should deal with our most important enemy, the PLO ... The minute Yassir Arafat says he recognizes Israel, I say OK, let's talk. What we need is another Six-Day War – on the political front.'

Such statements divorced Weizman from a new generation of Israelis who viewed the PLO as political anathema. Some of his colleagues in cabinet suggested he had taken leave of his senses. He no longer cared about the Jews, they said, but rather about the Arabs. It was a sad epitaph to a career born out of devotion to the state and Zionism. Weizman, mellowing in his later years, displayed in return both uncharacteristic phlegm and typical contempt.

'As a young man I was usually ahead of my contemporaries,' he concluded. 'So I look at it this way. I grew up after 1967. Israel didn't.'[20]

Left-wing Israelis and Palestinian supporters of the PLO tended to agree about politicians such as Muhammad Nasr. He was, they said, a fifth columnist, a quisling among Arabs of the West Bank. Nasr, a quiet, thoughtful figure, responded to such criticism. 'I stand for a generation which genuinely wants peace,' he said. 'But I am punished for doing so.' Like Ezer Weizman, Muhammad Nasr had undergone a conversion in the years after 1967. Just as Weizman changed his stance, so Nasr improvised in the face of Israeli occupation. Weizman represented Israel's second generation of leadership, baptized in the war of 1948, confirmed by the victory of 1967. Nasr symbolized a second generation of Palestinian which split from the traditional leadership in the hope of finding a compromise with the Israelis. It was no coincidence that both suffered the same fate: political limbo. Indeed, they contributed to each other's downfall. Weizman looked upon Palestinians like Nasr as turncoats, incapable of delivering the Palestinians to an agreement. For his part, Nasr learned to view moderates like Weizman as ineffectual. If Weizman felt it necessary to deal with the PLO, then Nasr believed that the Palestinians needed to tackle the Israeli right wing. In the process, two potential allies lost whatever common ground existed between Arab and Jew.

Nasr was born in the village of Dura outside Hebron in 1944, the son of a middle-class Palestinian family which could afford to send him abroad for an education. During the 1967 war, he was studying at the Moslem University in Karachi, Pakistan. In the years afterwards, he followed countless young Palestinians of the day into exile, first in Saudi Arabia and then in Colonel Gaddhafi's revolutionary Libya. In both countries, he worked for the government as an engineer, and spent his free time raising money and support for the nascent PLO. As the dedicated follower of a radical PLO faction led by George Habash, Nasr returned to the West Bank in 1974 to organize the movement from within the occupied territories. But, almost immediately, he found himself questioning the principles he had been taught while abroad.

'I had spent my entire life until then believing what I was told by the Arabs,' he recalled in an interview. 'Israel was the enemy, Israel would destroy us and so on. Yet I had returned from Libya, the most backward of countries, to find the West Bank had improved noticeably under the Israelis,' he explained. 'Palestinians had jobs. They had more freedom than there was in Libya. And the enemy wasn't some mythical figure of hatred. He was the Jew you worked for, the Israeli you saw in the street. The situation was by no means as bad or as gloomy as I had been led to believe.'[21]

Sadat's visit proved to be as seminal to Nasr's thinking as it had been for Ezer Weizman. In the Palestinian's view, peace with Egypt crystallized the options facing the Palestinians. 'There were only two choices: military or political. By taking Egypt out of the equation, the military option became implausible and fanciful. For me, the meaning of Sadat's initiative was clear,' he added. 'We had to take what we could get. There was no point in fighting the enemy of our imagination. We had to deal with the reality ... of Israel and Jewish settlement.'

During the late 1970s and early 1980s, Nasr helped establish the so-called Village Leagues of the West Bank. Funded and supported by Begin's government, they were called the 'vanguard of the peace movement in the West Bank ... committed to the battle against bigotry and terrorism'. Ariel Sharon was a leading patron, presenting figures such as Muhammad Nasr as the new, moderate leadership of the territories. Within months, the leagues, whose original aim was to improve the fortunes of the average Palestinian, had their own budget, armed militia, uniforms, prison cells and interrogation centres as well as a bi-weekly newspaper, *al-Mira* (the *Mirror*). Just as Weizman had been dismayed by the two-faced approach of the Begin government towards peace, so Nasr despaired of Sharon's tactics in manipulating a moderate Palestinian leadership.

'As time went on, I realized that the Israelis were not interested in peace,' said Nasr, who was arrested after breaking away from the leagues and setting up his own movement in 1983. 'What they wanted was a client leadership totally dependent on them. There was no shortage of Palestinians ready to make money and win favours. Any occupation makes quislings. But quislings can't make peace.'

By the mid 1980s, Muhammad Nasr was despised by many of his own people and by the most moderate Israelis. His had become the unacceptable face of Palestinian politics. In the eyes of Jewish liberals, he was tainted by his involvement with Sharon; to the PLO, he was an outlaw because he had compromised with the Israelis. He doubted that the Israelis truly wanted an alternative leadership; he suspected that the government sought only to maintain the status quo of hostility and hatred. 'Why is it that I have so few outlets for my opinion,' he declared, 'when those who support the PLO have newspapers and magazines openly tolerated by the Israelis? Is such a policy consistent with a search for a solution?'

Muhammad Nasr and Ezer Weizman had never met, yet they spoke a common language. They voiced the hope of a middle generation of Jews and Arabs who stood between a dogmatic past and a radical future. Their lives encapsulated a natural progression in the years after 1967. They were nationalists who came to terms with reality, adapting to the changes that took place in their respective societies. They both believed that the Palestinians were ready for compromise; they feared Israel was not. 'I can't change Gaddhafi,' remarked Weizman, 'but I'm not so sure I can change the Jews either.' Nasr put the dilemma another way. 'It's as if peace is a crime,' he said.[22]

In another world, David Ziso and Joanna Rayyes might have been friends, even a well-matched young couple. They were both born in the years leading up to the 1967 war; they grew up in the same city, Jerusalem. Their backgrounds were comparable. David's father was a businessman, firmly established in the Israeli middle class; Joanna's parents were teachers, members of the Palestinian intelligentsia on the West Bank. In the 1980s, such contemporaries encountered each other frequently. Young men like David had completed their army training on the West Bank before going to university. Along with virtually every other Palestinian student, Joanna had occasionally been stopped for interrogation by soldiers her own age.

As a matter of principle, they refused to be interviewed together. Yet, to talk to them separately was to sense the growing indifference of Jewish and Arab youth to each other – the way in which both were becoming more radical through the experience of occupation and the mutual sense of hostility. Few at either of their universities classified themselves as extremists or radical. Only a minority were followers of Rabbi Kahane or the Moslem Brotherhood. David and Joanna spoke for many young people in their respective societies. Their next generation voiced little hope of compromise in the years ahead. Indeed, both were preparing for decades of Israeli occupation on the West Bank.

Like most Palestinians, Joanna, a vivacious young woman in her final year of engineering at Bir Zeit University, admitted almost total ignorance of the Israelis. She had never met Israelis – whom she constantly referred to as Jews – except for soldiers at road-blocks. The impressions formed there were damning. 'I look upon them as mini-gods,' she remarked over a drink at a coffeehouse on campus. 'They can do whatever they want with someone like me. I try to bury it, but I feel a deep sense of inferiority in the presence of a Jew.' As a result, she consciously avoided all contact. 'To me a Jew means danger. You learn to stay out of their way. You try to block them out of your mind, but you can't ... It's fear mixed with loathing when I think about them.'

At 23, David was the same age. A keen student who was reading political science at Hebrew University in Jerusalem, he had moved to Israel and Morocco with his family when he was an infant. Honest and plain-speaking, he did not disguise his feelings towards the Palestinians. 'It's not the older generation of Arabs we have problems with. It's the Palestinians who are my age,' he explained. 'A lot of them look at us with hatred.' He found it difficult to look upon Palestinians as equals. 'However hard you try, you have this sense of superiority on the West Bank. It's part of your training. No one actually tells you to look down on Arabs. But you do.'

Joanna's family had little political experience; she called her parents 'political agnostics'. She had joined the majority at Bir Zeit in favour of the PLO. Much as she was disillusioned by the PLO's failure to achieve any tangible results, she saw no other option. She represented the new educated class of Palestinians who supported the politics of armed struggle out of duty as much as conviction. 'You don't really have a choice at a place like this,' she submitted. 'Without a flag, a movement or a cause, you would be at the mercy of the Jews. So you support the PLO.' She hesitated, pondering before she finished her thought. 'I wouldn't do anything violent myself,' she explained. 'But I don't condemn those who have the courage to attack the Jews. They don't seem to worry about attacking us.'

One of David's classmates, a Russian immigrant named Uri Purham, was imprisoned for seven months after refusing military service on the West Bank. 'For me it was the only way to keep my conscience clean,' Uri declared, provoking derision from David. 'I didn't leave the oppression of the Soviet Union to come here and suppress the Palestinians.' Such dissent was unusual among Israeli students, most of whom supported the mainstream parties. David was a member of the right-wing Likud and a follower of Ariel Sharon. Far from being isolated among educated youth, the right wing usually claimed the votes of 30 per cent of Israeli students. In many cases, military service in the occupied territories had created a constituency among the country's best and brightest. 'For me it's a simple equation,' said David. 'Likud advocates what I learned on the West Bank: the only way to handle the Arabs is to settle the land and deal firmly with anyone who causes trouble. Appeasement will lead only to chaos.' He curtly dismissed Uri's objections. 'The Palestinians have a choice,' he added, echoing a statement voiced by Ariel Sharon. 'Either to leave – or stay and live by the rules.'

As for the future, David foresaw 30 years of part-time military service with few qualms. The founders of Israel, he argued, had fought in 1948. His parents' generation had experienced the wars of 1967 and 1973. 'My generation has a very different conflict on the West Bank,' he concluded. 'But the issue is the same, namely survival.'

At Bir Zeit, Joanna Rayyes ruled out the possibility of seeking work abroad, as some of her colleagues had done. Her grandparents, she contended, had stayed on after 1948; her own parents had refused to leave after 1967. 'I'm like most people I know. I feel I have to make a contribution. My contribution will be to stay and have a family. Whatever happens, there must be another generation of Palestinians,' she concluded. 'It is for them that I have some hope.'[23]

CONCLUSION

*'It is the sad destiny of a prophet when, after working
20 years, he is no longer convinced himself.'*
– FRIEDRICH NIETZSCHE – HUMAN ALL-TOO-HUMAN, 1878

The way in which Israelis and Palestinians learned to grow apart
after 1967 was testament to man's insensitivity and prejudice. Of
all the peoples in the Middle East, they shared a common heritage.
Both had experienced the suffering of oppression. Both had known
the despair of exile. Both believed that they would cease to exist
without a physical homeland. What the Jewish people sought –
the security of an independent state – the Palestinians needed as
well. To recognize the aspirations of one represented an injustice
to the other. To ignore the right of the Palestinians to a home
undermined the long-term prospects for the survival of the Jews.
Theirs was a mutual tragedy, born out of the pursuit of common
territory which they claimed was granted by God. Their conflict
was an extraordinary combination of religion, race, territory and
nationalism. The world had never experienced anything quite like
it – and one way or another the world paid a price for the
deadlock in the rich yet desperate land of the West Bank.
  The destructive influence of the conflict for the land defied all
logic. A tiny enclave of 2,100 square miles – the size of the

215

American state of Delaware or the British county of Norfolk – had extracted a staggering human and financial toll. Neither did the West Bank represent an isolated struggle between Arabs and Jews. In so many unseen ways, the world also suffered for what had happened in Nablus, Hebron, Ramallah and Bethlehem. The price could not be measured only in the casualties of war, terrorism and counter-terrorism. The conflict also sparked the economic havoc created by the oil crisis of the 1970s and the rise of religious fundamentalism which threatened the survival of countless regimes in the Moslem world. Its impact was felt most starkly in a country such as Lebanon.

Seen from one perspective, Lebanon's civil war and anarchy could be viewed as a symptom of the Palestinian issue. For generations, the age-old conflict between that country's Christians and Moslems had created a political vacuum and instability. In the 1970s, the Palestinians, led by the PLO, exploited the void for their own ends and made Lebanon the front line in the Arab–Israeli dispute. In the 1980s, the confrontation between Syria and Israel centred on Lebanon, adding yet another dimension to the crisis: that of the superpowers. The Soviet Union supported Syria; the United States backed Israel. Each side had vastly different objectives and neither considered the aspirations of the Lebanese. The result was the dismemberment of Lebanon and the emergence of warring factions which made hostages out of both American civilians and the US administration.

Yet, whatever the dire consequences elsewhere, the root issue of the West Bank became more complex, the dispute more bitter, the two sides more irreconcilable as the conflict dragged on. Over the years, the world tried time and again to resolve the matter, but the land turned into a quagmire for peace missions that carried the names of world leaders, cities, countries and continents. There was the Yugoslav Plan (1967), the Johnson Plan (1972), the Venice Declaration (1980), the Fahd Plan (1981), the Brezhnev Doctrine (1981), the Franco-Egyptian Plan (1982) and the Reagan Initiative (1982). None of them even got started because no one could bridge the psychological gap of suspicion and animosity between Jew and Arab – and no mediator could reconcile the conflicting claims of Israeli and Palestinian to the same piece of land.

The danger of such protracted conflict was both domestic and international. In the local arena of the West Bank, a city such as

Hebron had been transformed into a potential battleground between Arab and Jew. There, as elsewhere, the Israelis had won the dispute over the land, yet their occupation had sharpened the conflict into a battle between two peoples and two nationalist movements. The years since 1967 had made the PLO the undisputed voice of the Palestinians. With a parliament, a diplomatic presence in many foreign capitals, its welfare institutions dotted throughout the territory and all the other trappings of nationhood, the PLO became a surrogate state for a people who knew that they faced a long uphill fight for the real thing. As the peace process of the early 1980s showed, the PLO retained a veto over any moves towards a negotiated settlement. After the military defeat in Lebanon, it was still capable of confronting the occupation of the West Bank and Gaza. The future bore the threat of the Palestinians mounting open resistance and uprisings against an Israeli population which boasted the weaponry to impose the rule of conquest – but not a sufficient number of settlers to make occupation an irreversible fact.

In the hiatus created by stalemate, the new generation of Arab and Jew turned increasingly to extremism. Young Israelis and Palestinians divorced themselves from the history of the conflict to seek ultimate solutions. The generation that grew up after 1967 experienced at first hand the consequences of that war. They became accustomed to Jewish exploitation of the Arab population, the double standards that applied to almost every aspect of life. Their parents saw the possibility of co-existence; the children spoke a different vocabulary, voiced different goals, espoused the politics of confrontation as the only way out. In 1967, it would have been unthinkable for a racist like Rabbi Kahane to mobilize support for the mass deportation and expulsion of Arabs. Likewise, the radical wing of the PLO and the Moslem Brotherhood could not have recruited Palestinian youth to their cause as they did in the late 1980s. The rise of fundamentalists on both sides signalled a future conflict which could be religious rather than secular, a holy war rather than a territorial dispute.

The lesson of such interminable struggle was that it had unleashed forces that could no longer be controlled by the mainstream of both societies. The past and present pointed to a future in which conventional leaders would be able neither to seek a solution – nor to deliver their people to any settlement. Just as the years since 1967 had created profound changes on the West Bank, so time passing had worked against any future compromise. Almost inevitably, given the modern history of the region, the stakes became higher, the potential for misunderstanding and further violence greater.

In the world at large, the deadlock over the West Bank made the Middle East the prime arena for rivalry between the superpowers. Until 1967, the Arab–Israeli dispute had been largely a regional conflict. In the years after, it became a focal point for the Soviet Union and the United States. In the nuclear age, Washington and Moscow found it convenient and safer to avoid direct confrontation. They challenged each other in the Third World, using indirect encounters to test the other's political will and military hardware. In Africa, they sparred over Ethiopia and Angola; in Asia the battleground had been Vietnam and Cambodia; in Central America it was Nicaragua and El Salvador. To some extent, however, the Kremlin and the White House could still control both the scale and the nature of those conflicts. Circumstances in the Middle East were different.

Syria and Israel were both fiercely independent. Neither paid much attention to the interests of their respective superpower when these did not coincide with their own plans. Both were eminently capable of using their most sophisticated weaponry without reference to their allies. Israel had nuclear arms; Syria acquired the Soviet Union's longest-range missiles. For the first time in the history of the Middle East conflict, an Arab power was capable of destroying Israel's air bases in the Negev desert, also the site of the country's nuclear reactor. Such an escalation of the arms race signalled a quantum leap in the struggle for control of the region. As long as this stalemate persisted, the threat remained of hostilities between Moscow and Washington rather than merely between their proxies.

The mutual interest in avoiding a future war might therefore seem to demand the pursuit of a solution on the West Bank as a prerequisite for world peace. But this is not what has happened. Even as the decades after 1967 made the problem ever more intractable, so did the passing years diminish both the prospects of effective mediation and the willingness of the major powers to gamble on peace. Having been humiliated in the war of 1967, the Soviet Union made its priority rehabilitation within the Arab world

218

rather than an overall settlement. For its part, the United States sought largely to expand its influence with both sides in the region. In doing so, Washington reinforced the status quo and became yet another of its victims. The lesson was clear. The Arab–Israeli conflict threatened all those who ignored it or became involved with it. The actions of the United States showed how the super-powers jeopardized the chances of peace by taking sides in the Middle East.

For most of his presidency, it seemed that Ronald Reagan, the most popular US leader in a lifetime, had defied the historical tide of corruption, double standards and disaster that had ruined his immediate predecessors. Whatever his limitations, his inattention to detail, Mr Reagan had retained the support and affection of most Americans with his advocacy of strength backed by righteous-ness. His vision, so often expressed with eloquence and conviction, depicted America as divinely placed, a shining city on the hill beaming out goodness to mankind. Such a belief echoed the claims made by many in modern-day Israel, who portrayed the Jewish state as 'a light unto other nations'. It was no mere coincidence that President Reagan's fall from grace should have revolved around the special relationship between Washington and Jerusalem. The scandal over arms for US hostages and secret dealings with Iran was the culmination of a Middle East policy which made the United States and Israel inseparable partners, notionally com-mitted to a war against international terrorism and so-called Soviet meddling.

American willingness to follow Israel's lead on policy in the region dated back to the 1967 war and President Johnson's quiescent acceptance of Jerusalem's tactics during the Six-Day War. The débâcle over Iran revealed, arguably as never before, the pitfalls of the special relationship between Washington and the Jewish state. By many accounts, Israel initiated the idea of arms for hostages and Israel was primarily responsible for its execution. The Iranian affair confirmed to some extent what America's Arab friends had been saying for years: that the United States was no longer a superpower in the Middle East but rather an ally of Israel, so supportive of Jerusalem that its claim to be impartial peace-maker was seriously undermined. The damage done to US standing in the region was one factor, but only a short-term consideration. The long-term implications lay in an American foreign policy that cast most Arabs as enemies and Israel as a reliable ally. This psychological landscape, fostered during the Reagan years, was likely to inhibit the chances for peace long after his administration had departed. 'It's not that Reagan was responsible for the crisis, or that he was to blame more than other Presidents,' remarked a senior Arab ambassador in Washington. 'It's that Reagan made a solution so much more difficult.'

At times, American policy in the 1980s seemed to be born out of benign neglect, a direct consequence of leadership which sought simple answers to complex issues. The fact of the matter was that the Reagan administration squandered its inheritance in the Middle East, and the reasons for this would dictate the prospects for a settlement in the years ahead. In 1981, Mr Reagan had come to power at a time of hiatus in the region. The Camp David Agreement, the only peace the region had ever known, was just three years old; Lebanon enjoyed a rare ceasefire in its apparently endless civil war. By the spring of 1982, moderate Arab states were haunted by the fear of an Iranian victory over Iraq, and their need for American weapons made them susceptible to US pressure on the Palestinian issue. On the West Bank, Menachem Begin and Ariel Sharon had not yet created irreversible facts of Jewish settlement and, in theory at least, Jerusalem was committed through Camp David to a measure of home rule for the Palestinians in the territories. In short, Jimmy Carter's administration had bequeathed a script of sorts for future negotiations between Arabs and Jews. Neither side expected miracles, but both believed that the dialogue had to be pursued.

The Reagan years symbolized regression on almost every count. After the President shelved his 1982 peace plan – primarily because of Israel's immediate rejection – confrontation rather than compromise became the abiding principle of his administration. The peace process enshrined in Camp David came to a virtual halt. By the late 1980s, Egypt was in grave danger of upheaval, with a dire, economic crisis prompting insurrection and the rise of an increasingly powerful Moslem Brotherhood. Lebanon, once proclaimed so vital to American interests throughout the region, was transformed during the US military presence into a state of abject chaos and unprecedented anti-Western fundamentalism. On the West Bank, the Israelis dismissed Reagan's 1982 demand for a freeze of Jewish settlement, creating precisely the facts that successive administrations had feared. The causes of this were not difficult to analyse.

In common with many of his predecessors, Reagan's philosophy on the Middle East was governed by three fundamental interests: preservation of the state of Israel, maintaining the flow of Gulf oil and preventing Soviet expansionism. Grafted on to those interests was the growing concern, at times to the point of obsession, with developments in terrorism. Under Mr Reagan, America came to regard terrorists almost exclusively as those who killed Westerners or took a hostile attitude to the West. Understandably, public opinion accepted the definition when Americans were killed on board cruise liners in the Mediterranean, gunned down in cold blood at airports in Rome and Vienna, murdered in West Berlin nightclubs. It was both comprehensible and consistent for a clear majority of Americans to support the bombing of Libya, a country led by a man described by the White House as 'the mad dog of the Middle East'.

Yet calling an enemy a 'mad dog' was the sort of thing Arab and Israeli leaders had done for decades. The President therefore now joined their ranks, making Washington sound and act like a regional power in the Middle East. Worse still, in regarding Israel as a fellow victim of attacks and an ally in the war against terrorism Mr Reagan destroyed America's claim to be the impartial umpire in the conflict between Arabs and Jews. Terrorism was never exclusive to one side or the other in the Middle East, and America's failure to acknowledge the fact became a cause of widespread distrust, particularly among its Arab allies. Above all, the crusade against Colonel Gaddhafi blurred the issue that made America a target in the first place: support for Israel. The bombing of Libya became a short-term palliative for a long-term problem which was then largely ignored. Extremists on both sides profited from America's obsession with a secondary issue.

Compounding its own crisis of credibility was the Reagan administration's unprecedented financial backing for Israel. As a second-term President, the first likely to complete eight years in office since Dwight Eisenhower in the 1950s, Mr Reagan enjoyed relative freedom from the constraints imposed by the electoral process and the powerful Jewish lobby in Washington. Since 1967, a political maxim on the Middle East had been that only a strong, second-term US leader would be able to pressure the Israelis into making territorial concessions for peace. Yet, under the Reagan administration, America's principal card in any such negotiations – US military aid and economic aid to Israel – increased by 40 per cent, with few strings attached. Before 1967, Israel had received $200 million a year from Washington, and none of it in military hardware. By 1987, the United States was giving Jerusalem $3,000 million annually, almost $1,000 for every Israeli man, woman and child. More than 60 per cent of this aid was designated for military purchases. While his predecessors had established the commitment, President Reagan was responsible for turning it into an unquestioning, uncritical acceptance of Israeli policy.

Such indulgence steadily eroded the US claim to be an honest broker in the Israeli–Palestinian conflict. It created a strategic-military alliance which made even-handed, impartial mediation on the Palestinian issue impossible. Even some Israelis were dismayed at the President's unwillingness to grapple with the problem that underpinned all else: the West Bank and Gaza.

'I predict that, in the long run, the Reagan days will be remembered as bad days for Israel, days of misunderstanding and disregard for our problems,' declared Yossi Sarid, a left-wing member of the Israeli parliament. 'True, the Reagan administration has been generous to Israel, generous to a fault. But its corrupting handouts recall the gifts that wealthy but light-headed parents lavish on their children – parents who have never bothered to find time for their children and never devoted any attention to their real problems.'

Inevitably, American foreign policy was paralysed by the scandal over arms for US hostages. Bereft of a clear mandate at home, the administration was loath to take risks abroad. The main goal for the Reagan White House, as it entered its last years, was to regain credibility in the region rather than seek new options for solving its crisis. 'There is no longer the political will to tackle an issue like the Middle East,' remarked a longstanding adviser on the region at the State Department after the Iran arms scandal. 'We have switched from being active to being passive ... We seem to believe, like Hippocrates, that doing nothing is sometimes a good remedy.' In the 20th year of Israel's occupation of the West Bank and Gaza, those Arabs and Israelis who sought peace were bound to be the ultimate losers in a climate of such disillusionment that it bordered on disinterest. As one Jordanian commentator noted: 'God help all of you who look to America for salvation.'

Moderates within Israel and the Arab world feared that the 'lost years' of the Reagan presidency would drive the Middle East headlong into another war. They pointed to profound changes taking place in the region, especially in those countries which had long relied on America for support: Jordan, Egypt and the Gulf states. In each country, religious fundamentalism was becoming a potent factor in policy formation. In Jordan and Egypt, the deepening economic crisis only exacerbated the frustration engendered by the state of perpetual deadlock. For such nations, America's obvious duplicity over Israel became a source of embarrassment and suspicion. Almost every Arab leader had to weigh the benefits of co-operation with the United States against the popular discontent it created at home.

Elsewhere, notably in Syria, Arab moderates predicted conflict with Israel as a way of deflecting public attention from the domestic unrest created by years of high inflation, unemployment and food shortages. The arms race between Israel and Syria escalated steadily after their confrontation over Lebanon in 1982; according to the Israelis, the Syrians produced and stockpiled chemical weapons, including deadly nerve gas, which were capable of being delivered by those long-range Soviet missiles. The prognosis of another round of war was shared by many in Washington. 'I have an existentialist dread of another holocaust in the Middle East,' said Roscoe Suddarth, a high-ranking official at the State Department. 'Every time the peace process goes on the back burner, the chances increase.' It all pointed not to a peaceful Middle East in which a powerful America supported a fair settlement, but to a region of mounting and ever more callous violence.

Yet the Reagan presidency had taught Arabs and Israelis one clear lesson. If the most powerful President of his generation had been reluctant to pursue a Middle East solution, then it was unlikely that any successor would gamble on peace in the immediate future. For the first time sine 1967, the parties to the Middle East conflict could no longer turn to Washington as the main powerbroker. The Arabs could not expect that any administration would eventually apply diplomatic and economic pressure on Israel. The Israelis had every reason to believe that they would

223

occupy the West Bank and Gaza for another 20 years or more. The Reagan presidency had shattered the illusion that America necessarily held the key to peace between Arabs and Israelis. Just as the United States had to face the reality of the status quo, so too did Israel and the Palestinians.

'I think if we gave back the territories, we could ultimately find ourselves at the mercy of our enemies, rather like Auschwitz,' said an Israeli journalist. 'But to keep them means apartheid. So we stand somewhere between Auschwitz or apartheid.'

In virtually every corner of Israel, you could hear a debate along these lines. In homes and offices, on street corners and at bus-stops, in the editorial pages and on national television, there would be the same discussion of the issue known quite simply as 'peace'. Every Israeli has an opinion: what to do about it, how much, if anything, to give for it. Yet few of these opinions were in agreement. Peace was the Achilles' heel of Israel. If the Arabs wanted to start a war among the Jews, remarked one of Israel's best-known political pundits, they had only to declare peace on Israel.

Ever since 1967, the parties to the conflict had perpetuated the myth that peace depended on Israel's willingness to return the occupied territories. Israel held the main card – the land. Therefore Israel alone could make the concessions that any solution entailed. But years of occupation had wrought profound changes in Israel's attitude towards the issue that so dominated national life. The days of waiting for the Arabs to seek negotiations had long since passed. Young Israelis had grown up fully aware of what Judaea and Samaria meant to Jews, yet ignorant of what the West Bank symbolized to Arabs. Their parents could well be contemplating a new home in the territories in preference to Tel Aviv or Jerusalem. Having lived longer with the land than without, many viewed the status quo as the most natural option for decades to come. For every Israeli who longed for release from the endless cycle of conflict, there was another who believed there could only be a military solution. In terms of lives and financial investment, the cost of occupation was bearable. Indeed, it was much lower than many had feared. To some extent, the status quo worked, and for the majority the alternative – a Palestinian state on Israel's border – was a far more dangerous prospect. One sure sign of the times was a Hebrew version of 'Monopoly' in which players could buy property in Hebron and Bethlehem as well as Haifa or Netanya. Mentally, as well as physically, Israel was digging in on the West Bank – for eternity.

Yet, much as semi-permanent occupation had created a new psychological map, the years that separated Israel from 1967 had been equally notable for those changes which had not taken place. Accordingly, the future would be affected by what had not happened as much as by the facts of Jewish settlement and Israeli occupation. Typically, few Israelis claimed that Arab and Jew enjoyed genuine co-existence or that they would learn to live together in the years ahead. Israel could hope to enjoy little respite from Palestinian guerrilla action either at home or abroad. Instead, the future threatened a more indiscriminate violence than the country had endured since 1967. Countless attempts to pass legislation formally annexing the territories had failed. There was little to suggest there could ever be a majority for such a move. So, Israelis could not agree to give up the land, neither could they unite on a policy to incorporate it into the Jewish state. But the status quo, which successive governments had sought as an end in itself, contained the seeds of future disaster.

In the late 1960s, Golda Meir confessed to having nightmares about the number of Arab children being born in the land of Israel. She did not live to see her worst dreams confirmed, but the facts guaranteed that future generations of Israelis would do so. By the late 1980s, more than two million Arabs lived under Israeli rule as opposed to 3.2 million Jews. Arabs under the age of 12 already formed a majority within their age bracket. The demographic clock suggested that there would, by the year 2008, be more Arabs than Israelis living in the area controlled by the Jewish state. By the year 2020, the Palestinians would boast a greater number of adults – perhaps very many more. To annex the territories and grant Palestinians equal rights would be to ensure a working Arab majority in the 21st century. To negotiate land for peace might open the way for a PLO-controlled state on the West Bank. And simply to leave the situation would inevitably create a country of two nations: a bi-national state divided between the two peoples. The Arab birthrate, significantly higher than the Israeli one, presented the Jewish state with a dilemma it ignored at its peril.

'We have two choices – bad and worse,' explained Yehoshafat

Harkabi, once a hawkish chief of Israeli military intelligence whose views underwent a dramatic change after 1967. 'Bad is leaving the West Bank. Worse is staying.' For Harkabi, the author of a devastating indictment of Israeli policy in the territories, the decision was purely selfish. 'Peace is in my interest. It's not something I seek as a favour to the Arabs, I merely seek the best deal for Israel. I look at the birthrate and I know I can't wait for the Messiah to come or for millions of Jews to move to the West Bank. The decision is here and we have to take it ... The alternative is national suicide.'

Fears of an Arab majority dictated that peace would remain the key issue in Israeli life for years to come. But it was naïve to expect any clear-cut decision on an issue that so divided the country. Opinion polls in the 1980s, conducted by the widely respected Institute of Hanoch Smith, consistently showed a narrow majority opposing the return of territory to the Arabs, but with up to 40 per cent in favour. Likewise, more than 50 per cent said they would refuse to negotiate with the PLO even if Yassir Arafat met the longstanding preconditions – recognition of Israel and a renunciation of terrorism against Israel. Significantly, however, more Israelis opposed any expansion of Jewish settlements on the West Bank and Gaza than those who supported it.

'My own reading of Israel is that our people hover between two impulses,' said President Chaim Herzog in an interview. 'More than any people in the world, we yearn for peace. So we keep our options open. But Israelis are frightened of having the PLO next door. So they hedge, they play safe.' He added: 'Unfortunately that isn't a solution.'

Leaders such as President Herzog were apt to cite the negotiations with Egypt and the return of the Sinai as evidence of the dramatic change that Israel could still undergo – if the Arab world made a genuine offer of compromise. Yet peace with Egypt had become a source of disillusionment for many. Egypt's conscious attempts to distance itself from Israel, particularly after the Lebanon war, created distrust and suspicion. 'We never knew our enemies before Sadat came to Jerusalem,' remarked former President Yitzhak Navon, 'but now we do. Before Sadat's visit, we had great illusions. Now we don't. Many Israelis feel we gave back land and got little in return.' He concluded, 'I don't agree but it's a sorry state of affairs when we have to defend the only peace we have.'

In such a climate of indecision, fear and growing indifference, Israel's own demographics became a key factor in determining future prospects. The nation might have been evenly divided over peace in the late 1980s, but every indicator suggested that those opposed to territorial concessions would muster a majority in years to come. Menachem Begin's constituency of Oriental Jews formed more than 50 per cent of the nation by the mid 1980s. Under Begin's leadership, they had been taught to consider land for peace as betrayal. Begin's successors, Shamir and Sharon, proposed a simple solution: peace for peace, the status quo in return for co-existence. Such leadership poured scorn on the prospects of negotiating with Yassir Arafat. 'What am I going to negotiate with Arafat?' shouted a right-wing parliamentarian, Geula Cohen, during an interview outside a Jewish settlement in Hebron. 'Not only is the man a murderer but he wants every bit of my home … Arafat is the negative to my positive. You don't negotiate with your negative.' Pointing to the Jewish enclave behind her, she insisted, 'The Zionist revolution goes on and we still have a long way to go. Why must we have peace?'

Alone, the right wing could probably never succeed with its plans for permanent occupation, leading to annexation and the expulsion of Arabs from the territories. What gave the right wing the edge was the emergence of a religious political movement after 1967. Victory in the June war and the capture of the holy sites of the West Bank and Jerusalem ignited the Messianic strain of Zionism. The religious movement, represented by a host of small parties, supplied many settlers for the cause of the West Bank. A new generation of Orthodox Israelis took the lead in establishing the new Biblical frontier for the Jewish nation; they settled the West Bank even as their parents and grandparents had been pioneers on the coastal plain of Palestine. By the late 1980s, they represented a crucial minority, more than 10 per cent of the nation. Almost any future government, of whatever political hue, was likely to require their support.

With nearly 150,000 Israelis living on the land captured in 1967 – almost 60,000 on the West Bank and Gaza, the rest in dormitory suburbs around Jerusalem – the settlers boasted electoral muscle in a country accustomed to hung parliaments and coalition govern-ments. Their political clout ruled out a repetition of the exchange – land for peace – which had been the basis of the Camp David

227

Agreement. Their ideology, combining Judaism with contemporary Realpolitik, presented a challenge no government would ever be able to ignore. 'Would the British ever negotiate Westminster?' the settlers asked. 'Would the Americans ever give up the Statue of Liberty?' It was a measure of how far the settlers had come since 1967 that a majority of Israelis saw Hebron and Nablus in such terms.

In the face of such opposition, the chances of any government relinquishing the West Bank receded with the years. Yet the moral, ethical and philosophical price which Israel paid for the status quo all the time increased. Jewish democracy was steadily weakened by the racism, discrimination and injustice endemic to military occupation. 'As much as anything else, I am concerned about the changes taking place in our society,' explained the Labour leader Shimon Peres. 'The Jews have never been a conquering people. Now it is difficult to imagine Israel any other way ... The occupation eats away at our principles and values. It is self-destructive.'

One incident in the 1980s reflected the damage Israel suffered as long as it remained the occupier. While Washington was obsessed with the 'arms-for-hostages' deal, the government in Jerusalem closed one of the most troubling chapters in the country's brief history. It had begun with the killing of two young Palestinians who hijacked a bus in Israel in 1984. Captured alive as the hijacking ended, the Palestinians were clubbed to death after being interrogated by agents of the Israeli security service, the Shin Beth. Such summary executions, in the aftermath of violent incidents, had taken place before, but had never been revealed publicly. The scandal showed how Israel was prepared to bend the rules of a democratic state.

When the attorney-general tried to investigate the matter, he was forced to resign by his opponents in government. Before the final commission of inquiry began, the men held responsible for the murders were given presidential pardons. The final investigation ended with the then Prime Minister, Yitzhak Shamir, being cleared of complicity to murder. Yet the verdict was hardly a cause for celebration. Some compared it to the Iran affair in the United States. Shamir, like Mr Reagan, might not have given any specific instructions. But how was he running the country? What were the principles and values which guided modern Israel? 'This whole affair stinks from top to bottom,' said the army general who conducted the initial inquiry. 'It is just not done in a proper country.'

Without a written constitution or a bill of rights, Israel had few checks and balances to counter such lawlessness. Unlike the United States, the mavericks did not operate out of the basement. They were in cabinet, the Prime Minster's office, the Defence Ministry; they had been flouting conventional rules for years. Such leadership explained the lack of public outcry over the murders of the two Palestinians, the arms shipments to Iran, the disclosures that Israel possessed hundreds of nuclear bombs. But such thinking did not justify the action taken, nor did it heed the consequences: the disintegration of the rule of law, the erosion of democracy, the deepening public cynicism.

In 1967, few Israelis foresaw the cost of victory. One who did was Yeshayahu Liebowitz, among the most respected philosophers of his day. Shortly after the June war, he wrote a newspaper article arguing that the 'liberation' of the West Bank and Gaza would be remembered as the starting-point for 'the decline and fall of the State of Israel'.

Two decades later, he insisted that his prediction was more valid than ever. 'Israel must find a way to liberate itself from the curse of brutally dominating another people,' he said in 1986. 'It is a matter of life and death. The moment the glory and the greatness of the nation becomes the highest value, man becomes a beast.' He added, 'If we do not get rid of these territories, the process will continue and Israel will become a fascist state.'

After two decades, Israel still held the territorial cards for a peaceful resolution of the conflict – but no government had the strength to play them any more. In the circumstances, the next 20 years would be determined as much by the Arabs as the Jews. If Israelis were either unwilling or unable to make peace, then arguably only the Palestinians could salvage the future. Or so it seemed.

In the despair that accompanied military defeat in 1982, one of Yassir Arafat's senior aides came up with a novel idea. During the siege of Beirut, he suggested that Arafat lead his fighters en masse to the Israeli front lines and surrender. His argument was that

Israel would be faced with the acute embarrassment of what to do with thousands of Palestinians who sought an end to the conflict. He maintained that the international community would have no option but to pressure Israel to negotiate with the PLO. He believed that opposition within Israel to the war would erupt, forcing the government to seek reconciliation with its enemy. Characteristically, Arafat slept on the proposal. In the days afterwards, he made no mention of it and the idea was dropped. Once again, Yassir Arafat had apparently avoided the question which he and the Palestinian people had faced ever since 1967: whether or not to recognize the enemy, challenge them on that issue of peace and so make the first decisive move towards settling the conflict between Arabs and Jews.

Arafat's political life had foundered on that issue of recognition of Israel; his fortunes and those of his people had been bedevilled by it. The question never changed, only the circumstances. Arafat's penchant for casuistry and semantic nit-picking enabled him to duck the matter whenever it was raised. But the longer the stalemate persisted, the greater the risk became of one man and his cause being destroyed by enemies such as the Syrians and the Israelis. Eventually the question had to be answered. If not, time would surely do it for him.

'I sometimes imagine that one day he will recognize Israel,' said a left-wing Israeli politician, Mordechai Bar-On, one of the few who had defied domestic public opinion and met Arafat. 'And I hear Israel saying, "So what?" Arafat wants peace, I'm sure of it, but he has to show us sooner rather than later.'

Of all the main actors on the Arab–Israeli stage, Yassir Arafat remained the most inscrutable, the most perplexing, the most frustrating. And, perhaps, the most powerful. 'As difficult as it is to include the PLO in any settlement,' noted Dr Aaron Miller, a policy planner at the US State Department, 'it is equally difficult to shut the PLO out.' The British Prime Minister, Margaret Thatcher, was more categoric. 'I continue to believe,' she said in a 1986 interview, 'that the PLO have to be associated with a settlement because of the wide level of support they enjoy in the occupied territories.'

Arafat's greatest achievement lay in the establishment of the PLO as the sole, legitimate representative of the Palestinian people. No organization had ever done as much for the Palestinian cause as his PLO. His people had gained the sympathy and recognition of much of the world at large: as many states maintained diplomatic relations with the organization as with Israel. The PLO had become the only non-governmental body to gain observer status at the United Nations, securing a platform from which it initiated anti-Israel resolutions in the General Assembly. More than anything else, the idea that a peaceful settlement of the Arab–Israeli dispute required a solution of the Palestinian problem had become an inescapable tenet of the world's thinking.

Yet the PLO had been unable to translate the support and sympathy it enjoyed into concrete results. Not one inch of Palestine had been 'liberated' in the years since 1967. Indeed, the aftermath of the war had seen increasing Israeli expansion in the land which Palestinians coveted. The longer Arafat went without tangible success, the greater the threat from radicals within his movement. The more the Israelis dug in on the West Bank, the less control Arafat wielded among Palestinians living under Israeli rule. The PLO's failure, to quote one of its leaders, had always been its tendency to split into 12 different factions, firing 12 different guns in 12 different directions. The danger was that Arafat would never be able to reunify the Palestinians and so form a common front for peace with Israel. Much as many Israeli leaders had sought the destruction of the PLO as an end in itself, it did not serve Israel's long-term interests. Without a leader of Arafat's stature, there was unlikely to be a comprehensive peace: only a repetition of Camp David, a partial settlement that bequeathed further conflict to the next generation. Those who predicted that Arafat's removal or death would provide the impetus for peace overlooked the fact that far more radical leaders waited in the wings to inherit leadership of the cause which Arafat had inspired. As Hanna Siniora, one of the PLO's leading spokesmen on the West Bank, remarked: 'The danger is that the Palestinian movement will split into even more factions in years to come. Then there will be no one for the Israelis to talk to.'

Arafat's influence was born not merely out of his popularity among the people of the West Bank and Gaza. However much the Israelis might accuse him of terrorism, his influence was not derived solely from the gun. Nor, given his fluctuating appeal in the Arab world, was it his ability to extract financial support from the oil-rich kingdoms and sheikhdoms of the Gulf. Arafat was a rarity in the Arab world: a self-made politician rather than the heir to a family dynasty or a general installed by the army. His strength lay in the independent leadership he had provided ever since the foundation of the PLO. His political authority rested on the fact that he alone could deliver the highest percentage of the Palestinians to any future agreement, and that, paradoxically, he alone could strike a deal which Jerusalem might accept and that the Arab world would sanction.

Aides to successive Israeli Prime Ministers recalled how King Hussein would constantly remind them, during secret meetings in the 1970s and 1980s, that Jordan could not even begin to contemplate peace with Israel unless the return of all the territory was guaranteed. The King had a common refrain: 'I am a partner for only 100 per cent. If you're going to talk about anything less than that you will have to talk to Arafat.'

In other words, the King had to be seen to get back everything, including Jerusalem (which was out of the question), since he would otherwise be accused of treachery. Arafat could take less because he could justify such compromise to the rest of the Arab world in the name of the Palestinians. As such, Israel's arch-enemy represented the most realistic hope of a solution which Jerusalem could sanction and that the Arabs would accept. To paraphrase Uri Avneri, another Israeli who had met the PLO leader down the years: Yassir Arafat was the only man in the world who could make Israel truly a part of the Middle East and put a stop to the conflict.

It was a power which presupposed that Arafat enjoyed the freedom to declare peace on Israel – and that he had refused to do so in the years since the 1967 war. The truth, as usual in the Middle East, was a good deal more complex.

Part of the legacy of those six days in June was that the Arabs and the Israelis effectively exchanged traditional roles. In August 1967, at a summit meeting in Khartoum, the Arabs issued an outright rejection of compromise with Israel. The communiqué delivered at the end was symbolized by a series of 'no's'. No peace with Israel, it read, no negotiations with Israel, no recognition of Israel. By the 1980s, the Israelis had adopted the same stance regarding the Palestinians. Politicians such as Yitzhak Shamir and Ariel Sharon would, in effect, parody the Khartoum declaration. No negotiations with the PLO, they said, no Palestinian state, no self-determination for the Palestinians. The result was a dispute in which first one side, then the other, had laid down preconditions that pre-empted any meaningful discussion.

In the circumstances, Yassir Arafat had little to gain and almost everything to lose by meeting the demands which the international community made for his inclusion at future negotiations, namely, acceptance of Israel and renunciation of violence. The rewards were far from guaranteed, the risk far too great. By accepting Israel, the PLO sacrificed its only trump card without any promise of a breakthrough. Time and again mediators pressed the PLO leader to make the fateful decision. Invariably, he managed to say both yes and no at the same time: yes to the general concept of peace and territorial compromise, no to the specific diplomatic concession that might have enabled talks to begin. Always, it appeared, Arafat presented an insurmountable obstacle while leaving the way open for peace.

Such prevarication obscured the fact that the PLO had shifted significantly from its original demands – for the return of all Palestine – in the years since 1967. From the mid 1970s onwards, Arafat accepted the principle that a homeland on the West Bank and Gaza was the only realistic prospect. In doing so, the PLO effectively acknowledged that 20 per cent of Palestine would have to suffice. He argued that he had already made the most substantial concession that could ever have been expected of him. He maintained that Israel was responsible for the stalemate by refusing to negotiate on those terms. He was apt to insist, as most Arab leaders did, that time was on the side of the Palestinians. 'Israel will crumble from within,' he said in a 1984 interview. 'We have waited this long. We can wait for as long as it takes.'

The reality suggested otherwise. The battle for the land had been lost. Israel had built enough settlements to guarantee both security and a permanent home for the Jewish people. The Palestinians were obliged to accept Israeli rule. If time was running out for anyone, then surely it was Yassir Arafat.

By the late 1980s, the Palestinians were as divided as the Israelis. Notionally at least, Arafat remained in charge of the PLO. But Syria backed those who challenged his leadership, Jordan sought to wean West Bankers away from his organization and the Gulf states expressed growing disenchantment with his inability to take a specific stand on the only issue that mattered, namely, peace. Hemmed in on all sides, Arafat reverted to the politics of the gun.

He reinvested men, money and weapons into rebuilding his bases in Lebanon as a springboard for attacks on Israel. Once again, survival became his main concern, and armed struggle provided the quickest route to re-establishing his claim to the support of the Palestinian people. The war of attrition between Israel and the Palestinians resumed. Attacks by the PLO on Israeli targets, both at home and abroad, rose steadily. As one American analyst, Bruce Hoffman of the Rand Corporation, wrote: 'The Israeli invasion of Lebanon had little effect – and, moreover, only an ephemeral one at that – on the level of Palestinian terrorist activity.'

Somewhat naïvely, the Israelis believed that Arafat's perennial crisis would herald the emergence of fresh Palestinian leadership on the West Bank. There were Palestinians who castigated Arafat for the years of indecision and indifference to the plight of those who lived under Israeli occupation. The PLO's mistake, they argued, was not that it had used violence in the past, but that it had never grown out of violence. Some charged that Arafat's leadership was bankrupt, out of step with the mood of people who had no choice but to accept Israel in all but name. Arafat, they said, had put his movement before the Palestinians. He had forgotten the dreams and aspirations of those who yearned for an end to occupation, whatever the price in terms of land and independence. Such voices, however, did not presage new leadership capable of negotiating a settlement with Israel which bypassed the PLO. As the murder of Zafer al-Masri proved, the different factions of the PLO silenced those whom they considered to be a threat to their supremacy. As al-Masri's funeral showed, the PLO remained the fulcrum of Palestinian politics because there was no viable alternative. 'Arafat is like the Pope,' admitted one former Israeli governor of the territories. 'Palestinians may disagree with certain aspects of his teaching, but the majority still look upon him as a God on earth.'

Not surprisingly, Yassir Arafat had always been more concerned about dealing with the Arab world than with Israel. His future preoccupation would be to reunite the PLO, renew his alliance with King Hussein and reach an understanding with enemies such as the Syrians. Seeking a solution with the Israelis was not necessarily high on his list of priorities. In the absence of any incentive for peace, he was bound to readopt the philosophy of

234

armed struggle. Arafat might have had it within his power to change the only variable left in the Middle East equation: Israeli public opinion.

But as long as he was categorized as a partner only for war, not peace, Arafat was under little pressure to play the card of accepting the Jewish state. If Israel was helpless to help itself out of the mire which occupation had become, then so too were the PLO and the Palestinian people.

Twenty years after the 1967 war, there was a powerful case to be made for believing that Israel's occupation of the promised land would last indefinitely.

No Israeli government was ever likely to enjoy a clear mandate for the exchange of territory for peace. Given that choice between Auschwitz and apartheid, Israel felt best served by the status quo. Indeed, that had always been the intention of many Israeli leaders. King Hussein was understandably more concerned about preserving his throne than gambling on the West Bank. A *fait accompli* which prevented another exodus of Palestinian refugees to Jordan and precluded a Palestinian state on his turf became the most attractive option. As for Yassir Arafat, the PLO would be hopelessly split if its leader did a deal with the Israelis on the occupied territories.

A growing number of Israelis and Arabs foresaw a future in which Israel would reach a de facto arrangement with its neighbour: no formal peace, yet no war either; a solution based on a tacit understanding rather than a negotiated armistice. They argued that it was too late to return territory for peace, that Israeli settlement had moved beyond the point of no return, that it was naïve even to suggest compromise. In the real world of Middle East politics, they admitted, a quiet understanding between Israel and the Arabs offered the nearest thing to a comprehensive settlement. Many Western diplomats, exasperated by the years of political impasse, concurred. In the words of one long-serving Western ambassador, 'Sometimes I think the Arabs and the Israelis deserve each other. They should be left to get on with it.'

But diplomatic retreat was not in the long-term interests of Jews, Arabs or the world at large. By accepting the status quo as the only workable solution, the international community condemned

Israelis and Palestinians to a future bereft of hope – and a conflict without end, likely to claim countless lives both in the Middle East and abroad. Ever since 1967, such Realpolitik had enabled politicians on all sides to maintain the state of war in preference to seeking a lasting solution. By ceasing to dream of a better tomorrow, they closed their minds to the possibilities of today. In dealing only with present reality, they ignored the necessity for future action. In truth, Realpolitik became a convenient excuse for both sides to avoid the decisions which, one day, would have to be made. Even though peace cost him his life, President Sadat buried the notion that fate, rather than man, dictated the course of Middle East history.

What was so urgently required was a drastic re-evaluation of the diplomacy applied to the Middle East after 1967. The jargon and formulas used since the June war no longer had any meaning. American envoys shuttled from one capital to another, talking a language that was increasingly out of touch with the realities on the ground of Israel, the West Bank and the Gaza Strip. The currency remained, in theory, territory. The equation was still 'land for peace'. The idiom was Arafat's recognition of UN Resolution No. 242, Israel's acceptance of the Palestinians' right to self-determination, or the so-called 'Jordanian option' which envisaged King Hussein negotiating alongside Palestinians acceptable to the Israelis. But such formulas ignored the changes that had taken place since 1967. As one Israeli expert remarked, American diplomats behaved like men speaking ancient Latin or Greek.

The fact was that there could not be a final, comprehensive solution to the aftermath of the 1967 war. Israel could not give back all the land. The Arabs could not promise absolute peace. The only 'permanent' solution had to be an 'interim' one, because the search for a definitive settlement was outdated by the facts on the ground of the West Bank and Gaza. What Arabs and Jews so desperately needed was a change in attitude, a recognition of the need for the kind of small, practical accommodations with one another that might ease the mutual sense of hostility and hatred. The only peace process with a future was one in which people on both sides could be persuaded, conditioned or bullied into taking their eyes off the map of the Middle East – and discover how to take a few first steps towards each other. Both shared more than a common heritage. They shared the experience together of the years since 1967. The lessons of that period were all too evident, if unpalatable.

Much as settlers on the West Bank argued otherwise, redemption proved as elusive for the Jewish people after those six days in June as it had before. Israel was still surrounded by notional enemies, some capable of inflicting yet another disaster. Within its new borders, the country suffered moral attrition. The Jewish people violated their own standards, compromised their democracy, denigrated the values of humanity and common decency which had traditionally set them apart from other nations. They drew on their past to justify the present. 'Never again!' – the *cri de coeur* Menachem Begin had turned into a slogan after the holocaust – remained an abiding principle of Israeli thinking. But it could not explain or vindicate occupation, oppression and the very tactics of terror they sought to condemn in others.

The Palestinians experienced something far worse. They became the 'Jews of the Arab world', as the Egyptians called them. They adopted a Hebrew saying to define their plight: caught between the hammer and anvil, they said, between the Jews and the Arabs. The lesson of 1967 was that they had to rely on themselves, to forge a new nation capable of challenging both Israel and the Arabs and with justice on its side. Within the old borders of Palestine, they achieved that. Yet their leadership in exile jeopardized the future by relying on the tactics of the past. In the late 1960s and early 1970s, guerrilla warfare and terrorist tactics had a certain logic. The Palestinians were trying to force their way back into the consciousness of the West and of the Israeli public. To apply the same thinking indefinitely only reinforced the Israeli fear that they were not after a settlement but rather a war without end.

The questions remained. When and how would both sides purge themselves of the past? At what point would they learn the lessons of history instead of blindly pursuing the animosity and prejudice which their history had created? Those who lived almost exclusively with the past, as so many Palestinians and Israelis did, were bound to re-enact it. The replay of history brought neither side security and peace. That was the supreme lesson of the years since 1967.

Had they stopped to look at the future, both sides might have seen that they had a new potential enemy: the religious fundamentalism that engulfed the Moslem world in the years after 1967 and spread to the land occupied by the Jews. Israel could have diagnosed that the long-term threat lay in Islam as well as Palestinian nationalism. The Palestinians could have foreseen that they might be trapped once again, this time between Israel and the forces of revolutionary Islam. If Jerusalem was truly the goal of the ayatollahs, then the Israelis and the Palestinians shared a common interest in preserving their claim to the Holy Land. If the super-powers were unable to provide sufficient incentives for a territorial compromise, Jews and Arabs had to recognize that they were obliged to live together in pursuit of mutual survival. The stalemate served only to deepen the despair and misery which gave rise to religious zealots. Worse still, fundamentalism raised the spectre of the secular strife between Arab and Jew turning into religious conflict, a holy war in which only the extremists could succeed.

There was, however, one positive lesson to be drawn from the occupation of the promised land after 1967. It lay in the experi-ence, attitude and achievements of both Israelis and Palestinians. If it was possible for the Jews to wait 2,000 years for a return to Jerusalem, to believe in a Temple that no longer existed, it was surely possible to work towards a peace that was not yet there either. If the Palestinians could cling on to their land despite the excesses of Israeli rule, then they were certainly capable of the courage which the battle for peace demanded. The years together had shown that each had the strength and determination to perpetuate the deadlock for ever – or fight for peace.

'You see, the Middle East doesn't have to be a curse on the world,' remarked Rabbi David Hartman, one of the few on either side who looked to a future free of the past. 'If we recognize each other for what we are, it could be an example for the world to follow.'

Given the history of the years since the 1967 war, and the potential for further conflict, it seemed a forlorn hope. Yet a necessary ambition.

NOTES

CHAPTER ONE

1. See *Battle for Jerusalem*, Mordechai Gur, Popular Library, New York, 1974, pp. 279-80
2. See *Fall of Jerusalem*, Abdullah Schleifer, Monthly Review Press, New York, 1972, pp. 190-1
3. Interview with author
4. Diaries provided by Moghrabi family
5. Interview with author
6. Interview with author
7. Interview with author
8. Diary provided by family
9. Interview with author
10. Interview with author
11. *Book of Chastisement and Faith*, Uri Zvi Greenberg, Tel Aviv, 1938
12. Koran Sura
13. Interview with author
14. Interview with author

CHAPTER TWO

1. *Ha'aretz* 14.1.83
2. *Jerusalem Post* 24.8.76
3. *Koteret Rashit* 16.5.84
4. *Guardian* 5.11.82
5. *Story of My Life*, Moshe Dayan, Weidenfeld and Nicolson, London, 1976, pp. 298-9
6. Genesis 22-9
7. Dayan speech supplied by Rafi Levy

8. Interviews with author
9. Interview with author
10. Hadassah House newsletter, Issue 1
11. *Village Voice* November 1985
12. Interview with author
13. Interview with author
14. Interview with author
15. Interview with author, Amman 1986
16. *Jerusalem Post* 8.2.83
17. Interview with author
18. Israeli Radio 15.8.84
19. *Ha'aretz* 14.2.85, 11.3.85
20. Interview with author
21. Shamir speech, Government Press Office
22. Interviews with author

CHAPTER THREE
1. See *Israel's Lebanon War*, Zeev Schiff and Ehud Yaari, Simon and Schuster, New York, 1984, pp. 198-205
2. Interview with author, 13.5.86
3. *New York Times* 2.11.86
4. Interview with author
5. Interview with author
6. Interview with author. See also *Occupier's Law*, Institute for Palestine Studies, Washington, 1985
7. Interview with author
8. *Jerusalem Post* 20.8.80
9. From commission verdict provided by Felicia Langer
10. Interview with author
11. Interviews with author
12. Arafat interview with author, Tripoli, November 1983
13. Interview with author
14. Interview with author
15. Interview with author
16. Interview with author, May 1984
17. Interview with author, July 1986
18. Interviews with author
19. Interview with author, 13.5.86

CHAPTER FOUR
1. *New York Times* 24.3.80
2. Ibid
3. Reagan press conference 27.1.81
4. Interview with author, Washington DC
5. Reagan speech, 1.9.82

6. Ibid
7. Interview with author, Washington DC
8. *The Times* 16.9.82
9. *New York Times* 12.9.82
10. *Time* magazine 20.9.82
11. Interview with author
12. Address to nation 27.10.83
13. Interview with author
14. Interview with author
15. Interview with author
16. Interview with author
17. *Shimon Peres*, Matti Golan, Weidenfeld and Nicolson, London, 1984, p. 207
18. ABC News interview 22.3.84
19. Interview with author
20. Interview with author, Damascus, November 1984
21. *Al-Mussawar*, Cairo, July 1985
22. Interview with author
23. Interview with author, Aqaba, September 1985
24. ITN 3.10.85
25. *New York Times* 11.11.85
26. *Al-Fajr* 14.12.85
27. *Jerusalem Post* 24.1.86
28. King's speech, Amman, 19.2.86
29. *Davar* 28.2.86
30. Jordanian television 1.3.86
31. PFLP communiqué issued Damascus 3.3.86
32. Interview with author

CHAPTER FIVE
1. Interview with author, 1.5.85
2. Interview with author
3. Interview with author
4. Interview with author
5. *Jerusalem Post* 12.4.78
6. *Arab–Israel Wars*, Chaim Herzog, Arms and Armour Press, London, 1982, p. 165
7. *Warriors for Jerusalem*, Donald Neff, Linden Press, 1984, pp. 329-33
8. Interview with author
9. *Sharon*, Uzi Benziman, Adama Books, New York, 1985, p. 116
10. Interview with author
11. *Maariv* 2.2.73
12. Interview with author
13. Interview with author
14. Interview with author
15. Interview with author
16. Gaza Citrus Growers' Association report 1986

17. Interview with author
18. Military court verdict 8.12.79
19. Interview with author
20. Gaza Strip survey, *Jerusalem Post* publications, 1986
21. Interview by phone, July 1986
22. Interview with author
23. See *Guardian* 30.9.85
24. Interview with author

CHAPTER SIX
1. *Kol Hair* April 1986
2. Interview with author
3. *New York Times*
4. Interview with author
5. Interview with author
6. Interview with author
7. Interview with author
8. Interview with author
9. Israeli central bureau reports 1980-5
10. Interview with author
11. Interview with author
12. Interview with author
13. Interview with author
14. Shamir speech, Government Press Office
15. Dekel interview, *Haaretz* 24.9.82
16. Interview with author
17. Interview with author
18. Interviews with author

CHAPTER SEVEN
1. Translation by Abdul Lattif Barghouti
2. *Haaretz* 8.12.86
3. Interview with author
4. IDF figures released 25.2.86
5. Interview courtesy of Jamil Hamad
6. Interview with author
7. *New York Times* 12.1.87
8. Speech, Haifa University, 12.3.86
9. Interview with author
10. Interview with author
11. Interview with author
12. Interview with author
13. Interview with author
14. Interview with author
15. Interviews with author

16. Interviews with author
17. Interview with author
18. Interview with author
19. Interview with author
20. Author's interview. Also *Davar* 25.7.86
21. Etzion, 'To fly, at last, the flag in Jerusalem', *Nequda* 93
22. Interview with author
23. Livni confession, 6.5.84
24. Interview with author
25. Interview with author
26. *Davar* 12.2.85
27. Interview by phone with author
28. *Washington Post* 10.11.86
29. *Jerusalem Post, Haaretz* 12.12.86
30. Interview with author
31. Rabin speech to Knesset, 9.12.86
32. Interview with author
33. Interview with author

CHAPTER EIGHT
1. *Newsweek* 14.4.86
2. Ibid
3. Interview with author
4. Interview with author
5. Interview with author
6. Interview with author
7. *Newsweek* 14.4.86
8. *Ma'ariv* 18.6.86
9. Interview with author
10. Interview with author
11. Interview with author
12. Interview with author
13. Interview with author
14. Interview with author
15. Interview with author
16. Interview with author
17. *The Six-day War*, Randolph and Winston Churchill, Houghton Mifflin, New York, 1976, p. 65
18. Interview with author
19. *On Eagle's Wings*, Ezer Weizman, Steimatzsky, Tel Aviv, 1974 (extract in Hebrew version only)
20. Interview with author
21. Interview with author
22. Interview with author
23. Interview with author

INDEX

A-Shabiba, 176–7, 185
Abdallah, Mahmoud (Osama Tukan), 115–16
Abdullah, King of Transjordan, 122
Abou Tor, 153
Abraham, 4, 44–5, 48
Abu-Dhra, Mahmoud, 125
Abu-Dhra, Mohammed, 125
Achille Lauro, 116
Acre, 83
Addik, Jihad, 94
Aderet carpet factory, 160–1
Africa, 45, 62, 218
African National Congress, 87
Afula, 62
Ahmed, 136
al-Alami, Sheikh Saad al-Din, 39, 196–7
Albades, Haim, 37, 38
Albeck, Plia, 77–9, 80–1, 89
Algeria, 10, 179
Ali, Brigadier Ata, 19
Allon, Yigal, 134
Aloni, Shulamit, 199
Amer, Mahmoud, 173–4
Amman, 19, 89, 112
Amos, 44

an-Nahar, 186
Anathoth, 44
Angola, 10, 218
al-Ansar, Shafiq Risa'a, 115
Antonius, 141
Arab Legion, 19
Arabia, 141
Arafat, Yassir, 23, 29, 49, 83, 87, 169; leadership of Palestinians, 31, 35; deportation of West Bank Mayors, 50; and the Israeli invasion of Lebanon, 94, 102; relations with King Hussein, 106, 111–13, 119–22, 234; PLO's loss of support on West Bank, 122–3; and al-Masri's murder, 124–5; support in Gaza, 138, 143; support network, 175, 177; and Akram Hanniye, 185; Israel tries to neutralize PLO in West Bank, 186; Weizman advocates negotiations with, 208–9; future prospects, 226, 227, 234–5; siege of Beirut, 229–30; expulsion from Beirut, 98; inability to recognize Israel, 230–3; achievements, 230–2; failures,

245

231; re-arms, 233–5; and
  Resolution 242, 236
Araj, Farah, 84
Arens, Moshe, 59–62, 144
Argov, Shlomo, 100
Ariel, 89–94, 95
Ashkelon, 10, 130, 131, 137, 203
Ashour, Khalil, 176
Asia, 62, 218
al-Assad, Hafez, 102–3
Atamoun, 178
Atarot, 32
Athens, 115
Auschwitz, 5, 43, 224, 235
Avneri, Uri, 232
Awad, Arabi, 93
Ayesh, Abdullah Ahmed, 94
Azmona, 203, 204
Azzul, Izzat, 107

Baal, 153
Babylonians, 4, 27, 37
Baghdad, 120, 177
Balata refugee camp, 125, 171–2,
  189
Balfour, Arthur, 5
Balfour Declaration, 26–7
Bank Leumi, 56
Baq'aa, 114
Bar-Lev, Chaim, 60–1
Bar-Oh, Mordechai, 230
Barghouti, Abdul Lattif, 196
Bashan, Eleizer, 203–5
Bashan, Gidon, 203–5
Basle Congress of Zionists, 26
Be'eri, Dan, 182–3
Begin, Menachem, 24, 29, 35–6, 64,
  77, 84, 96, 106, 208, 220, 237;
  Camp David Agreement, 28, 90–1,
  109, 192; and the Temple Mount
  demonstrators, 39; settlement of
  West Bank, 25–6, 27–8, 48, 78,
  88, 164, 167; moves settlers into
  Hebron, 50; and Jewish terrorism,
  58–9; and the Oriental Jews, 62–
  3, 227; siege of Beirut, 70;
  invasion of Lebanon, 99; American

support for, 100; reaction to
  Reagan's proposals, 103; Reagan's
  relations with, 104; massacre of
  Palestinians in Lebanon, 105;
  Sadat's visit to Jerusalem, 90,
  108–9
Beilin, Yossi, 124
Beirut, 49, 199; Israeli siege of,
  11, 70, 94, 95, 99, 101, 111,
  229–30; expulsion of PLO from,
  97–8; peace-keeping force, 101,
  104; US marines withdrawn from,
  105
Beit Fejar, 84–5
Beit Hanun, 140
Beit Jala, 84, 160
Beit Romano, 169
Beit Shean, 62
Belgium, 10
Ben-Aharon, Yitzhak, 134
Ben-Eliezer, Binyamin, 48, 189
Ben-Gurion, David, 5–6, 23–4, 25,
  62–3, 84, 91, 119, 141–2
Ben-Gurion airport, 184
Ben-Shachal, Yehoshua, 43
Ben-Yosef, Avraham, 63
Benvenisti, Meron, 87–9, 96, 146–7
Bergen-Belsen, 5, 119
Berlin, 221
Beth-el, 44, 48
Bethlehem, 71, 79, 158, 188–9,
  216, 225
Bible, 25, 27, 155–6, 180, 194, 195
Binur, Yoram, 152
Bir Zeit University, 185, 188, 200,
  212, 213
al-Bireh, 51, 126
Black September, 31, 115
Boers, 89
Boim, Avi, 91
Boorsin, Ghassan, 176
Brezhnev Doctrine (1981), 216
Britain, 32, 142; control of
  Palestine, 5, 55; and the Six-Day
  War, 2; Jewish emigration, 82;
  Mrs Thatcher's visit to Jordan,
  113–14; and Peres's peace plan,

246

119; denounces deportation of
Akram Hanniye, 185
Buchenwald, 5
Burg, Yosef, 50
Byzantium, 45, 131

Cairo, 2
Cambodia, 218
Camp David Agreement, 28, 90, 109
192, 208, 220, 227–8, 231
Canaanites, 4, 131, 153, 194
Cape Town, 86
Carter, Jimmy, 99–100, 101, 220
Casablanca, 29
Castro, Fidel, 144
Central America, 218
Chaiken, Yona, 168–70
Chatilla, 96, 103–4, 105, 108, 130
Chroulmay, Ayyoub, 163
Citizens' Rights Movement, 163–4
Cohen, Geula, 227
Cohen, Merle, 86, 87
Cohen, Ramon, 86
Cohen, Selwyn, 86–7
Coles, John, 113–14
Communist Party, 93
Cordesman, Anthony, 12–13
Council of Jewish Settlements, 73,
156
Crusaders, 4, 5, 18, 45
Cyprus, 98, 114–16, 141

Dakkak, Ibrahim, 199–200
Dam, Kenneth, 104
Damascus, 3, 125
David, King, 45, 48, 52, 60
Davidson, Ian, 114–16
Dawani, Yacoub, 125
Dayan, Moshe, 48, 49, 54, 56, 62,
63, 84, 145, 173, 200, 207; Six-
Day War, 1, 24–5; capture of
Hebron, 44–7; and Gaza, 133
Dead Sea, 153
Deir Sharaf, 156
Dekel, Michael, 165
Dhra, Abdullah, 171–2
Dhra, Majed Abu, 171–3, 174, 189

Dura, 174
Durban, 86

Eban, Abba, 33, 34, 35–6, 175
Efrat, 79–83, 84–6, 90, 95
Egerton, Stephen, 114
Egypt, 19, 45, 220; War of
Independence, 6; Six-Day War, 1–
2, 25, 206; Yom Kippur War, 12,
31; Sinai returned to, 28, 226;
Sadat's visit to Jerusalem, 33–4,
108–9, 114; Camp David
Agreement, 90–1; and the Israeli
invasion of Lebanon, 102; and
Gaza, 130, 131–3, 139; Islamic
fundamentalism, 198, 223
Eisenhower, Dwight, 221
El Salvador, 218
Elon Moreh, 77, 78, 80
Engels, Friedrich, 144
Ephron the Hittite, 44
Eretz Israel, 25–6
Erez, Colonel Shaike, 149
Eshkol, Levi, 8–9, 23–4, 25, 72, 77
Ethiopia, 64, 218
Etzion, Yehuda, 179–84, 188
European Economic Community, 113,
142

Fahd, Kind of Saudi Arabia, 102–3,
111
Fahd Plan (1981), 102–3, 216
Fahoum, Walid, 178
al-Fajr, 174
Fatah, 49, 177–8, 199
Fayez, 136
fedayeen, 132, 133, 143, 145, 150
fellahin, 67
Fez Plan, 102, 103, 111
Fiad, Abu, 97
Force 17, 23, 94, 115
Foreign Office (Britain), 113, 114,
185
France, 10, 116–17, 179
Franco-Egyptian Plan (1982), 216
Freij, Elias, 157–8, 178
French Hill, 71, 72

247

Friedman, Thomas, 174

Gaddhafi, Colonel Muammar, 3–4, 210, 211, 221
Gai Ben Hinom, 153
Galilee, 83
Galilee Triangle, 91
Galloway, Alexander, 132
Gandhi, Mahatma, 23
Gaza, Islamic University of, 195–6, 198
Gaza city, 132, 148
Gaza Strip, 8, 12, 13, 28–9, 34–6, 70, 130–50, 196–9, 203, 226
Gazit, Shlomo, 47, 173, 190
Geneva Convention (1949), 78, 100
Germany, 7, 55, 119
Ghanem, Raja, 93
Ghazala, Hatem Abu, 130
Ghraith, Taleb, 168–70
Gideon, 64
Gilboa, Amos, 179
Gilo, 72, 73–6, 77, 88–9, 95
Golan Heights, 2, 13, 182
Goodman, Marvin, 81, 82
Goren, General Shlomo, 22
Goren, Shmuel, 123
Graham, Sir John, 113
Greece, 4, 7, 98
Grenada, 105
Grunzweig, Michael, 73–5
Grunzweig, Naomi, 73–5
Gulf states, 223, 233
Gur, Motta, 17–18, 19–20, 22, 23–5, 28, 32, 44, 132–3, 146
Gush Emunim, 26, 38, 50, 54, 62, 181
Gush Etzion, 27, 203, 204

Ha'aretz, 42, 173
Habash, George, 111, 125, 143, 144, 210
Habib, Philip, 98
Habla, 167
Hadassah House, Hebron, 48, 49, 50, 51, 56, 60, 63
Haddad, Wadi, 4, 115

Haetzni, Elyakim, 52–4, 55–6, 157, 162
Haganah (Jewish Defence Force), 52–3, 75
The Hague, 119
Hague Convention (1907), 77
Haifa, 83, 89, 203, 204, 206, 225
Haig, Alexander, 100, 103
Halhoul, 50
Hanini, Jawad, 65
Hanniye, Akram, 184–7
Harel, Israel, 73, 156, 181
Harkabi, Yehoshafat, 225–6
Hartman, Rabbi David, 154–6, 193, 238
Hassan, Crown Prince, 124
Hassan, King of Morocco, 102
Heathrow Airport, 2
Hebron, 41-67, 95, 123, 126, 150, 161–3, 169, 170, 175, 181, 197, 206, 216, 217, 225
Heineman, Benzion, 50
Herod the Great, 45
Herut, 62, 64
Herzl, Theodor, 26, 53, 62, 84
Herzliyya, 73, 160
Herzliyya Pituach, 137
Herzog, Chaim, 226
Hirbawi, Idris, 54–6
Hitler, Adolf, 29, 52, 55, 78, 119, 132
Hitler Youth, 195
Hoffman, Bruce, 234
Holland, 119
Hollywood, 3
Holy Roman Empire, 7
Horn of Africa, 64
Hurewitz, Captain Eli, 148–9
Hussein, King of Jordan, 13, 89 139, 200, 235; Six-Day War, 19, 25, 33; and the Yom Kippur War, 31; relations with Palestinians, 31–2, 34–5, 95; secret negotiations with Israel, 32–4; and the occupied territories, 34–5, 36; control of West Bank, 93; and the Israeli invasion of

Lebanon, 102; relations with
Arafat, 106, 111–13, 234; Peres
seeks agreement with, 109, 110,
116–19, 232; and Resolution 242,
110–11, 236; Mrs Thatcher visits,
113–14; negotiations with PLO,
119–22; and al-Masri's murder,
124; tries to break PLO's control
of West Bank, 186
Hussein, Saddam, 102
Husseini, Faisal, 189

Ibrahim, Haider, 178
Institute of Hanoch Smith, 226
Iran, 43, 62, 99–100, 105, 197–8,
219, 220
Iraq, 2, 6, 19, 62, 65, 220
Isaac, 45, 48
Islam: fundamentalism, 3, 196–9,
216, 223, 237–8; importance of
Jerusalem to, 18, 37–8
Islamic University, Hebron, 57
Israel: history, 4–7; War of
Independence, 6; Six-Day War, 1–
4, 7–9, 13–14, 17–27; expels
Palestinians, 6–7; Palestinian
refugees, 7–11; military
expenditure, 12; Yom Kippur War,
12; secret negotiations with King
Hussein, 32–4; settlement of West
Bank, 41–67, 70–96, 104; invasion
of Lebanon, 11, 12, 13, 58, 94–5,
98–101, 102–3, 105, 112, 149,
197, 216; siege of Beirut, 70;
Camp David Agreement, 90–1;
massacre of Palestinians in
Lebanon, 96, 103–4, 105; and
American proposals for
Palestinians, 101, 103; Fez Plan,
103; Peres seeks agreement with
King Hussein, 109, 110, 116–19;
and Resolution 242, 110–11; bombs
PLO in Tunisia, 116; and Arafat's
negotiations with King Hussein,
119–21; and al-Masri's murder,
125–6; Gaza problem, 130–50;
Jewish and Arab co-existence,

151–70; economics, 158–61;
Palestinian resistance movement,
171–9; Jewish underground, 50–1,
180–4; tries to neutralize PLO in
West Bank, 186–7, 189; and the
West Bank riots, 187–9; political
views of younger generation, 191–
205, 212–14, 217; and Islamic
fundamentalism, 196–9;
Palestinian civil disobedience
advocated, 202; relationship with
America, 218–22; future
prospects, 224–8, 235–8;
Palestinian hijackers murdered,
228–9; PLO attacks, 234
Israeli Aircraft Industries (IAI),
90
Israeli Marketing Board, 142

Ja'abari, Sheikh Mohammed Ali, 46
Ja'abari, Nabil, 47
Jabari, Zeyad, 41–2
Jaber, Adnan, 49–50
Jabotinsky, Vladimir, 25
Jacob, 44, 45, 48
Jaffa, 64, 83
Janoun, Abu, 184
Jenin, 46, 188–9
Jeremiah, 44
Jericho, 8, 71
Jerusalem, 46, 62; Six-Day War, 2,
3, 17–25, 27; Sadat's visit to,
33–4, 35, 90, 108–9, 114, 208,
210, 226; Temple Mount
demonstrations, 37–9; Israeli
settlements around, 71–6, 95;
Jewish and Arab co-existence,
151–6; Jewish underground plan to
destroy the Dome of the Rock,
180, 182–4; Islamic
fundamentalism, 199
Jerusalem Electricity Company, 200
Jerusalem Post, 43, 187
Jesse, 60
Jewish Agency, 2
Jewish underground, 50–1, 180–4
Jihad, 198–9

Jihad, Abu, 49, 56–7, 115, 124–5, 169
Johannesburg, 86
Johnson, Lyndon, 3, 219
Johnson Plan (1972), 216
Jordan, 93, 131, 200, 201–2, 232; Six-Day War, 1–2, 19, 25; Palestinians in, 28–9, 30–1, 35, 95; growth of PLO, 29; and the Yom Kippur War, 31; secret negotiations with Israel, 32–4, 109, 110, 116–19; West Bank boundaries, 72; and the Israeli invasion of Lebanon, 99, 102; and American proposals for Palestinians, 101; and Resolution 242, 110–11, 236; relations with Palestinians, 111–13; Mrs Thatcher visits, 113–14; negotiations with PLO, 119–22; tries to neutralize PLO in West Bank, 186–7, 189, 223; Islamic fundamentalism, 223
Jordan Radio, 21
Jordan River, 110, 132
Joshua, 4, 44, 194
Jounieh, 11
Judaea, 25, 155, 182, 183, 224
Judaism, 192, 228
Justice Ministry, 61

Kach, 195
Kaddoumi, Farouk, 120
Kahane, Rabbi Meir, 38, 193–5, 198, 212, 217
Kalandia refugee camp, 198–9
Kamal, Zahera, 178–9
Karp, Yehudit, 58
Kawasmeh, Fahd, 50
Kemp, Geoffrey, 102, 105
al-Khader, 79–81, 84, 85
Khader, Wajiha Abdul, 92–3
Khader, Yusuf, 93
Khalag, Karim, 51
Khaled, 199
Khalil, 135–8, 140, 146
Khan Younis, 132, 150

Khartoum Declaration (1967), 232
Khatib, Anwar, 18–20, 23, 28–9, 31–2
Khomeini, Ayatollah Ruhollah, 43, 197–8
Kiel, 52
Kiryat Arba, 41–2, 47, 48, 50, 60, 64, 66, 77, 156, 162–3, 169, 181
Kiryat Shmona, 62, 63
Kissinger, Henry, 119
Klein, Rachel, 63
Klibi, Chedli, 103
Kollek, Teddy, 88, 154, 158
Kook, Rabbi Avraham Ha-Cohen, 26–7, 43, 53
Kook, Rabbi Zvi Yehuda, 27, 204
Koran, 198,199
Kuttab, Jonathan, 141

Labour Party (Israel), 23–4, 25, 28, 106, 108
Langer, Felicia, 81
Larnaca, 115–16
Lasch, Dr Eli, 147
League of Nations, 5
Leah, 45
Lebanon, 131; Israeli War of Independence, 6; Israeli invasion, 11, 12, 13, 58, 94–5, 98–101, 102–3, 105, 112, 149, 197; growth of PLO, 29; massacre of Palestinians in, 96, 103–4, 105; expulsion of PLO from Beirut, 97–8; Islamic fundamentalism, 197, 198, 199, 220; civil war, 216, 220
Lenin, 189
Leor, Dov, 50–1
Levinger, Miriam, 43, 48–9, 60, 63
Levinger, Rabbi Moshe, 52, 53, 73, 74, 90, 161–2, 165, 169, 181; settlement of West Bank, 43, 47–9, 60–4, 77; and the Jewish underground, 50–1, 57; uses PLO terrorism as weapon, 175
Libya, 103, 210, 221
Liebowitz, Yeshayahu, 229
Likud Party, 24, 96, 108, 167,

168, 213
Lincoln Square Synagogue,
  Manhattan, 81–2
Livni, Menahem, 50, 59, 182
London, 32, 100, 119
Loney, Naomi, 92

Maaleh Adumim, 71, 73
Ma'ariv, 196
Machpela, cave of, 44, 45
Maghreb desert, 29
Malaysia, 179
Mamelukes, 4
Mandela, Nelson, 87
Marighella, Carlos, 144
Marx, Karl, 144
al-Masri, Raghda, 123
al-Masri, Taher, 124
al-Masri, Zafer, 106–8, 109, 112–
  13, 117, 118, 121, 123–6, 234
Massada, siege of, 205
Massuot Itzchak, 203, 204
Mecca, 37
Medina, 37
Meidad, Ettie, 63-4
Meir, Golda, 8–9, 23–4, 77, 134,
  225
Mesopotamia, 45
Middle East Journal, 13
Milhem, Mohammed, 50
Miller, Dr Aaron, 230
Minawi, Shehadeh, 178
al-Mira, 210
Modai, Yitzhak, 122, 159
Moghrabi, Hassan, 21–3, 28, 29–30
Moghrabi, Insaf, 21, 22
Moghrabi, Mahmoud, 22–3, 30–1
Mohammed, Prophet, 9, 18, 37, 45
Morocco, 19, 29, 62, 102
Moses, 4
Moshav Nahalim, 165
Moslem Brotherhood (Al-Mujaama),
  196, 198–9, 212, 217, 220
Mossad, 116
Mozambique, 10
Mubarak, Hosni, 13
Al-Mujaama (Moslem Brotherhood),

196, 198–9, 212, 217, 220
Murphy, Richard, 111, 113, 118,
  119
Mustafa, 199

Nabi, Halima Abdul, 76
Nablus, 46, 51, 71, 77, 106–7,
  112, 118, 121, 123, 125–6, 150,
  167, 171, 189, 216
Nachman, Ron, 89–92, 94
an-Najah, Arab University of, 175–7
Napoleon, Emperor, 131
Nasr, Muhammad, 209–11
Nasser, Fuad, 93
Nasser, Gamel Abdel, 2, 19, 25,
  110, 131–2, 201
Nasser, Victor, 160, 161
Nassif, Ali (Salah Nassif), 115–16
Nathanson, Natan, 50, 51, 183
National Security Council, 102
Navon, Yitzhak, 193, 226
Nazis, 27, 52, 54, 98, 131, 180,
  195
Ne'eman, Yuval, 61, 193
Neemanei Har Habayit, 38–9
Negev desert, 69, 91, 218
Netanya, 10, 89, 225
Netherlands, 10
Netivot, 62
Neve Ya'acov, 71, 73, 74
New York, 2, 81–2
New York Times, 100, 117, 118, 174
Newsweek, 8, 195
Nicaragua, 218
Nidal, Abu, 4
North Africa, 29
Norway, 142
Nusseibeh, Anwar, 200–3, 207
Nusseibeh, Sari, 200–3
Nusseibeh family, 200, 205

Odeh, Ahmed, 167–8
Ofakim, 62
Ofra, 50, 180, 188
'Operation Moses', 64
Oranit, 168
Oriental Jews, 62–3, 227

251

Ossaileh, Khaled, 66–7
Othman, Samir, 85
Ottoman Empire, 7, 78, 79, 83,
   131, 141
Ozeri, Nati, 195

Palestinian Liberation Organization
   (PLO), 58, 67; Force 17, 23, 94,
   115; rise of, 29, 31; in Hebron,
   47–50; and the West Bank Mayors,
   50, 51; attacks Ariel, 94; and
   the Israeli invasion of Lebanon,
   12, 94–5, 98–101; siege of
   Beirut, 11, 97–8, 229–30;
   Reagan's view of, 100;
   negotiations with King Hussein,
   109, 110, 117, 119–22; and
   Resolution 242, 110–11; British
   relations with, 113–14; Larnaca
   murders, 115–16; *Achille Lauro*
   hijack, 116; Tunisian
   headquarters bombed, 116; support
   on West Bank, 122–3, 175, 176–9;
   and al-Masri's murder, 124–6;
   support in Gaza, 133, 139–40,
   143–5; and co-existence with
   Jews, 157; Israeli conspiracy
   theory, 174–5, 183, 189–90;
   finances, 177; as a surrogate
   state, 177–9, 217; and the
   deportation of Akram Hanniye,
   185–6; Israel tries to neutralize
   in West Bank, 186–7, 189; Weizman
   advocates negotiations with, 208–
   9; and the Lebanese civil war,
   216; future prospects, 226;
   achievements, 230–2; inability to
   recognize Israel, 230–3;
   failures, 231; attacks Israeli
   targets, 234
Palestinians: history, 4–6; turned
   into refugees, 6–11; nationalism,
   9, 29, 30; in Jordan, 28–9, 30–1,
   35; leadership, 31, 35; and the
   Israeli settlement of the West
   Bank, 41–67, 70–96; and the
   Israeli invasion of Lebanon, 11,
94–5, 98–101; massacre in refugee
   camps, 96, 103–4, 105; American
   proposals for, 101–2, 103;
   divisions amongst, 111; relations
   with Jordan, 111–13; and Arafat's
   negotiations with King Hussein,
   120–2; in the Gaza Strip, 130–50;
   co-existence with Jews, 151–70;
   economic position, 158–61; land
   scandal, 163–8; resistance
   movement, 171–9; and the Jewish
   underground, 180–4; Israel tries
   to neutralize PLO in West Bank,
   186–7, 189; West Bank riots, 187–
   9; political views of younger
   generation, 191–205, 212–14, 217;
   attitudes of young Israelis
   towards, 191–5; Islamic
   fundamentalism, 196–9; generation
   gap, 200–3; civil disobedience
   advocated, 202; and the Lebanese
   civil war, 216; future prospects,
   224–8, 235–8; hijackers murdered,
   228–9
Paris, 3, 32, 116–17
Peres, Shimon, 13, 82, 112, 144,
   208, 228; advocates returning
   West Bank, 53–4; forms government
   of national unity, 108; and
   Sadat's visit to Jerusalem, 108–
   9; seeks agreement with King
   Hussein, 109, 110, 116–19; and
   Arafat's negotiations with King
   Hussein, 121; and al-Masri's
   murder, 124; on problem of Gaza,
   130
Petah Tikva, 165
Philistines, 4, 44, 131
Poland, 5, 25, 119
Popular Front for the Liberation
   of Palestine (PFLP), 111, 125,
   143, 144
Porat, Hanan, 20–1, 23, 26, 27–8
Portugal, 10
Prisoners' Friends Association,
   178
Progressive Federal Party, 87

Purham, Uri, 213

Qalqilia, 160, 165, 207
Qarnei Shomron, 160

Ra'anana, 73
Rabat, 19
Rabin, Yitzhak, 77, 82, 108, 189
Radio Cairo, 2, 21, 110
Radio Jordan, 1
Radio Mecca, 132
Rafah, 132, 150
Raizmann, Yaacov, 160–1
Ramallah, 46, 51, 126, 150, 180,
    184, 188–9, 216
Ramat Eshkol, 71, 72
Ramat Hasharon, 73
Ramat Mamre, 66
Ramle prison, 184
Rayyes, Joanna, 211–14
Reagan, Ronald, 113, 117; and the
    Six-Day War, 3; support for
    Israel, 99–100, 103, 221–2; peace
    initiative, 101–2, 103, 110, 216,
    220, 221; intervention in
    Lebanese civil war, 101, 104–5,
    109; inability to find Middle
    East solution, 104–5, 220–4; and
    the *Achille Lauro* hijack, 116;
    and the deportation of Akram
    Hanniye, 185; Iran affair, 219–
    20, 228; attitude to terrorism,
    221
Rebecca, 45
Red Cross, 104, 184
Resolution 242, 110–11, 120, 236
al-Rifai, Zeid, 120
Riskin, Rabbi Shlomo, 81–3, 84,
    85–6, 89, 90
Romans, 4, 5, 9, 18, 37, 45, 131,
    205
Rome, 221
Rothschild family, 5
Rubinstein, Dani, 184
Ruth, 153

Saba, Yussuf, 75

Sabra, 96, 103–4, 105, 108, 130
Sadat, Anwar, 102, 174, 236; Camp
    David Agreement, 28, 192; visit
    to Jerusalem, 33–4, 35, 90, 108–
    9, 114, 208, 210, 226
Saifan, Hamdan, 176
Saladin, 55
Salameh, Fatima, 75, 76
Salameh, Musa, 75–6
Salfit, 90, 92–4
al-Salfiti, Fahmi, 93
Salomon, Gershon, 38, 39
Sama, 140–1, 142
Samaria, 25, 48, 50, 90, 160, 165–
    6, 173, 180, 182, 183, 224
Samuel, 44
Sanniriya, 168
Santayana, George, 11
Sarah, 44
Sarid, Yossi, 164, 222
Saudi Arabia, 46, 103, 210
Saul, 44
Schnell, Chaim, 82
Schnell, Sima, 82
Schurab, Ahmed, 140
Schurab family, 140–1, 142
Sebastia, 48
Seneca, 13
Shaka'a, Bassam, 51, 107, 157, 166
Shaleev, Michael, 134–5
Shalev, Aryeh, 179, 190
Shamir, Yitzhak, 28, 77, 82, 84,
    96, 227, 232; settlement of West
    Bank, 60, 112; and the Jewish
    settlement of Hebron, 64–5; in
    government of national unity,
    108; and Arafat's negotiations
    with King Hussein, 121; and the
    land scandal, 165; support for
    Jewish underground, 183; and the
    murders of Palestinian hijakers,
    228–9
al-Shara, Farouk, 13
Sharafat, 72, 75–6
Sharm el-Sheikh, 3
Sharon, Ariel, 69–70, 77, 84, 111,
    121–2, 124, 168, 213, 220, 227,

232; settlement of West Bank, 48, 70–1, 72, 78, 80, 89, 95–6, 104; and the settlement at Ariel, 90–1; invasion of Lebanon, 11, 13, 70, 94–5, 101, 112, 149; desire to be Prime Minister, 96; massacre of Palestinians in Lebanon, 96, 105; expels PLO from Beirut, 98; American support for, 100; in government of national unity, 108; and Arafat's negotiations with King Hussein, 121; operation in Gaza, 133; support for Jewish underground, 183; popularity amongst young, 192; and the Village Leagues of the West Bank, 210–11

Sharon, Lily, 71
Sharon, Sonya, 122
Shawa, Rashad, 138–40, 143, 197
Shehadeh, Raja, 78–9
Shemesh, Zamir, 61
Sheve Shomron, 156
Shifa hospital, 146–7
Shi'ite Moslems, 197, 199
Shiloh, 44, 48, 50, 156
Shimon, Yitzhak, 162–3
Shin Beth, 184, 228
Shubaki, Mohammed, 49
Shultz, George, 103, 111, 114
Sidon, 199
Silwan, 153
Sinai, 2, 4, 28, 226
Siniora, Hana, 121, 174, 186, 231
Sinjul, 156
Six-Day War (1967), 1–4, 7–9, 11, 13–14, 17–27, 44, 132, 155, 167, 206–7
Sneh, Colonel Ephraim, 178
Sourani, Raja, 143–5
South Africa, 82, 86–7, 89, 131, 134–5, 174
Soviet Union, 99–100, 111, 213; pogroms, 5; military aid to Syria, 12; Jewish emigrants, 64; and the Lebanese civil war, 105, 216; and Peres's peace plan, 117;

inability to find Middle East solution, 218–19
Spain, 10
Subeih, Fathi Ismail, 79–81, 84
Subeih, Mariam, 79
Subeih, Zaimab, 79
Suddarth, Roscoe, 223
Suez Canal, 3, 207
Suez crisis (1956), 131
al-Suiri, Abdullah Ahmed, 65–6
Sunni Moslems, 197
Supreme Moslem Council of Jerusalem, 196
Suzman, Helen, 87
Syria, 13, 19, 131; War of Independence, 6; Six-Day War, 2, 3; Yom Kippur War, 12, 31; military expenditure, 12; growth of PLO, 29; PLO driven into, 94; and the Israeli invasion of Lebanon, 102–3; US planes bomb, 105; and the Lebanese civil war, 216; relations with Soviet Union, 218; arms race with Israel, 223

Tamir, Avraham, 186
Taqatqah, Ali Murshed, 85–6
Tawil, Ibrahim, 51
Tehiya, 193
Tekoa, 44
Tel Aviv, 6, 10, 53, 55–6, 62, 73, 89, 136–7
Tel Rumeida, 60–1, 63–4, 65
Tezion, Yehuda, 50
Thatcher, Margaret, 89, 113–14, 115, 116, 119, 230
Tiran, Straits of, 3
Toledano, Shmuel, 192
Transjordan, 6; see also Jordan
Tukan, Osama (Mahmoud Abdallah), 115–16
Tulkarem, 160, 188–9
Tulscinski, Dr Ted, 147–8
Tunis, 23, 116
Tunisia, 62, 116
Turks, 4

Uganda, 62
Umm el-Jamal, 204
United Nations, 5–6, 35, 117, 130–
1, 139, 185, 231; Security
Council, 110, 185
United Nations Relief and Works
Agency for Palestine Refegees
(UNRWA), 131, 132
Unna, Yitzhak, 174
US Eastern Analytical Assessments
Center, 12–13
US State Department, 103, 104–5,
111, 125–6, 185, 222, 223, 230
United States of America: and the
Six-Day War, 2, 219; and Arab
terrorism, 11; support for
Israel, 12, 218–22; Jewish
emigration, 81–3; and the Israeli
invasion of Lebanon, 99–101, 105;
and the West Bank settlements,
100, 104; and the Lebanese civil
war, 101, 104, 216; Reagan's
peace initiative, 101–2, 103,
110, 216, 220, 221; economic aid
to Israel, 104; Middle East
policies, 105; Achille Lauro
hijack, 116; and Peres's peace
plan, 117, 119; and the Gaza
Strip, 142; anti-Semitism, 169;
Vietnam War, 179; and the
deportation of Akram Hanniye,
185; inability to find Middle
East solution, 218–19, 220–4,
236; attitude to terrorism, 221;
Iran affair, 219–20, 222, 228

Venice Declaration (1980), 113,
216
Vienna, 221
Vietnam War, 133, 179, 218
Village Leagues of the West Bank,
210–11
Vollek, Ernst, 160

Wafa, 124
Wahid, 136
Waldman, Eliezer, 50–1

Walid, 146
War of Independence, 6
Wazir, Khalil see Jihad, Abu
Weinberg, Joel, 149–50
Weiss, Daniella, 181
Weizman, Ezer, 130, 144, 206–9,
210–11
Weizman, Shaul, 207–8
Weizmann, Chaim, 7, 84
West Bank: under Jordanian rule,
93; Six-Day War, 3, 4;
Palestinian refugees, 8; Israeli
occupation and settlement of, 12,
13, 26, 27–9, 34–6, 41–67, 70–96,
104; Jewish terrorism, 51, 56,
57–60, 180–4; Reagan accepts
settlements as legal, 100;
American proposals for, 101;
Peres seeks agreement with King
Hussein, 117–18; PLO's loss of
support on, 122–3; Zafer al-
Masri's funeral, 125–6; Jewish
and Arab co-existence, 156–70;
economic position, 158–61; land
scandal, 163–8; Palestinian
resistance, 171–9; Israel tries
to neutralize PLO in, 186–7, 189,
233; riots, 187–9; and the
political views of the younger
generation, 192–5; Islamic
fundamentalism, 196–9; peace
missions, 216; future prospects,
224–8
Williams, Angela, 130–1
World Health Organization, 148
World War One, 5
World War Two, 5, 55
World Zionist Organization, 5

Yassin, Ahmed, 198, 199
Yemen, 6, 46, 62
Yom Kippur War (1973), 11–12, 31
Yugoslav Plan (1967), 216
Yussa, 153–4

Zaar, Moshe, 165–7
Zagazig, 2

Zaibak, Ali, 115
Zeitan, Ramadan, 189
Zemach, Mina, 192
Ziad, 199
al-Zir, Hassan, 93

al-Zirr, Hamza, 93
Ziso, David, 211–13
Zucker, Dedi, 163–4
Zürich, 185